Epic Journey

Epic Journey

The 2008 Elections and American Politics

James W. Ceaser,
Andrew E. Busch,
and John J. Pitney, Jr.

ROWMAN & LITTLEFIELD PUBLISHERS, INC.
Lanham • Boulder • New York • Toronto • Plymouth, UK

ROWMAN & LITTLEFIELD PUBLISHERS, INC.

Published in the United States of America
by Rowman & Littlefield Publishers, Inc.
A wholly owned subsidary of The Rowman & Littlefield Publishing Group, Inc.
4501 Forbes Boulevard, Suite 200, Lanham, Maryland 20706
www.rowmanlittlefield.com

Estover Road, Plymouth PL6 7PY, United Kingdom

Copyright © 2009 by Rowman & Littlefield Publishers, Inc.

British Library Cataloguing in Publication Information Available

Library of Congress Cataloging-in-Publication Data

Ceaser, James W.
    Epic journey : the 2008 elections and American politics / James W. Ceaser, Andrew E.
Busch, and John J. Pitney, Jr.
        p.   cm.
    ISBN 978-0-7425-6135-9 (cloth : alk. paper)
    ISBN 978-0-7425-6136-6 (pbk. : alk. paper)
    ISBN 978-0-7425-9968-0 (electronic)
    1. Presidents—United States—Election—2008.   2. United States—Politics and
government—2001–   I. Busch, Andrew E.   II. Pitney, John J., 1955–   III. Title.
JK5262008 C43   2009
324.973′0931—dc22

                                                                                    2009002250

Printed in the United States of America

⊗ ™ The paper used in this publication meets the minimum requirements of American
National Standard for Information Sciences—Permanence of Paper for Printed Library
Materials, ANSI/NISO Z39.48-1992.

Contents

Acknowledgments

We would like to thank the following individuals for their assistance and advice in preparing this manuscript: Emily Charnock, Tyler Clarkson, Daniel DiSalvo, John Gardner, Lloyd Green, Hans Hassell, Byron Koay, Zachary Courser, Dylan Laslovich, Rob Saldin, Steve Schier, and Jeremy Shane.

Prologue

Near the end of 2007, well before the presidential nominees had been selected, political observers found themselves in uncommon agreement about the likely results of the upcoming election. With President Bush's approval rating at near record lows, with the number of voters identifying with the Republican Party sinking rapidly, and with Americans believing by wide margins that the nation was on the wrong track, it was shaping up to be a pretty good year for the Democrats. And that was just where things ended up on November 4, 2008. A Democrat was elected president by an impressive seven-point margin (53 percent to 46 percent), with Democrats making solid gains in both the Senate (seven seats) and the House (twenty-one seats).

Yet to describe the 2008 election in such a perfunctory way does not begin to do this event justice. It would be akin to summarizing Homer's *Odyssey* by saying that Odysseus set out after the Trojan War to return home and got there. Yes, he did get there. But it was what happened along the way—the astonishing twists of fate, the uncanny detours, and the remarkable surprises—that turned an ordinary voyage into an epic journey. Just so with the 2008 election: The nation reached the destination that most foresaw, but it did so by a path that defied every expectation and that produced a story of classic dimension.

Consider first an institutional matter. The schedule of primaries and caucuses for the nomination was stacked with contests right at the beginning, or "front-loaded" in campaign speak. This arrangement led everyone to predict that the nominations would be decided earlier and more quickly than ever before, most likely by the first week in February. But fate had something else in mind. While the Republican race went only slightly longer than anticipated, concluding in early March, the Democratic contest turned into a marathon. Having eliminated the broader field of contenders, Hillary Clinton and Barack Obama went head-to-head until the full schedule of contests had ended. After threats to take the struggle to the convention, Mrs. Clinton finally conceded in the first week of June. It was the longest active contest in modern times. The three-part "structure" of the presidential campaign that had evolved over recent elections—a nomination race with an early decision, a long "interregnum" period, and a final election campaign—gave way this time to an essentially direct transition from the primaries to the general election campaign.

It was the results of the nomination contests themselves, however, that produced the journey's greatest surprise. For one political party in American politics to select a long shot as its nominee is rare, but for both parties to do so in the same year is unprecedented. Yet this is exactly what happened. The Republicans chose John McCain, a very early front-runner who by the end of the summer of 2007 had fallen almost completely out of the picture. Journalistic accounts of the Republican race sometimes left him off the list of serious prospects altogether. The Democrats selected a young and inexperienced first-term senator from Illinois, Barack Obama, who many originally thought was running to burnish his credentials for a future race. Democrats were preparing to celebrate a "historical first" by selecting a woman, Hillary Clinton; they ended by breaking a more unlikely barrier of choosing an African American.

The twists and turns of this journey did not stop with the nomination phase. The general election campaign brought its own surprises. The contest was fought between two candidates known as advocates of reform, including reform of the political process itself. Yet the race between them produced a billion-dollar presidential contest that shattered all previous records for campaign spending. This was primarily the consequence of Barack Obama's stunning decision in June to forgo public funding for his campaign, enabling him to raise and spend without any limits, which he quickly proceeded to do. This particular precedent places a half-century's worth of effort—aimed at controlling the money spent in presidential campaigns—in jeopardy.

One aspect of the contest did play out according to expectation. Just as the Democrats hoped and planned, the campaign focused largely on the record of the Bush administration—on whether, in Obama's words, Americans wanted to give a "third term" to George Bush. Yet in another challenge to prediction, attention was not focused on the part of Bush's record that everyone in 2007 had expected. As early as the spring of 2008, Democrats began to shift their fundamental campaign strategy, altering the main subject of the race from foreign affairs and the Iraq War, which had been the 2007 game plan, to domestic affairs and, above all, the economy. Here came another surprise that sealed this effort to make 2008 an election about the economy: the sudden onset, beginning on September 14, of a severe crisis in the nation's financial institutions, which spread worldwide and which signaled a sharp global economic downturn. This event was one of the most decisive "outside" occurrences ever to have intervened during an American presidential campaign, rivaled perhaps only by the French surrender to the German blitzkrieg two days before the opening of the Republican convention in June 1940. Immediately, government action on an unprecedented scale came under discussion. For the rest of the campaign, anxieties over economic security that escalated after "9-14" eclipsed the national security fears that had dominated since 9-11.

Whether this event fundamentally altered the outcome of the election can never be known. Yet it was the case that in early September John McCain had taken his first, and arguably only *real*, lead in the national polls since June, bolstered by the controversial but successful "rollout" of the Republicans' vice presidential candidate, Governor Sarah Palin of Alaska. The surge in public opinion for the Republican presidential ticket was accompanied by a jump in the polls for congressional Republicans. It seemed that the race could possibly be about to turn. But then Poseidon blew a gust of wind, the sails flapped, and the ship turned back on course toward its original destination.

The longest active presidential campaign of modern history concluded with the triumph of a most improbable candidate, secured amidst numerous unexpected events, yet whose victory in the end seemed logical and natural. The nation passed a historical milestone with the election of the first African American president. Barack Obama assumed office backed by large majorities for his party in both houses of the Congress and under circumstances of a major economic crisis—that rare combination of conditions in American politics that provides a warrant for extensive presidential leadership in the domestic arena. One epic journey was over. Time alone would tell whether another had begun.

Chapter One

The Scope and Meaning of the Democratic Victory

People commonly exaggerate the magnitude of events taking place in their day, probably to flatter themselves about the significance of their own lives and times. This particular kind of inflationary tendency was on vivid display in many interpretations of the Democrats' 2008 electoral victory. Descriptions ranged from the relatively mild claims that it was "unprecedented" to the bold, unqualified assertions that it was "a genuinely realigning election." *Time* magazine went so far as to suggest a parallel with Franklin Roosevelt's 1932 victory, printing a cover that morphed Barack Obama's head onto an iconic photo of FDR, sporting his thirties style "lid" and driving a convertible.[1]

The 2008 Democratic triumph was no doubt impressive—how much so will be seen in a moment—but it was far from being massive, or even unusual, by historical standards. A brief review of the record provides some perspective. There have been twenty-nine presidential contests since 1896, a year many scholars use as the starting point of "modern politics." Barack Obama won the presidency with a popular vote share of just under 53 percent, which ranks fourteenth, or almost at the median (table 1.1). His margin of victory over his rival (6.9 percent) was the nineteenth largest, or slightly below the median. Finally, his electoral vote percentage (always magnified relative to the popular vote) was 67.8, or seventeenth among the twenty-nine contests.

The most helpful figure for considering the magnitude of a presidential victory is the popular vote margin, because it "controls" for the problem of third-party candidacies. On this basis, presidential elections can be sorted into five different categories: (1) the overwhelming landslides (more than 13 percent), the largest and also the least memorable of which was Warren G.

1

Table 1.1 Magnitudes of Presidential Victories

Margin of Victory (%)	Election	Winning Candidate	Losing Candidate	Winner's % of Total Vote	Winner's % of Electoral Votes	Change since Last Midterm Election		Change since Last Presidential Election	
						Senate Seats	House Seats	Senate Seats	House Seats
Landslides									
26.2	1920	Harding (R)	Cox (D)	60.3	76.1	10	62	17	88
25.2	1924	**Coolidge (R)**	Davis (D)	54.0	71.9	1	22	−5	−55
24.3	1936	**F. Roosevelt (D)**	Landon (R)	60.8	98.5	7	12	17	21
23.2	1972	**Nixon (R)**	McGovern (D)	60.7	96.7	−2	12	−1	0
22.6	1964	**Johnson (D)**	Goldwater (R)	61.1	90.3	2	36	4	32
18.8	1904	**T. Roosevelt (R)**	Parker (D)	56.4	70.6	1	44	2	51
17.8	1932	F. Roosevelt (D)	**Hoover (R)**	57.4	88.9	12	97	20	149
17.7	1984	**Reagan (R)**	Mondale (D)	58.8	97.6	−1	16	0	−10
17.5	1928	Hoover (R)	Smith (D)	58.2	83.6	8	32	2	23
15.4	1956	**Eisenhower (R)**	Stevenson (D)	57.4	86.1	0	−2	−1	−20
14.4	1912	Wilson (D)	**Taft (R)***	41.8	82.0	7	61	19	119
Big Wins									
10.8	1952	Eisenhower (R)	Stevenson (D)	55.2	83.2	1	22	6	50
10.0	1940	**F. Roosevelt (D)**	Willkie (R)	54.7	84.6	−3	5	−10	−67
9.7	1980	Reagan (R)	**Carter (D)**	50.8	90.9	12	34	15	49

Moderately Competitive

8.5	1908	**Taft (R)**	Bryan (D)	51.6	66.5	−1	−4	2	−32
8.5	1996	**Clinton (D)**	Dole (R)	49.2	70.4	−3	2	−12	−52
7.7	1988	G. Bush (R)	Dukakis (D)	53.4	79.2	0	−2	−8	−7
7.5	1944	**F. Roosevelt (D)**	Dewey (R)	53.4	81.4	0	20	−9	−25
6.9	2008	Obama (D)	McCain (R)	52.9	67.8	7	23	12	54
6.1	1900	**McKinley (R)**	Bryan (D)	51.7	65.3	0	13	7	−6
5.6	1992	Clinton (D)	**G. Bush (R)**	43.0	68.8	1	−9	2	−2

Squeakers

4.5	1948	**Truman (D)**	Dewey (R)	49.6	57.1	9	75	−3	21
4.3	1896	McKinley (R)	Bryan (D)	51.0	60.6	5	−48	9	−12
3.1	1916	**Wilson (D)**	Hughes (R)	49.2	52.2	−2	−16	3	−77
2.5	2004	**G. W. Bush (R)**	Kerry (D)	50.7	53.2	4	3	5	11

Dead Heats

2.1	1976	Carter (D)	**Ford (R)**	50.1	55.2	1	1	5	50
0.7	1968	Nixon (R)	Humphrey (D)	43.4	55.9	7	4	11	52
0.2	1960	Kennedy (D)	Nixon (R)	49.7	56.4	−1	−20	13	29
−0.5	2000	**G. W. Bush (R)**	Gore (D)	47.9	50.4	−5	−2	−5	−7

Note: Incumbents in bold.
*In 1912, although Taft was the incumbent, Theodore Roosevelt actually came in second to Woodrow Wilson. Wilson's margin of victory is thus calculated for the differences between him and Roosevelt.

Harding's twenty-six-point thumping of James M. Cox in 1920; (2) the big wins (10–12 percent), with Ronald Reagan's 1980 victory over Jimmy Carter being the most recent; (3) the moderately competitive races (6–9 percent); (4) the squeakers (a margin of 3–5 percent), of which George W. Bush's 2004 victory was the squeakiest; and (5) the dead heats (a margin of less than 2 percent), which must include George W. Bush's election of 2000, when he lost the national popular vote.[2]

Obama's victory fits into the moderately competitive category. This designation also happens to correspond to the "feel" of the race as experienced by the American public. As the election neared, all the major polls had Obama ahead, but a few were at or near to the margin of error. A last-minute swing of only two or three points, in just the right places, could have produced an upset, a possibility that kept many riveted to the press coverage and blogosphere until the very end.[3] But the result, when it was finally called, came as no surprise. When the television networks reported that Obama had won Pennsylvania, Ohio, and Florida, everyone knew the race was over. Unlike 2004 there would be no waiting until the wee hours of the morning for Ohio's results to be known, or as in 2000, until five weeks later, when the contest in Florida was resolved by the Supreme Court of the United States. It was an even greater relief this time to be spared all talk of recounts and litigation. The armies of lawyers that were at the ready, their briefs fixed like bayonets, were demobilized and sent back to their barracks. Something yet to be experienced by Americans coming of political age since 1996 came to pass: the election of a president without accusations of perfidy or ballot manipulation.[4]

In judging the scope of Barack Obama's victory, it is also helpful to narrow the focus to more comparable events and look at the subset of *first-term* presidential victories. Not surprisingly, the larger victory margins have tended to occur in cases where a popular incumbent is reelected, such as Ronald Reagan in 1984 or Franklin Roosevelt in 1936, while narrower margins, including all of the "dead heats," have mostly occurred when candidates ascend to the office for the first time. In this more limited group, Obama fares slightly better on the magnitude scale, ranking tenth among the sixteen first-term presidents. His victory was not as large as Ronald Reagan's in 1980 or George H. W. Bush's in 1988, but it was greater than Jimmy Carter's in 1976, Bill Clinton's in 1992, and George W. Bush's in 2000. Indeed, Obama had the largest victory margin of any incoming *Democratic* president since FDR in 1932. Perhaps he should have been in that convertible after all.

Analyzing the scope of congressional victories in historical perspective is trickier. Much depends on the position from which a party begins; it is obviously more difficult to pick up seats when a party already has a large proportion of them than when it is starting from a low base. Also, the system of congressional elections has changed significantly across time, including the direct election of senators, which began in 1914, and the rules and practices governing the drawing of district boundaries for House seats. Bearing this in mind, however, the Democratic congressional gains, relative to the previous midterm election (2006), falls in the upper range of such congressional victories in a presidential year, ranking the sixth largest in the Senate and the tenth largest in the House.[5] There have been only six presidential election years in which a party has either held its own or won more seats in both the Senate and the House (1912, 1920, 1928, 1932, 1948, 1980). In four of these six (all but 1928 and 1948) party control of the presidency changed, just as in 2008.

Another statistic of interest is the congressional gains for the president's party since the previous presidential election, meaning where the Democrats stand today after the 2008 election relative to where they were after the 2004 election. This is a measure of how the party in Congress fared in *consecutive* elections (see the final two columns of table 1.1). There are even more caveats that could be introduced about this figure, but when all is said and done the 2008 Democratic gain for consecutive elections (with gains in both elections) is striking. It should be ranked about the fifth largest, attaining rough parity with what Republicans achieved with Reagan's victory in 1980, but well short of the party gains that occurred at the time of FDR's triumphs in 1932 or 1936, Harding's in 1920, or Wilson's in 1912. The huge progress for Democrats in consecutive elections takes us to a larger point about the scope and meaning of the 2008 election.

THE BIGGER STORY

The statistics just discussed portray a substantial victory for Democrats. Yet to grasp the full significance of the 2008 election, it needs to be looked at in light of what has happened since the previous presidential contest. The combined impact of the 2008 contests with the 2006 midterm elections dramatically transformed the political scene, turning a red nation into a blue one.

This reversal of party fortunes is all the more important because of what the 2004 election meant for the Republican Party. It produced the high-water mark for GOP performance since 1952, when Dwight Eisenhower was chosen, or arguably since 1928, when Herbert Hoover was elected. Granted, Republicans have won the presidency by much greater margins, including the three landslides of Eisenhower (1956), Nixon (1972), and Reagan (1984). But unless one counts 2000, when the Republicans limped into control of all three institutions while losing the popular vote for the presidency and managing only a tie in the Senate, the 2004 election was the first since 1952 in which

Republicans emerged holding a majority in all three branches. It was the first time in this period that they could truly be called the "governing party." (Democrats by contrast have held majorities in all elected federal institutions five times, following the elections of 1960, 1964, 1976, 1992, and now, of course, 2008.) And 2004 was the only time since 1952 that Republicans won each branch *and* gained ground in each institution. In 2004, Republicans were in a stronger position in the Congress than at any time since 1929.[6]

The Republican victory in 2004 thus fulfilled, at long last, one of the hopes of the "new" Republican Party forged under Ronald Reagan in 1980. Beginning in that year, Republicans achieved some notable victories: Reagan's own election along with a Republican Senate (but still a Democratic House), then the stunning 1994 GOP congressional victory in both the House and Senate during Bill Clinton's first presidential term. Yet Republicans never, as has been noted, achieved a majority across the board. Many analysts viewed 2004 as a threshold election, a launching pad from which the GOP would ascend to win a more commanding majority status. A brief glance at book titles published after the election, among them *One Party Country* and *Building Red America*, were indicative of this assessment.[7] Speculation abounded that the GOP could win that most coveted and elusive of prizes in American electoral politics (if it exists at all), the electoral equivalent of the Holy Grail—a favorable partisan realignment. Karl Rove, whom President Bush called "the architect," had the blueprint on his desk.

But as the Biblical verse so aptly puts it: "O how the mighty are fallen." By 2006 Republican hopes of realignment had become little more than fond memories, and following the 2008 elections they were distant memories as well. Republicans have fallen to their lowest point since the beginning of the Reagan era. They have begun to dig in for the long haul, looking to figure out a recovery strategy while taking cover in their foxholes. And Karl Rove has traded in his architectural license for a post as a television commentator.

American elections are much more than contests between political parties. Our political system, in contrast to those in most other advanced liberal democracies, retains important elements of the "classical" understanding of political representation, in which candidates are chosen on the basis of their individual qualities, their own political viewpoints, and, in the case of legislators, their record in helping their constituencies—not simply on the basis of their partisan affiliation. That said, the partisan dimension of electoral contests remains important. It is of special interest to students of elections because, unlike individuals who come and go, the parties endure and their records can be compared across different time periods.

To describe party strength in the most comprehensive terms, taking account of both the federal and the state levels, it is necessary to look at election results for the six major offices in the American political system: the President, the Senate, and the House at the national level, and the governor and each of the two legislative chambers at the state level. (Only Nebraska has a unicameral legislature, in which there is no formal partisan division.) Table 1.2 shows the standing of the two parties across the range of these six institutions following the elections of 2004 and 2008.

In writing this series of books over the years, we have boldly gone where none have gone before, experimenting with the use of a single number, the Major Party Index (MPI), to chart the strength of the parties at two-year intervals, based on their electoral performance across these six offices.[8] The MPI can be thought of as the Dow Jones Index of politics, a rolling average of party strength. (Though, since not all offices have elections every two years, a few assumptions and statistical artifices must be introduced.) Like any such index, it pulls together diverse areas that, for many purposes, are better analyzed separately. But it does provide a good starting point and a bird's-eye view of the political landscape. The MPI shows the sweeping changes of party fortune over the entire period and the notable rise of the Democrats since 2004. A cautionary note, however, is in order, especially after the stock market crash of 2008. Like the Dow Jones average, the MPI is a descriptive index, not a tool for prediction. Pollsters beware.

WHERE ARE WE?

Two questions flowed from the results of the 2008 elections and the more general upsurge of Democratic strength since 2004: first, did the election of Barack Obama spell the end to nearly a three-decade period commonly referred to as the "Reagan era"? and second, did this election signal the beginning of a long-term electoral realignment in favor of the Democrats?

Historians have adopted the "Reagan era" label not for partisan reasons, but in recognition of the Reagan presidency's deep influence, which stretched beyond its own years and helped define the categories of much modern political debate. It has been said that all elections are equal, except that some are more equal than others. Reagan's 1980 victory over Jimmy Carter is one of those contests that historians place into the elite club of "key" elections.

Certainly, this is how Republicans looked at the historical record. Ever since Reagan led a broad-based conservative movement that took control of the GOP in 1980, Republicans have viewed him as an icon. All Republican presidential candidates in this period sought to claim his mantle, from George H. W. Bush in 1988 and 1992, to Bob Dole in 1996, to George W. Bush in 2000 and 2004. John McCain, though a self-described maverick, was no

Table 1.2. Strength of Parties, 2004–2008

| | Presidential | Congressional | | Gubernatorial | State Legislatures* | |
		House	Senate		Lower	Upper
2004						
Republicans	51%	232	55	28	25	24
Democrats	48%	202	44	22	23	25
2008						
Republicans	46%	178	41	21	16	20
Democrats	53%	257	58**	29	32	28
Swing to Democrats	+5%	+55	+14	+7	+9	+3

Note: Ties (one in each chamber in both years) are not counted.
*Expressed in numbers of chambers held. Nebraska is excluded because of its nonpartisan legislature.
**Excludes Minnesota's disputed Senate seat.

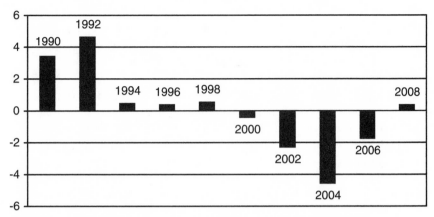

Figure 1.1.   Major Party Index, 1992–2008 (higher number indicates greater Democratic Party strength)

exception. He regularly reminded his audiences during the primary contests that he had been "a foot soldier in the Reagan Revolution."

Reagan's influence has also been felt on the Democratic side, though obviously in a different way. Democratic candidates, unable to ignore his figure looming in the background, have sought either to measure up to him or to displace him. In a comment that generated a huge controversy during the Democratic primary contest, Barack Obama acknowledged Reagan's continuing presence in American politics: "I think Ronald Reagan changed the trajectory of America. . . . He put us on a fundamentally different path. . . ."[9] Obama's opponents pounced on him for violating his party's commandment to speak no good of Ronald Reagan, but the vehemence of their protests only seemed to confirm Obama's point.[10]

The Reagan era might be defined in a number of interlocking ways. Reagan built and bequeathed a potent electoral coalition that made Republicans much more competitive for the presidency, both houses of Congress, and state governments than before his presidency. Conservative policy departures were much more likely to be considered and adopted, as well; indeed, there was a general conservative thrust to policy, though liberals were hardly without their own victories. Governance under Reagan improved the public's perception of Republican performance in both the foreign and domestic arenas. And Reagan himself remained a figure who was affectionately remembered by a majority of Americans and served as the most recent transformative president. In each of these respects, 2008 showed the potential to mark the end of the era.

Reagan remained widely popular, but the simple passage of time erodes memory. Young voters, who went overwhelmingly for Obama, had scant recollection of "The Gipper" or of the crises of his day. New crises, and a new commanding figure, have filled the vacuum for them.

The Reagan coalition, if it was not shattered, at least shrank in 2008, and many analysts believe that it is destined to continue shrinking. Republicans themselves now suspect that the old coalition might no longer be enough, even in circumstances more auspicious for the GOP than 2008.

The public agenda has turned, at least for a time, toward greater regulation, more centralized government, and greater confidence in federal activism—a trend which, it should be noted, predated Obama's victory and undoubtedly contributed to it. A certain intellectual exhaustion seems to have set in among conservatives.

Perhaps most importantly, the Republican reputation for competence in both foreign and domestic affairs won during the Reagan years—arguably the basis for the strength of their coalition and their influence on the policy agenda—lay in shambles. The progression of this process is important to grasp, because it explains not only 2008 but much of electoral history since 1980. In sum: Reagan, who was elected in a moment of both foreign and domestic crisis, resolved both crises to the satisfaction of most voters. By his departure from office, the United States was on the verge of total victory in the Cold War, and a growing, noninflationary economy had replaced the stagflation of the 1970s. George H. W. Bush, if anything, enhanced the Republicans' edge on national security with the final denouement of the Cold War and the U.S. victory in Kuwait, but a mild recession dampened (but did not destroy) the Republican reputation on the economy.

Precisely because of this success in foreign affairs, which resolved most feelings of threat and left the United States in a commanding position, Americans ceased to cast their votes on the basis of foreign policy. Every election, national and congressional, from 1992 through and including 2000, was based on domestic politics. This fact helped account for the Democrats' resurgence under Bill Clinton. Nevertheless, Republicans retained a sufficient domestic reputation to seize control of Congress and force Clinton to the right on spending and welfare.

Everything changed with the attack of 9-11. The foreign policy and national security dimension returned to national consciousness and was the dominant, though not the exclusive factor, in the elections of 2002, 2004, and 2006. In 2002 and 2004, the return of this dimension worked overall to the benefit of the Republicans, helping to account for their surge. George Bush and the Republicans were seen as the better protectors of national security, even if by 2004 there were widespread doubts about the Iraq War that galvanized the Democratic Party. By 2006, the general security concern was over-shadowed by dissatisfaction with the Iraq War.

The sequence of events in George W. Bush's second term, playing out in the elections of 2006 and 2008, represented a collapse of the Republican reputation on both fronts. Republicans lost control of Congress in 2006 primarily because of a loss of public confidence in Republican foreign policy in Iraq, though domestic mismanagement in Hurricane Katrina and congressional corruption played a part. Then they lost control of the presidency when the economic crisis destroyed public confidence in their domestic stewardship. Each of these elections took place at a high point of public dissatisfaction with (or a low point in confidence in) the Republicans, first in foreign affairs and then in domestic affairs. Aside from the inexorably increasing distance from Reagan and 1980, it is the loss of confidence in both of these realms that bodes ill for a continuation of the Reagan era.

Yet, even the end of a transformative president's dominance seldom means the end of his influence. The American ship of state does not usually turn on a dime, and new policy must take old policy as a starting baseline. The Reagan coalition, while battered, is not dissolved, and much will depend on whether Obama and the Democrats provide it with a diet of solvent or glue, taking actions that entice some elements away or that drive the coalition back together. And Obama himself undoubtedly noticed that one of his most potent promises was to cut taxes for most Americans, hardly a position indicative of the demise of Reaganism.

Of course, the Reagan era could come to a close without a new era of Democratic dominance necessarily taking its place. The concept of party realignment is one of the most contested ideas in political science today. Some argue that it should be retired altogether, while others hold that, shorn of certain outsized connotations, it still adds something to an understanding of electoral history.[11] Whatever the state of the academic debate may be, journalists and political commentators have swallowed the concept whole. Their only battles have been over when and where the last realignment has taken place. The 2008 election provided a rich field for speculation. Scarcely had the ballots been counted than many were ready to declare the Obama victory a realignment. According to *Washington Post* columnist Harold Meyerson, Obama's margins "among decisive and growing constituencies make clear that this was a genuinely realigning election."[12] For John Judis of *The New Republic*, the election "is the culmination of a Democratic realignment that began in the 1990s, was delayed by September 11, and resumed with the 2006 election."[13]

A modest understanding of realignment would conceive of it as a major shift in the relative support for the two parties within the electorate. And since voters' party support is ordinarily durable, resisting many temporary ups and downs, the pattern established in the realignment is likely to continue for some time. A realignment in which the parties change majority status is also likely to be accompanied by a shift in the reigning political ideas, those that set the government's agenda, as well as by a major change in the direction of public policy. To what degree a shift in partisan dominance leads to a shift in reigning ideas, and to what degree a shift in ideas precedes and contributes to the electoral shift, is not easy to untangle.

By this definition, a realigning *election* is probably a misnomer. An election may provide the opportunity for change, but the resulting shift in party support is only solidified afterwards, in the people's judgment of the performance of the party that has won power. Realignment is, at least partly, a function of governing. It follows that a realigning election is something that can only be determined retrospectively. It is a status projected back on an election in light of what happens afterwards. This fact helps account for why 1932 (FDR's election), but not 1920 (Warren G. Harding's election), is usually counted as a realigning election.

Yet even if there are such things as realignments, their significance for electoral outcomes can be—and has been—greatly exaggerated. A realignment is only part of the story of electoral politics. It is not a guarantee—nowhere close to it—that the stronger party will *win* any given future election. Presidential elections are influenced both by the alignment (meaning the tendency of partisans to vote their party preference) *and* by a relatively freestanding assessment made by many voters at each election on the performance of the incumbent and the incumbent party, weighed against the merits of an alternative. With the exception of perhaps one or two periods in American history, when the alignment may have provided one party with a truly commanding lead over the other, the aligned portion of the electorate is too small relative to the assessing portion to decide the outcome. Students of elections indirectly confirm this fact every four years. In the models used to predict elections, the relevant factors focus on various aspects of the voters' assessments of current conditions and candidates. The alignments will have some influence on that assessment for much of the electorate, but it is the *assessment* itself that is the most reliable predictor.[14]

What an alignment in a party's favor provides, therefore, is an advantage, all other things being equal. But all things rarely are equal in politics. Politics is often the realm of the new, the unpredictable, and the unique, be it the attack of 9-11 or a financial shock of massive proportions. How long an alignment itself will last is always dependent on political events. Even the advantage that an alignment bestows is slightly countered by the tendency of the party holding power to accumulate, over time, more grievances than new support.

Without being able to judge the performance of a president in office, talk of realignment would seem to be premature—though this proves to be no deterrent, of course, to commentators offering their speculations. Those making the case for 2008 as a realigning election emphasize the "growing constituency" argument. As early as 2002, John Judis and Ruy Teixeira contended that the demographic outlines of a new Democratic era were becoming visible, and that this majority would assert itself by 2010.[15] Obama, it is said, captured the parts of the electorate that are growing on their own: Latinos, the youth vote, and professionals. Obama won 66 percent of the Hispanic vote, a group that proved even more important in some key states, such as New Mexico, Colorado, and Florida, that flipped to Obama; he won 66 percent of voters between the ages of 18–29, which can accrue long-term payoffs, as these voters will come to constitute a larger portion of the electorate, and as first-time voting also often establishes a long-term pattern of allegiance; and he did remarkably well among the highly educated (or at least long-schooled).[16] In total, Obama was the first Democratic candidate for president to win more than 50.1 percent of the vote since Lyndon Johnson in 1964, as nine states shifted from Republican to Democrat from 2004 to 2008. Indeed, Obama was only the second non-southern Democrat in U.S. history to receive more than 51 percent of the vote (FDR was the other).[17] Democratic pollster Peter Hart, looking particularly at the lopsided win for Obama among young voters, contended, "This was a transformational election. Whatever used to be true is not going to be true for the future. We are headed towards a potential center-left nation of tomorrow."[18] The summary, in the words of Harold Meyerson, is that "the future in American politics belongs to the party that can win a more racially divided, better educated, more metropolitan electorate."[19] That party is the Democrats.

This prophecy, others suggest, is based on nothing more than reading the results of the current election into the future. There is another way of looking at 2008. Despite the burdens of a highly unpopular incumbent, a financial crisis, and a massive disadvantage in campaign resources (all temporary factors), John McCain was in a competitive race until the end. The size of Obama's win was solid but not overwhelming, coming in a bit under Bill Clinton's 1992 showing in electoral votes. Most groups that had voted Democratic in 2004 did so again in 2008, just more so; most groups that voted Republican in 2004 did so again in 2008, just less so. Few groups actually switched allegiance, and it was hard to identify a new cross-cutting issue basis for a radically new partisan alignment. Is it not possible to imagine, under different circumstances, a swing (or a swing back) of 3 or 4 percent of the electorate to the Republicans? For one thing, the gap in voter identification that opened up between 2004 and 2008 was due much more to a decline of Republicans than to a gain of Democrats. Furthermore, while a bare majority of 51 percent said they thought government should be doing more, there was no evidence of a decisive ideological shift in Americans' thinking. The proportion of voters describing themselves as liberal, moderate, and conservative stayed roughly the same as it was four years ago. It is possible, of course, that a Democrat could capture more moderates, but there is no guarantee of such a result. As pollster Andrew Kohut of the Pew organization argued, "There's no indication that ideology drove this election. It was driven by discontent with the status quo."[20] For his part, commentator Michael Barone held Obama's election to be, first and foremost, a victory of unflappable temperament in unstable times, saying, "The Democrats' victory—and Barack Obama's—was overdetermined and underdelivered."[21]

In short: It depends on what happens. Kohut predicted, "Everything will depend on the success Obama has. If the new administration takes us left and it works, then people will be won over."[22] Quite a prediction. Change the words "Obama" to "Bush" and "left" to "right" and the same thing could have been said after the election of 2004. One Democratic consultant wrote, "We will not know if 2008 was a realigning election until we know if the Obama administration has been successful enough to keep its majority coalition intact. Our nation faces daunting domestic and foreign challenges, and Obama's success is not assured."[23] Analysts David Brady, Douglas Rivers, and Laurel Harbridge contend that a Democratic realignment is the more likely scenario, but that it is also possible that events or Democratic mistakes will produce a new swing in fortunes.[24] In short, Obama's performance "could determine whether the 2008 election turns out to be a long-term Democratic realignment for Democrats or a one-time repudiation of an unpopular Republican president at a time many Americans are unnerved by economic turmoil."[25] As Republicans discovered after 2004, four years is a long time in the political world. The definitive pronouncement on the realignment must await the election book of 2016. Orders are now being accepted.

THE CHOSEN ONE: SIX KEYS TO THE
SUCCESS OF BARACK OBAMA

Given widespread dissatisfaction with the Republican administration, the Democratic nominee (whoever it was) was bound to enter the race as the favorite. For Barack Obama, winning the nomination was therefore a greater challenge than winning the general election. Capturing the nomination required him to topple a formidable and well-established candidate, Hillary Clinton, who had a national political "machine" attached to her and her husband. The general election, by contrast, was Obama's to lose. His task was to pass a threshold of acceptability for an electorate prepared to make a change. This required, in his case, allaying concerns about his political inexperience and demonstrating that he possessed the judgment and maturity to be president. In this task, it was critical to avoid the rookie mistake or the major error. That he managed to do.

The factors that help explain success in the nomination and general election are not identical. It is possible nevertheless to identify six "keys" that operated throughout the campaign and that helped Obama to achieve victory.

Key #1: Barack Obama articulated the dominant themes of the 2008 election, which were "change" and "post-partisanship."

Presidential campaigns can appeal to the electorate on as many as four different levels: They speak of the personal qualities of the candidates ("experienced," "a hero," "intelligent," "steady"); they talk about the candidates' records and positions on major issues (the economy, national security, proposals for health or for taxes); they can stake out a general programmatic or ideological direction ("conservatism," "a New Democratic agenda," "compassionate conservatism"); and they can elaborate general themes ("outsiderism" or "change"). The first two—personal characteristics and issue positions—are always present. The other two appear at the discretion of the candidates.

The 2008 campaign was notable for the absence of any appeals at the programmatic level. Neither Obama nor McCain adopted an ideological label akin to Clinton's "New Democratic agenda" or to Bush's "compassionate conservatism." Obama's slogan, "Change You Can Believe In," provided little clue as to his general policy direction, much like McCain's boast of being "a maverick." McCain did step into ideological territory toward the end of the campaign, but did so in a "negative" way, accusing Obama of having "the most liberal voting record in the United States Senate." But McCain did not go on to characterize himself as a conservative. What provided coherence to the 2008 campaign was not a general ideological program, but a set of thematic appeals. And it was Barack Obama who supplied those themes. He managed, almost exclusively, to frame the race.

Imitation is the sincerest form of flattery. Candidate after candidate went up against Obama, attempting to frame the election on his or her own terms, only to accept in the end the themes that Obama had introduced. First, there was the idea or mantra of "change." How often did Hillary Clinton say, "I have for thirty-five years been an instrument and agent of change," or John McCain declare that Obama "hasn't been willing to . . . risk criticism from his supporters to bring real change to Washington. I have."?[26] This theme even

dominated where Obama was not in the race! Following Obama's victory in
Iowa, Mitt Romney arrived in New Hampshire with a hastily constructed ban-
ner of "change" as his visual backdrop. Change then became the theme of
his campaign: "The message I got out of Iowa is that people said they want
change. . . . There's no way Sen. McCain can come to New Hampshire and
say he can be the candidate to change Washington. . . . He is Washington."[27]

Post-partisanship was Obama's other major theme, though he used the
concept more than the word. The term seems to have originated with the
"Governator," Arnold Schwarzenegger, who pledged to eviscerate partisanship *and* bipartisanship in California and move to "post-partisanship," where
"Democrats and Republicans actively give birth to ideas together."[28] Obama
spoke in the same vein, declaring that "we need a new kind of politics, one
that can excavate and build upon those shared understandings that pull us
together as Americans." Like change, post-partisanship—understood more
conventionally as bipartisanship—found its way into the speeches of candidates in both nomination races. Unless a candidate's arm was outstretched,
full-length, reaching across the aisle, he or she was not a bona fide pretender
for the presidency in 2008. And unless a journalist demanded to know how
quickly and how far that arm was really extended, he or she was not a certified member of the Fourth Estate. The post-partisan theme tapped into a
fatigue among many voters with the bitter partisan disputes of recent years;
it expressed a desire for unity. It did not matter that most of those applauding
loudly for an end to partisanship wanted it ended on their own terms; what
counted was the sentiment.

To say that Obama first articulated the main themes of this campaign is not
to say that he always controlled them or that they always worked to his advantage. Beginning with post-partisanship, it is clear that the theme proved helpful to Obama in the Democratic nomination contest. Many Democrats were
concerned from the outset that Hillary Clinton, who had participated in many
of the bitter partisan fights of the nineties, might be too polarizing a figure to
win the general election. Her persistent inability to pass the 50 percent threshold of support within her party, despite being the apparently prohibitive early
favorite, reflected this uneasiness. Obama used the theme of post-partisanship
to attract wavering Democrats, on the grounds that he would have greater
appeal to independents in the general election. It also proved advantageous to
Obama by making a virtue out of necessity. His lack of experience, in comparison to the other candidates, could be recast as a lack of involvement in
the previous partisan wrangling in Washington. Post-partisanship was a way
of saying that he could come into office untainted and begin anew. It was
code for being an "outsider" without carrying unhelpful connotations of
inexperience.

Post-partisanship would prove less helpful to Obama in the general election campaign. The reason lay in that most inconvenient of obstacles: the record. If there was one individual in American politics who had made a reputation for reaching across the aisle, and who had earned the disfavor of many in his own party for doing so, it was John McCain. McCain could convincingly claim—and did regularly—that he had not only "talked the talk but walked the walk"; and he pressed Obama to say when he had actually broken with his own party leadership. McCain's advantage on this point was real, but it never proved decisive. Obama executed what in military parlance would be called a tactical retreat, never fully abandoning this flank but parrying the enemy as he withdrew. But he continued to attack on the other flank.

Change was the theme that defined the 2008 race. It worked on many different levels for Obama, from the metaphysical to the inspirational and all the way down to the practical. Change became something greater than the sum of its parts. As a purely political theme, it served with great effect in the primary contest. Though ostensibly the chief object—that from which we had to change—was the person and policies of George Bush, the real target at this stage was the Clintons—both of them. Hillary Clinton's fate was partially tied to Bill's, offering as she did a return to the Clinton years, absent certain extracurricular activities. As much as most Democrats appreciated Bill Clinton, and felt unable to attack him or his administration head-on, many were also slightly ashamed of his actions as president; and some on the Left intensely disliked his policy moderation. Many were looking for a way, without ever openly admitting regret, to turn the page from the Clinton era. Obama's call for change served as code for Democrats to begin anew and close the book on the Clinton era in the Democratic Party.

This theme also worked well for Obama in the final election campaign. Now the target could really shift to George Bush and the "last eight years" of Republican rule (conveniently obscuring the fact that the Democrats had controlled Congress for the last two). The goal became the inextricable linkage of John McCain to George Bush by way of asking Americans whether they wanted a "third term" for George Bush. Of course, John McCain made every effort to slip this association. Separating himself from the president was one of the chief objectives of his campaign, exhibited in the carefully prepared line (one of his best) in the final debate: "Senator Obama, I am not President Bush. If you wanted to run against President Bush, you should have run four years ago."[29] (Imagine the charges of Obama's inexperience if he had run then!)

But breaking away from his connection to the Republican administration proved a difficult task. McCain not only made a concerted effort to establish distance from the administration, but also attempted to capture the theme of change when he selected Sarah Palin as his vice presidential nominee. The plan was to position the two of them together as a "reform" ticket, two mavericks willing to take on the establishment in Washington and "shake things up." *Reform* was meant to be change on steroids, a replacement agenda that both incorporated and went beyond "mere" change. It was a bold gambit, perhaps under the circumstances a reasonable one, although the conservative columnist, Charles Krauthammer, did not think so: "A fool's errand from the very beginning. It defied logic for the incumbent-party candidate to try to take 'change' away from the opposition."[30]

A potential threat to the theme of change was its very vagueness, opening it to the charge of being an abstract concept without substance. (Alexis de Tocqueville, the great political theorist, once likened an abstract concept to "a box with a false bottom; you may put in it what ideas you please, and take them out again without being observed.") The classic case of exposing a rival's vagueness occurred in 1984, when Walter Mondale attacked Senator Gary Hart's "new ideas" theme with a punch line borrowed from a Wendy's commercial (launched against its fast-food competitors): "Where's the beef?" This example was on the minds of many in Mrs. Clinton's camp when she set about criticizing Obama for being "all talk, no action." The flaw in her approach was that having herself already bought into the concept of change, she had one foot in the door to McDonald's.

Obama thus survived the campaign with his theme of change intact, but with many still asking what it really meant. Besides its purely political uses, it certainly expressed the progressive impulse that has been at the root of the modern Democratic Party since Woodrow Wilson. Change is an appealing idea to a party whose leading thinkers have made "progress" their foundational idea; change, in Obama's lexicon, does not mean just change, but change for the *better*. But a thematic campaign necessarily leaves the country wondering about the specifics, so it came as no surprise that on the day after his election, even Obama's followers were wondering in what direction he intended to take the nation. In certain respects, the emphasis on "change" invited voters to see in Obama what they wanted to see, an invitation made more plausible by his slender public record. The campaign certainly did not fill in all the dots, and the darkening economic conditions left room for even more discretion. Still, when it came to determining the content of change, Obama made it clear, in one of his first press conferences as president-elect, that this remained his prerogative: "Understand where the vision for change comes from, first and foremost. It comes from me. That's my job, to provide a vision in terms of where we are going, and to make sure, then, that my team is implementing it."

Key #2: Barack Obama was a compelling individual candidate who, by the end of the campaign, displayed remarkable flexibility.

The 2008 election stood out in large part because of its distinctive candidates. Recent candidates for the presidency—Bob Dole, Al Gore, John Kerry, and George W. Bush—were all skilled politicians with strong support in their respective parties. But none of them could be accused of being compelling or charismatic. (If some today think of Al Gore, post–Nobel Prize, as a kind of star, it should be recalled that entering the 2000 campaign he had a reputation, justly deserved, for being wooden and boring.) By comparison with these men, both candidates in the 2008 election had "big" stories and personalities: John McCain as a full-blown war hero and Barack Obama as an extraordinary candidate with a distinctively contemporary American success story.

Barack Obama had to stand out. There was no other way an inexperienced first-term senator could take the nomination away from a heavy favorite like Hillary Clinton (and from a former vice presidential nominee, John Edwards, known as a formidable orator). Looking back at all the individuals who have sought their parties' nomination for the presidency, Obama is one of a very few to have won almost entirely on the basis of what they showed of themselves in the campaign itself, as a candidate. Obama first impressed a national audience as the keynote speaker at the 2004 Democratic convention. That speech, along with William Jennings Bryan's Cross of Gold speech at the 1896 Democratic convention, count as the most important addresses in American history for launching a political career in presidential politics. Bryan secured the nomination of his party only a few days later, while Obama had to wait four years. Yet the speech prefigured Obama's appeal as a candidate by showcasing his oratorical skill and message of unity. Next to Obama, John Edwards looked like an understudy.

Obama had the capacity to inspire his audiences. His high-minded oratory seemed to mesmerize listeners, leaving them spellbound. One commentator, Ezra Klein, described the experience as follows:

> Obama's finest speeches do not excite. They do not inform. They don't even really inspire. They *elevate*. They enmesh you in a grander moment, as if history has stopped flowing passively by, and, just for an instant, contracted around you, made you aware of its presence, and your role in it. He is not the Word made flesh, but the triumph of word *over* flesh, over color, over despair.[31]

Although this encomium may sound a little hyperbolic, it was not unusual to hear observers repeat its basic message. The term finally coined to describe the enthusiasm displayed at his appearances was "Obamamania." Audiences reached sizes never before heard of in nomination contests. If it was Austin, it was 20,000; Philadelphia, 35,000; and Portland, 75,000. Everywhere Obama went, he met a sea of supporters; everyone wanted to see him. The conservative writer Byron York, after attending an Obama rally early on (and after surveying the possible Republican opponents), echoed the conclusion of the local sheriff in the movie *Jaws*: "We're gonna need a bigger boat."

But this story did not end where one might have expected. While Obama's rise seemed tied to his inspirational oratory, it was not this quality that won him the nomination or the general election. Almost the contrary. The great risk of an appeal of this kind is that it could not be sustained—either the bubble surrounding the cult of personality would burst or it would provoke an equal or greater reaction. Hillary Clinton began to count on and cultivate this prospect, deriding Obama as a "messiah" who preaches that the "celestial choirs will be singing, and everyone will know we should do the right thing, and the world will be perfect." Her hope was that the spell would be broken and that his believers would cease to believe.

The bubble, however, did not burst in time for Mrs. Clinton. But it almost did during the summer, at the apex of Obamamania, when the phenomenon went global. In July, Obama took a highly publicized foreign trip, visiting the troops in Iraq and then meeting with European leaders on his way back to the United States. The trip was capped off with a public address in Berlin, which drew a vast crowd of 200,000 people. Though hailed internationally as a great triumph, a testimony to Obama's global appeal, there remained another consideration—how did it play in Peoria? What did the folks back home in America think of a candidate for presidency being engaged in such an unusual event? The McCain campaign raised the issue, with a heavy dose of sarcasm, in an ad showing Britney Spears and Paris Hilton and charging Obama with cultivating celebrity over substance. The ad seemed to have hit its target, and the Obama campaign was deeply shaken.

This mistake, however, may have ultimately saved the race for Obama because it occurred early enough to allow for a midcourse correction. Obama concluded that it was time to pull back and curb his grandiloquence. It was a case of less being more. Superman slipped into a telephone booth, took off his cape, and came out as Clark Kent. The image Obama projected for the general election campaign was strikingly different from the one he had presented in the spring. His demeanor was now sober and understated. It was his good fortune, too, that he recaptured the lead after the financial crisis hit in mid-September. Every candidate, of course, prefers to be in the lead, but in Obama's case it was doubly helpful. It spared him the necessity of continually attacking his opponent and answering every charge. He could *afford* to be calm and cool. And it was just these qualities—the qualities of a mature statesman under fire—that enabled Obama to dispel any concerns about his inexperience. The closing "argument" from the Obama campaign on personal characteristics was that Obama was calm under fire, while McCain was volatile and erratic.

Accompanying this flexibility on a grand scale was flexibility on a more mundane scale. After securing the Democratic nomination, Obama quite openly shifted his positions on guns, revision of the Foreign Intelligence Surveillance Act, and other issues, always to a more conservative position. Somehow, he succeeded in doing so without losing the enthusiasm of his liberal base.

Key #3: Barack Obama had an unusually strong—and unusually innovative—campaign organization.

A problem with crediting the victor with possessing a superior organization is that a version of this claim is found in virtually every account of a political campaign ever written. The winning candidate's organization is depicted as a smooth-running operation (with allowance usually made for one critical shake-up along the way); the organization's main strategists—it could be a Dick Morris, a Karl Rove, or a David Axelrod—are heralded as political geniuses, men or women of vast political acumen beyond that possessed by nearly all mortals (sometimes even including their own candidate). On the other side, the defeated candidate's organization is described as weak, chaotic, and dysfunctional; its managers—who even remembers their names?—as mediocre operatives, lacking in skill and imagination.

It defies reason to think that this description is always true. Just as there are candidates with monetary disadvantages who still manage to win, there must be candidates who win despite weaker organizations. The more surprising point, however, is that the claim that organizational superiority breeds victory holds true as often as it does, although not exclusively for the reason that most think. It is not just that a good organization contributes to success, but that enjoying success contributes to a good organization. If a campaign continually performs well and exceeds expectations—which was the case, except for one or two brief periods, for Obama's campaign—this helps to build morale and promote cohesion. The reverse is even more true. Let a campaign fall short of expectations or experience the pressure of falling behind, and things can quickly begin to implode. Every decision is scrutinized by the media, campaign staff begin to lob blame and accusations at each other, and higher-level strategists start to protect their own reputations for the future. The Clinton and McCain organizations both became textbook examples illustrating this point. The wheels simply fell off the Clinton campaign following her defeat in Iowa. There were shake-ups at the top, followed by bitter sniping among factions and a huge public controversy over the salary of one of her key campaign strategists, Mark Penn. John McCain rearranged his staff several times over the course of the campaign, and the final lineup seemed to hang together fairly well until October. But at that point, the pressure of making high-risk decisions that bore no fruit began to take its toll. By the end of the race the organization was in turmoil. Key tactical decisions, meant to remain private, were being announced to the press, and leaks about alleged problems with Sarah Palin—including her "diva" persona, spending habits, and lack of familiarity with basic geography—were coming straight from "unnamed" sources within the campaign.

Yet even discounting for the effects of success, the soundness of Barack Obama's organization stands out. Obama paid a great deal of attention to organization from the start, recruiting quality staff members early on and creating an integrated campaign network across regions, and his upper echelons enjoyed remarkable stability over the long haul. It was commonplace in the campaign for Obama's critics to make light of his leadership credentials by pointing to his chief job experience as that of "community organizer." Obama's supporters could take great satisfaction in their revenge, announcing: "And now you know what a community organizer is!"

The importance of organization as a factor in the Obama's victory was also evident during the nomination phase. For all of Obama's appeal before large audiences, his victory was won in the "trenches," in caucus states, more so than in the primaries. Hillary Clinton narrowly edged out Obama in primary voting, but Obama crushed her in the caucuses.[32] It is in caucus states that organization is at a premium. Had Obama knocked Hillary from the race at the beginning, as he appeared to be on the verge of doing with a (predicted) double-digit victory in New Hampshire, the superiority of his organization might never have become fully evident. But the fact that the race continued, and included caucus contests in many out-of-the-way places (for Democrats), such as Idaho, Montana, and Texas (the caucus portion of that race), meant that the quality of Obama's organization could shine. Obama defeated Hillary Clinton by outorganizing her.

The Obama campaign had certain advantages in building its organization in these caucus states. Obama's constituency included elements that were more readily available to be organized, such as college youth, highly educated professionals, and issue activists who opposed the Iraq War—in brief, those with the skills, tools, time, and money to get involved. Mrs. Clinton's constituency, more working class, downscale, or rural, could not compete. She complained directly of this fact, attacking "the activist base of the Democratic Party . . . [and the] gusher of money that never seems to slow down."[33] The complaints were on target, but to what point? They added up to a concession that Obama's campaign organization was doing a better job than her own.

As for the final election campaign, it is more difficult to say if and how much organization really mattered. Obama's "fifty-state strategy" in the nomination contest (less Florida and Michigan) enabled him to build up organizations throughout the country, though in many cases these were constructed in solidly Republican states that remained Republican in the final election. Still, Obama did flip some states with the help of a very formidable ground game and organization.

Obama's campaign built on some of the breakthroughs pioneered by the Howard Dean campaign in 2004. That campaign had been especially adept at making use of some of the newer methods of communication. Obama's campaign took this to a new level—showing innovation in the use of social networking websites such as Facebook, in text-messaging, and in the reliance on YouTube videos, which brought cyber-celebrity to the amply endowed, postracial "Obama Girl." The Obama campaign had a hip approach to cutting-edge technology, which both reflected and appealed to the huge youth constituency that supported Barack Obama. The McCain campaign could only appear stodgy and square by comparison. Obama was Apple; McCain, PC.

Key #4: Barack Obama demonstrated an unprecedented capacity to raise money—and raise (and spend) it he did.

Barack Obama did not just break records, he shattered every fundraising record for a candidate in a presidential election, in either phase of the campaign. To compare his feat to the annals of sport, it looks like the equivalent of Bob Beamon's long jump at the 1968 Olympic games in Mexico City, a record that bested the previous one not by inches but by feet, and went on to last twenty-three years. There is a good chance that Obama's record, measured in constant dollars—feet and inches are not subject to inflation—could last that long. Obama succeeded in spending his major opponents (both Hillary Clinton and John McCain) into the ground, reducing them both to pleading the virtue of poverty and complaining of their opponent's financial prowess. There is little evidence that these arguments helped. Especially in the nomination contest, where Hillary Clinton began the race as Goliath, complaining about David's advantage won her little sympathy.

A capacity to raise money in presidential contests is important, not just for the things money can buy, such as television and radio ads and salaries for campaign staff, but for its symbolic value. In the early stages of a nomination contest, raising money is, *by itself*, a prime indicator of the seriousness of a campaign, especially in the case of lesser-known candidates who are trying to establish their credentials. Polls are of little utility at this point. Barack

Obama scored a huge coup in the first months of 2007 by far out-raising all of Hillary Clinton's other competitors, and then, in the second quarter of 2007, by out-raising Clinton herself. This put Obama on the map, earning him a cover on *Newsweek* in July 2007 and lifting him to the status of a major challenger.

Obama may also have gained stature when he opted out of accepting public funding for the final election. Although this choice meant Obama forfeited $84 million in public money, it freed him to continue to raise and spend funds without limits. (By accepting public funding, a candidate must agree to spending limits.) When Obama made this decision in June, reversing his earlier commitment to take public financing, it looked like it could jeopardize his claim to be a different kind of politician. He would now be charged with slaying the sacred cow of the reform agenda, public campaign financing (that cow had already been partly dispatched for Democrats when Howard Dean and John Kerry opted out of public funding for the nomination phase in 2004). Obama justified his decision on the grounds that the existing system was broken, that Republicans had proven more adept at getting around it, and that his fundraising program was, in effect, a system of public finance due to the vast number of citizens contributing to it.

There is no evidence, however, that this decision cost Obama much more than a debating point. To be sure, modern-day reformers who had championed campaign finance reform over the years all issued stern protests. But one will search in vain for a single one of them who abandoned Barack Obama to vote for John McCain. The McCain campaign sought to make it an issue, immediately declaring that this decision "revealed [Obama] to be just another typical politician who will do and say whatever is most expedient" for his election.[34] But the charge never gained much traction. For most voters, if they paid the matter any attention, Obama may even have gained ground, showing that for all his high-minded rhetoric he was a tough politician who was bent on winning.

In the end, the most valuable thing about money is still its monetary value. The enormous advantage helped—how decisively one can never say—but it provided resources to pour into key contests in the nomination race and into the battleground states in the general election. Obama was able to outspend his rivals wherever and whenever he chose, which included the luxury of buying air time for a thirty-minute prime time broadcast only days before the election. No campaign manager would ever disdain such an advantage.

Key #5: Barack Obama is an African American.

The issue of race had effects so various and complex—and so important— that they will never be fully fathomed. Race was only occasionally right at the surface (as in Obama's Philadelphia speech addressing his relationship with Reverend Wright), sometimes just beneath the surface (as in the symbolic date chosen to deliver his nomination acceptance, the anniversary of Martin Luther King's "I Have a Dream" speech), and most often beneath the surface of the surface (as in the constant agonizing among McCain staffers over what ads to run or what photos to use, so as to avoid provoking charges of racism). A noted historian, Wilfred McClay, aptly observed that "in the guise of being a post-racial election, [2008] was entirely and almost exclusively a racial one, although in ways that were rarely stated, since acknowledging them explicitly would break the spell and banish the magic."[35]

It is best, ultimately, to think of the question of race in the campaign as a bundle of different issues, but the sum total of all of them seems, on balance, to have worked in Obama's favor. It did so, however, not automatically and alone, but through the application of much political skill on Obama's part. This positive effect needs to be compared to the role that race played in the case of the other African American candidate who ran with some success for the Democratic nomination in 1984 and 1988, Jesse Jackson. Jackson received mass support from the African American community, a fact which clearly helped his candidacy; but race also placed a ceiling on the heights he could attain. Jackson was first and foremost a black leader who had never held an elective office; and his formidable rhetorical skills were most clearly those of a black preacher (as was the case with Al Sharpton in 2004). Barack Obama, by contrast, was a politician who had broken through to be elected senator of a major state. More important, his image and demeanor were different. His rhetorical style was inspirational but not directly in the sermonizing mold, and in debate and interview appearances he sounded just like the Harvard-educated lawyer that he was, only much better. Commentators looked carefully for ways of saying that Barack Obama was the first "serious" African American candidate for the presidency without seeming to disparage the accomplishments of Jesse Jackson. What they meant was that Obama could be accepted by white Americans more as a politician than as a black leader: he could be nominated and elected president, while Jesse Jackson could not have been. No one said it better—or more maladroitly—than Joe Biden, Obama's eventual vice presidential pick, who characterized Obama in early 2007 as "the first mainstream African American who is articulate and bright and clean."[36]

Barack Obama did not, however, seek chiefly to acknowledge and then transcend race, as Colin Powell might have done had he run for the Republican nomination in 1996. Race was essential to Obama's advancement. It could not be otherwise within the Democratic Party, where group identities play so prominent a role. The question of identity, as stressed in Obama's memoir *Dreams from My Father*, was the central theme in the story of his personal development. The child of a white mother and an African father who was raised mostly by his white grandparents, Barack Obama had to make important decisions as a young man about his identity. He could have insisted on a multiethnic label, but he consciously chose an African American identity; this choice was reinforced by his marriage to Michelle Robinson, whose heritage was tied directly to slavery, and by his entrance into politics in Chicago. The important point here, however, is not a biographical, but a political, one. At the outset of the 2008 campaign, many in the African American community raised questions about his status as an African American, whether he was "authentically black enough."[37] Obama had to deal effectively with these questions because the support of the African American community was a crucial component to gaining the nomination. He could not hope to win without it.

Yet, at the same time, Obama needed to be seen as a politician who also happened to be black, rather than as a black politician. Americans were looking for a *president*, and for that role, the race question was secondary. Overemphasizing race would not help Barack Obama be nominated or elected. This element of the equation became clear in the eruption of the "Wright affair" in March, the first genuine crisis in the Obama campaign. Jeremiah Wright Jr., Obama's longtime pastor and spiritual advisor, was seen in video footage distributed to his own church membership expressing an extensive array of anti-white and anti-American ideas and sentiments. Race now moved center stage, with Obama being called upon to define his relationship to Wright and his views. After demurring for some time, Obama decided to address the matter in a speech that was widely credited for its care and depth. Obama disassociated himself from Wright's views, but would not repudiate him entirely.

Obama's speech was considered by commentators and intellectuals as an occasion for inaugurating a great "conversation" about race in America. This intellectual enthusiasm for a dialogue illustrates the vast disconnect between culture and politics: from a political standpoint, a continuing "conversation" about race was the very last thing that the Obama campaign wanted or needed. The Wright affair made clear that, for Obama, the optimal position for race in the campaign was largely beneath the surface. When incorporated in a favorable way, such as celebrating the accomplishment of an African American and congratulating voters (or voters congratulating themselves) for making progress on racial questions, it could be beneficial; and it also proved useful in warding off certain kinds of criticisms that might be made of Obama. But in the end, it was not the Philadelphia speech, the launching of the conversation, that saved him. Rather, the opportunity came when Wright himself deepened the crisis by publicly reiterating some of his themes. Obama was then able to break with him definitively, thus ending the speculation over their association.

Race worked as a positive factor for Obama in two important ways. First, it provided him with a crucial base of support inside the Democratic Party, helping him in many of the primary contests, including such decisive victories as South Carolina early on and North Carolina toward the end. South Carolina was the critical early test, and the African American vote had to be wrenched away from Hillary Clinton. But for every action in politics there is a reaction. Obama's gains in the black community were partially offset by losses among working and downscale white voters, whom Bill Clinton courted on his wife's behalf. The racial aspect of this division was later exacerbated by a self-inflicted error, when Obama, in a "closed" speech given in San Francisco, spoke of Americans in small towns who "get bitter, they cling to guns or religion or antipathy to people who aren't like them . . . as a way to explain their frustrations." These people were of course white, but the point was taken to be not so much about race as about "class," with "class" understood in terms of educational status and sophistication. The anti-Obama sentiment that emerged as a result was demographically racial, but it was inspired by what was seen as a "class" slight coming from the elite.

Second, race provided an enormous reservoir of goodwill and a source of moral authority for Obama with large parts of the educated white professional classes. To look to an African American as a leader (and for this group, a multiracial person was just as important) was a way of participating in historical progress. Indeed, Obama played on this aspiration rather openly. To be part of the movement for Obama was to become part of the "religion" of humanity, to help overcome past (and present) injustice. The religion of humanity represents the secular idea of where the progressive instinct now found in advanced societies is destined to be taking us, if only the correct views are heeded. The sense of riding a wave into the future, a future for the world as well as America, was also strongly felt in Europe. Though present throughout the contest, these sentiments were best expressed in the post-election international commentary. The French newspaper *Le Monde* welcomed his election with the headline, "Happy New Century." The columnist E. J. Dionne noted, "For large parts of the world, his middle name will be an icon, proof of America's commitment to religious pluralism. . . . He is not post-racial. He is multi-racial. The word defines him as a person. It also describes the broad coalition that he built and the country he will lead."[38]

It was such feelings, so strong among large segments of the Democratic professional class, that helped ignite Obama's campaign in the Democratic contest and that led many to abandon Hillary Clinton. Despite embodying the cause of gender equality, the feelings she evoked paled in comparison to this sentiment in favor of progress and the religion of humanity. The power of this sentiment was evident in this part of the electorate's reaction to Sarah Palin. Forget that she was a woman; the important point was that she represented *opposition* to the religion of humanity. To the Democratic professionals, Obama may have *looked* different to many of them (being African American or multiracial), but he spoke the same language; while Sarah Palin might look the same (at least in terms of her race), her language was alien. In the most extreme version of this dichotomy, Palin emerged as disgusting, vulgar, the worst kind of American, while Obama was sophisticated, cool, and verging on European. Sarah Palin was premodern; Obama was postmodern.

Race was therefore far more on the surface during the intra-Democratic nomination contest than it ever was in the interparty final election campaign. In fact, race was rarely mentioned directly by either side in this latter stage, except to commend the historic milestone the Obama campaign represented. The McCain campaign went out of its way to avoid anything vaguely touching on the subject, to the point of banning any mention of the Wright affair. Obama issued one or two preemptive "warnings" regarding the negative use of race, but interestingly, coming directly from the candidate, they seemed to do his campaign little good. Yet the warnings and general suspicions continued from other sources. McCain's ads were heavily scrutinized and often accused of utilizing racially coded appeals. Racism could be present "symbolically" even where it was not immediately apparent or intentional. The overlap between race and class (elitism) that had appeared in the spring resurfaced, as Sarah Palin's populist appeals to middle America were said to be racially charged. There was no avoiding the question of race.

Yet the almost complete absence of this issue on the surface was one of the most remarkable—and important—aspects of the general election campaign. Of course, race played a role in voting behavior. The African American community, already overwhelmingly Democratic, voted even more Democratic in 2008 and turned out in larger numbers. Many others undoubtedly voted against (or for) Barack Obama for reasons related to his race. But, emerging from the contest, there were no visible scars of racism attached to the nation or to the Republican Party. This result leaves open the possibility that, like the question of Catholicism after the 1960 election (where John Kennedy's religious affiliation was considered), race will diminish as an issue in national electoral politics in the future.

It is impossible in speaking of race not to digress and say a word about gender, for as fate would have it both of these issues figured prominently in the 2008 election. Presidential campaigns are of interest chiefly for their political consequences—for which candidate and party wins and loses. But in the midst of these events, and as a by-product of them, cultural themes emerge and are aired in interesting ways. The political stakes involved sharpen the discussions, but they also distort them, forcing people to make their cultural views fit their political preferences. Gender had two "moments" in the campaign. In the first, during the nomination contest, race and gender competed for preeminence. Hillary Clinton had the bad fortune to mount her campaign to be the first woman elected president at the same time that Barack Obama was seeking to become the first African American to be so. As mentioned earlier, within the professional classes of the Democratic Party and among the young, race carried the day over gender. Some feminists expressed bitterness at the result, viewing the contest more in terms of male imposition of the glass ceiling.

The second moment occurred with the choice of Sarah Palin as the Republican vice presidential nominee, a "first" for the Republican Party. She made a direct appeal to some of the disappointed followers of Hillary Clinton, but the real story from the cultural standpoint became the internecine warfare that broke out between feminists. On one side, and in a distinct minority, were those who wanted to recognize the accomplishments of a woman who had achieved a position of high standing in American politics. On the other were those who deplored Sarah Palin's political views and her strong antiabortion and pro-family choices. The merits of Sarah Palin as a candidate aside, she became a symbol in this cultural struggle and found herself subjected to the type of attacks Clarence Thomas received from some in the civil rights community when he was nominated to the Supreme Court. This battle raged on and might have continued for the entire campaign had it not been overshadowed, like everything else, by the onset of the financial crisis. It will undoubtedly continue to stimulate debate in the future, if only as a case study for academic courses in cultural studies.

Key #6: Barack Obama enjoyed very positive coverage by the major media.

It was not so long ago that the major media—consisting of the news divisions of the three television networks, the principal national news weeklies (*Time* and *Newsweek*), and the recognized national newspapers (the *New York Times* and the *Washington Post*)—were far and away the main source of news and information for presidential campaigns. Information passed through these sources and was filtered and interpreted by them. The editors, managers, and journalists who held the key positions in these organizations were conscious of their collective power, often referring to themselves as the Fourth Estate.

The near monopoly once enjoyed by this estate is no longer. Cable television, talk radio, and now the Internet (with its own variety of blogs, sites, and postings) have opened alternative pathways for receiving and transmitting information. More and more individuals learn about the campaign from these sources, and the campaigns also make use of them on a regular basis. The influence of the major media has declined accordingly and along with it a good part of their prestige. Perhaps to their chagrin, a room may no longer fall silent when entered by a reporter from the *New York Times*. Added to the woes of the major media has been an economic crunch due to falling circulation and advertising revenues—leading to budget cuts, staff reductions, and restructuring in many of these organizations.

These changes in the system of communication have been accompanied by changes in the *character* of the information that is transmitted. The major media claimed, in the past, to be disseminating objective analysis and "news," understood as a neutral account of events. This information was meant for the public at large, not for those of one political persuasion or the other. The major media outlets also produced opinion and commentary, but they were explicitly labeled as such and kept separate from the news. In the newer media, much of the interpretive material comes in the form of commentary and opinion writing, and not necessarily designated as such. Readers are generally aware of the persuasion of different sources and select them in accordance with their preferred position. The Internet has clearly brought more information to more people, but it has also further freed them to pick and choose as they wish. The result has been to segment audiences into different groupings, like a series of anthills, rather than gather them together under the unifying umbrella of the old media stalwarts, such as the network news broadcasts.

Such changes, however, should not be exaggerated to the point of dismissing the importance of the major media. Less influence does not mean little influence. Of all of the pieces or parts of this complex system, the major media are still at the center. Even when they are not being watched or read directly, they do the most to fix the subject matter of what is commonly discussed; other media outlets pay attention to them and set their news agendas accordingly. Much of what is found in blogs or on talk radio is commentary on, or complaints about, the output of the major media. The best way to get something talked about—and talked about in a way that others will virtually be compelled to address it—is still to place it in the *New York Times* or the *Washington Post*.

This overview brings us back to the discussion of the sixth key, which is that the major media were partial to Barack Obama. In recent years, it has been increasingly argued by critics that the major media have abandoned their objectivity (though still claiming to possess it) and have slanted news and analysis in favor, overall, of the Democrats. But this time the claim was made that it was slanted, almost as never before, to one individual, Barack Obama, both in the nomination contest against other Democrats and in the general election campaign against John McCain. Analytic studies, themselves subject to disputes, have provided some confirmation.[39] For critics of the major media, a proliferating group, the claim was made more strongly. According to Mark Halperin of *Time* magazine, "It was extreme bias, extreme pro-Obama coverage."[40] Former CBS correspondent Bernard Goldberg published a book entitled *A Slobbering Love Affair*. The title stung, but a few in the media whose conscience is still troubled by professional standards have admitted to awakening to feel some remorse on the morning after.

The reasons for this favoritism toward Obama are not hard to discern. The most innocent would be his newsworthiness; Obama was the new kid on the block, the one initially who was "coming on" from behind (feeding into reporters' never-diminishing love for horse-race coverage), and the one who generated the most interest. John McCain himself had been the beneficiary of this kind of attention in his 2000 nomination race against George W. Bush. But that was eight years before; his Straight Talk Express was now an old story, and he was not campaigning against a conservative. Liberal ideological preference among journalists would be another reason, at least in the case of the race against McCain in the general election. This point has less explanatory punch when considering the Democratic contest itself, where all the candidates were liberal, although Obama was the candidate with the strongest antiwar credentials. But the simplest, and no doubt most important, reason for the journalistic lovefest is that they found in Obama the fulfillment of a collective vision—of what was right for America and for the world. In this they expressed entirely the views of the educated class to which they either belonged or hoped to belong.

Putting these six keys together, it becomes clearer why, in what was already a Democratic year, Obama would not be denied the presidency. Some of the keys were instruments wholly of his own making, others were advantages that came as "gifts" from the outside. But it takes a superior candidate to capitalize on every advantage, and that candidate was Barack Obama. Obama had the ship (unprecedented funds), he had the crew (his organization), he had strong sails (his theme), he had wind to his back (prevailing conditions), and he had his own character and skills as a captain. His course would not take him, however, straight to his destination.

NOTES

1. *Time*, vol. 172, no. 24, November 24, 2008; Ryan Lizza, "How Obama Won," *The New Yorker*, November 17, 2008.

2. For a categorization of presidential elections on a similar basis, see Lee Sigelman and Emmet Buell, *Attack Politics: Negative Campaigning in Presidential Elections since 1960* (Lawrence: University Press of Kansas, 2007).

3. None of the major polls had McCain ahead, but a few of them had him within or just beyond the margin of error. For those interested in the polling industry, solace could be found in the fact that an average of the polls, taken by RealClearPolitics, reflected almost exactly the election result. But individual polls were spread out widely.

4. In 1996, Republicans complained that Bill Clinton's legally dubious fundraising tilted the field; in 2000, Democrats complained about a number of circumstances surrounding George W. Bush's election; and in 2004 the close race in Ohio led to (unsubstantiated) charges of voting-machine fraud.

5. The comparisons between 2006 and 2008 are derived from the CNN Election Center, http://www.cnn.com/ELECTION/2006 and http://www.cnn.com/ELECTION/2008/results/main.results/#val = H.

6. With fifty-five senators, Republicans equaled their largest number in that chamber since 1929 (the GOP had achieved that number on three other occasions, from 1987 to 1989, 1997 to 1999, and 1999 to 2001), and they secured their largest majority in the House since 1929.

7. Tom Hamburger and Peter Wallsten, *One Party Country: The Republican Plan for Dominance in the 21st Century* (New York: Wiley, 2007); Thomas Edsall, *Building Red America: The New Conservative Coalition and the Drive for Permanent Power* (New York: Basic Books, 2006).

8. For a full explanation of the MPI, see James Ceaser and Robert Saldin, "A New Measure of Party Strength," *Political Research Quarterly* 58: 245–56 (2005).

9. Comments made January 16, 2008, in an interview with the *Reno Gazette-Journal* can be found at http://www.openleft.com/showDiary.do?diaryId = 3263.

10. There have been some exceptions to this Democratic rule, notably at Reagan's funeral and when positive invocation of Reagan could be used to attack George W. Bush.

11. David Mayhew, *Electoral Realignments: A Critique of an American Genre* (New Haven: Yale University Press, 2004); James W. Ceaser and Andrew E. Busch, *Red Over Blue: The 2004 Elections and American Politics* (Lanham, MD: Rowman & Littlefield, 2005). Mayhew, in particular, launched a vigorous attack on the idea of realignment, especially in its more rigid form. Instead, Mayhew advised election scholars to free themselves of the bonds of realignment theory in order to see the importance of each election. American political history, Mayhew urged, was not divided into a handful of important realigning elections and a mass of unimportant elections in between. Nor was American political history, or crucial shifts in voting coalitions, tied solely or even primarily to the narrative offered by many of the realignment theorists, a constant struggle between (as Al Gore put it in 2000) the people versus the powerful. Mayhew identified three alternative narratives that explained electoral history much better: war, race, and economic growth. The 2008 election featured all three of Mayhew's alternative themes.

12. Harold Meyerson, "A Real Realignment," *Washington Post*, November 7, 2008, A19.

13. John B. Judis, "America the Liberal," *The New Republic*, November 5, 2008.

14. Of all eight election models published in the political science journal *PS* and a ninth long touted by economist Ray Fair, only one—constructed by Helmut Norpoth—includes any variable to account for realignments.

15. John B. Judis and Ruy Teixeira, *The Emerging Democratic Majority* (New York: Simon & Schuster, 2002).

16. See Curtis Gans, "African-Americans, Anger, Fear and Youth Propel Turnout to Highest Level since 1960," AU News, December 17, 2008, http://www.american.edu/ia/cdem/csae/pdfs/2008pdfoffinaledited.pdf. See also Stephen Ansolabehere and Charles Stewart III, "Amazing Race," *Boston Review*, January/February 2009, http://www.boston review.net/BR34.1/ansolabehere_stewart.php. As Ansolabehere and Stewart point out, "Had Blacks and Hispanics voted Democratic in 2008 at the rates they had in 2004, McCain would have won."

17. There were several non-southern Democratic nominees in the nineteenth century who came close: Samuel Tilden of New York (50.9 percent in 1876), Franklin Pierce of New Hampshire (50.8 percent in 1852), and Martin Van Buren of New York (50.8 percent in 1836).

18. Robert G. Kaiser, "Pollsters Debate America's Political Realignment," *Washington Post*, November 23, 2008, A2; see also Harold Meyerson, "A Real Realignment," *Washington Post*, November 7, 2008, A19.

19. Exit polls accessed at http://www.cnn.com/ELECTION/2008/results/polls/#USP 00p1.

20. Kaiser, "Pollsters Debate"; see also Eric Fehrnstrom, "The Case of the Vanishing GOP Voter," *Boston Globe*, December 17, 2008, A19. Fehrnstrom, a Republican consultant, argued that "The good news is that the worst for Republicans did not happen. There was no major political realignment."

21. Michael Barone, "Triumph of Temperament, Not Policy," TownHall, November 8, 2008, http://townhall.com/columnists/MichaelBarone/2008/11/08/triumph_of_tempera ment,_not_policy.

22. Kaiser, "Pollsters Debate."

23. Bruce N. Gyory, "Is this a moment of shifts made to last? Obama's victory breaks away from past voting trends, making political realignment possible," *Newsday*, November 9, 2008, A54.

24. David Brady, Douglas Rivers, and Laurel Harbridge, "The 2008 Democratic Shift," *Policy Review*, December 2008 & January 2009, http://www.hoover.org/publica tions/policyreview/35390034.html.

25. Susan Page, "In Congress, a Democratic Wave," *USA Today*, November 5, 2008, 1A.

26. YouTube debate July 23, 2007, http://campaignspot.nationalreview.com/post/?q=MTM5ZmRmZTM3ZDhiMmQwODFjNDliYTBmODUwN2E2MTM=. "McCain's 'Change' Speech," http://www.newsweek.com/id/139906 delivered on June 3, 2008.

27. January 4, 2008, remarks delivered at Portsmouth, New Hampshire, http://www .swamppolitics.com/news/politics/blog/2008/01/a_changeed_romney_hits_new_ham.html.

28. Mort Kondracke, "Schwarzenegger's 'Post-Partisanship' Is Model for D.C.," *Laurel Leader-Call*, March 1, 2007, http://www.leadercall.com/cnhi/leadercall/opinion/local_story_064092311.html?keyword=topstory.

29. Final presidential debate at Hofstra University, October 15, 2008, http://latimes blogs.latimes.com/washington/2008/10/debate-transcri.html.

30. Charles Krauthammer, "The Campaign Autopsy," *Washington Post*, November 7, 2008, A19.

31. Ezra Klein, "Obama's Gift," *The American Prospect*, January 3, 2008, at http://www.prospect.org/csnc/blogs/ezraklein_archive?month = 01&year = 2008&base_name = obamas_gift.

32. Jay Cost, "How Obama Won the Nomination," *Policy Review*, August/September 2008.

33. Celeste Fremon,"Clinton Slams Democratic Activists at Fundraiser," *Huffington Post*, posted April 18, 2008, http://www.huffingtonpost.com/celeste-fremon/clinton-slams-democratic_b_97484.html.

34. Michael Muskal, "Obama Rejects Public Financing for Campaign; McCain Attacks Decision," *Los Angeles Times,* June 20, 2008, http://articles.latimes.com/2008/jun/20/nation/na-campaign20.

35. Remarks made by Wilfred M. McClay, Georgetown University, November 21, 2008.

36. "Biden's Description of Obama Draws Scrutiny," CNN, February 7, 2007, http://www.cnn.com/2007/POLITICS/01/31/biden.obama.

37. This phrase came from a question asked of Obama at the CNN/YouTube debate, July 25, 2007. It reflected widespread questions in the African American community.

38. E. J. Dionne, "A New Era for America," *Washington Post*, November 5, 2008, http://www.washingtonpost.com/wp-dyn/content/article/2008/11/04/AR2008110404476.html.

39. See Pew Foundation study, which examined more than 2,400 campaign stories from forty-eight news outlets. It found negative McCain stories outnumbered positive ones by 57 percent to 14 percent in the six weeks from the end of the conventions to the last presidential debate on October 7. Press treatment of Obama was more positive than negative—36 percent favorable to 29 percent unfavorable. Project for Excellence in Journalism, "Winning the Media Campaign: How the Press Reported the 2008 Election," Pew Research Center, October 22, 2008, at http://www.journalism.org/node/13307.

40. Alexander Burns, "Halperin at Politico/USC Conf.: 'Extreme Pro-Obama' Press Bias," *Politico*, November 22, 2008, http://www.politico.com/news/stories/1108/15885.html.

Chapter Two

George W. Bush: The Other Candidate

George W. Bush was not on the ballot in 2008, but he might just as well have been. A central element in Barack Obama's campaign strategy—it would have been the same for any Democrat—was to make the election a referendum on Bush's presidency. According to an in-depth analysis of the Obama campaign written by *The New Yorker*'s Ryan Lizza, Obama's chief strategists, David Axelrod and David Plouffe, believed that, from a tactical view, "all that was wrong with the United States could be summarized in one word: Bush."[1] A referendum in presidential politics, however, is never exclusively a matter of looking *back* and punishing; it must also look forward, treating the past as prelude to the future. As Obama put it, "The biggest gamble we can take is to embrace the same old Bush–McCain policies that have failed us for the last eight years."[2]

There were two premises in this argument: that the Bush presidency failed and should be rejected, and that McCain was Bush. The first (and major) premise went largely unchallenged in the final election campaign, as McCain sought to separate himself from George Bush and become an agent of change in his own right. There were accordingly *two* campaigns in 2008 running against President Bush. Few presidents have been so repudiated in an election year.

Although never extremely popular personally, George Bush nevertheless began his second term in 2004 with a reasonable reservoir of public support. He consequently suffered a precipitous fall from grace. What happened? The Chinese have a concept, dating all the way back to the Zhou Dynasty, known as "The Mandate from Heaven." It refers to the mysterious conferral of favor on the ruler, which, once withdrawn, is irrevocable. Sometime early in his second term, George Bush lost his "Mandate from Heaven," at least as far as public approval was concerned. His approval ratings plunged in such a way that, by the middle of 2006, a reversal seemed impossible, even to the president himself. Yet Bush bore his fate stoically, never complaining of his low standing. Even without public approval, he did not cease entirely to lead. Following the 2006 election he took one of the most important steps of his presidency by ordering an increase of troops in the Iraq War, a decision credited with turning defeat into victory.

Defenders of President Bush argue today that his record, like that of President Truman, will receive a kinder judgment at a later time. Perhaps so. For understanding the 2008 election, however, the question is not the lofty one of the verdict of History, but the more mundane one of the verdict of public opinion. In the realm of politics, the old adage still applies: *vox populi, vox Dei* (the voice of the people is the voice of God).

THE 2004 ELECTION

On the day after the 2004 election, Republicans felt as much relief as satisfaction with the previous day's results. Until the very end, opinion polls for the presidency remained within the margin error, and the outcome of many Senate and House seats also hung in the balance. The results all ended in the Republicans' favor. In an election in which voter turnout increased enormously, President Bush became the first presidential candidate since 1988 to receive more than 50 percent of the vote, and Republicans expanded their majorities in Congress. As always following a presidential contest, a debate immediately ensued about the election's broader "meaning." This debate is part of a politics of interpretation that seeks to create a dominant opinion about how much leeway belongs to the victor.

For some participants in this debate, meaning was best discerned by the method of looking back and analyzing voting patterns and voter opinions. Bush's 51–48 percent win was solid but also unspectacular, the narrowest margin for a winning incumbent since Woodrow Wilson's in 1916. He had coattails, but short ones by historical standards. As many commentators emphasized—mostly in an effort to diminish the victory—Bush issued a strong appeal to the Republican base to eke out every last vote from among his potential supporters. (Democrats were pursuing the same strategy on their side.) But as others pointed out, this strategy applied, as they say in economics, largely at the margins, meaning in the effort to attract the last slice of voters. Looked at in a different light, from the perspective of Bush's effort to attract all of his voters, his strategy was not so narrow or partisan. Bush improved his vote over 2000 among a wide range of Democratic-leaning groups, including women, blacks, Hispanics, and urban dwellers.

The election campaign emphasized national security more than domestic politics. The debate on national security broke down into two dimensions: first, fighting terrorism and keeping the nation safe; and second, the Iraq War. The public trusted Bush more than Kerry on the first dimension, while it showed considerable doubts about the war, where Kerry was preferred. At the same time, and especially in the appeal to partisans, a set of domestic issues focusing on cultural issues (moral values) also figured prominently. Included were questions related to abortion, same-sex marriage, stem-cell research—and therefore, since the Supreme Court is always likely to be involved in these issues, the character of future judicial nominees. Many voted for Bush on the basis of these issues, just as some opposed him for the same reasons. Finally, Bush himself expounded a number of controversial domestic proposals such as the revamping of Social Security.

Viewing the 2004 election in a larger historical perspective, many argued that 2004 was the culmination of a "rolling realignment," in which Republicans had become (albeit narrowly) the governing party by gradually gaining ground at varying levels of government. But setting the flow of history aside, and with it all of the attendant academic questions, for those who were operating in the real world seeking to build and extend this possibility—and this included both President Bush and his chief strategist, Karl Rove—it was well understood that everything hinged on successful governance. That alone could cement a broad coalition whose parts would come to see their interests fulfilled by the ideas and policies of the Republican Party. Creating this coalition meant extending support out beyond the existing voter base of 2004, which afforded only a narrow and precarious lead, and broadening it to include a larger share of Hispanics and an increasing segment of the professional class that would become part of an "ownership society." The key to securing this additional support would not come from the realm of foreign affairs. President Bush had to succeed in this realm or else lose ground, but to win the new majority would depend on the implementation and success of a new domestic agenda.

To the victor goes the spoils, and in the modern age one of the main spoils is getting the first crack at interpreting the meaning of the election. President Bush moved quickly to take advantage of this opportunity at a press conference following the election. His analysis focused less on voting behavior than on a selection of matters he had spoken about during the campaign. Interpretation was the means by which he would win support for what he planned to do in the future. The election, he believed, had conferred "political capital" on him, which he intended to use to push for significant policy change in domestic politics, beginning with Social Security:

> I earned capital in the campaign, political capital, and now I intend to spend it. It is my style. . . . I'm going to spend it for what I told the people I'd spend it on, which

is—you've heard the agenda: Social Security and tax reform, moving this economy forward. . . . For those of you who actually listened to my speeches on a daily basis—you might remember, every speech I talked about the duty of an American President to lead. And we have—we must lead on Social Security because the system is not going to be whole for our children and our grandchildren.

As it turned out, Election Day 2004 was the high point of President Bush's fortunes. Very shortly thereafter it became apparent that either the capital Bush thought he had earned never existed in the amount he thought, or else it was being rapidly depleted by ill-advised political investments and the cruel vagaries of the political market. By the time of the 2006 election, George Bush found himself facing a severe credit crunch.

COLLAPSE OF THE
SECOND-TERM AGENDA: 2005

George Bush's second term was buried early under the wreckage of dashed hopes in Iraq, a series of early setbacks and miscalculations in domestic affairs, and the mishandling of the response to Hurricane Katrina.

The Iraq War was almost always at the forefront of public concern, even when the president would have preferred to have it elsewhere. Bush had staked his all on the war, mortgaging his presidency and his reputation to its outcome. However bold or attractive his new program in domestic affairs might be, the measure of his public standing was certain to be determined more by what was happening in Iraq. As the presidential scholar Richard Neustadt pointed out long ago, a president's standing is a "whole" and cannot be broken into foreign and domestic pieces. Lose that standing, and the entire program of the administration can suffer.

The events in Iraq were now beyond the president's control, at least by the current war strategy to which he was committed. But Bush may inadvertently have upped the ante in his inaugural address, which set forth in lofty terms the aspirations of American foreign policy: "It is the policy of the United States to seek and support the growth of democratic movements and institutions in every nation and culture, with the ultimate goal of ending tyranny in our world." Of course, ending tyranny in our world was a long-term goal, not an immediate guide to policy in every case. But given the context of the problems at hand, it was bound in some measure to be read as the working assumption of the administration. Had the United States gone to war in Iraq for this reason? Having opposed Bush earlier for his allegedly cynical reasons of fighting a war to extend American power, his critics now depicted him as a misguided idealist, out of touch with the realities of international relations. Bush's policy was "Wilsonian."

The great problem for Bush became the mismatch between deeds and words; and the loftier the rhetoric, the greater the mismatch. A growing gap between word and result is fatal for any democratic leader. And this became the stark reality of the Bush presidency. As the matter was later put by Michael Gerson, Bush's chief speechwriter: "Hopes that the war had turned a corner—repeatedly raised by Iraqis voting with purple fingers and approving a constitution—were dashed too many times, until many Americans became unwilling to believe anymore."[3] Those "unwilling to believe anymore" began to grow almost from the moment of the election and continued growing steadily throughout the next two years. Despite administration assurances to the contrary, the U.S. position worsened. Enemy activity increased, as did U.S. casualties. Iraq looked to be a quagmire, not on the scale of Vietnam, but one that was heading to the same conclusion: withdrawal followed by collapse of the government in power. Put more simply, it was defeat, and many asked, "Why prolong the inevitable?"

If there was some hope of slogging through in Iraq and of seeing the situation stabilize or improve, it was dashed by new developments that took place in Iraq in 2005 and culminated in 2006. The fight was really three battles: a war against al Qaeda in Iraq, a fight against the Sunni Baathists who hoped for a Saddamite restoration, and a fight against the Iranian-backed militia of Shiite cleric Moqtada al-Sadr (the Mahti Army). It became the deliberate strategy of al Qaeda in Iraq (AQI) to take advantage of this complicated situation and to provoke a full-fledged civil war along sectarian lines of Sunnis versus Shiites. To this end, AQI began directing a larger and larger proportion of its fire against Shiite civilians, in hopes of initiating a cycle of recrimination and murder. The culmination of this effort came on February 22, 2006, when terrorists blew up the al-Askari Shiite shrine of the golden dome in Samarra, setting off a wild orgy of revenge killings across Iraq. Iraqi civilian deaths skyrocketed from approximately twelve hundred in November 2005 to approximately three thousand in November 2006, and the nation seemed poised on the brink of civil war and social collapse.[4]

Bush, as noted, wanted his second term to focus on his domestic agenda. Under his self-proclaimed "style" of leadership, he urged his administration to think big and take risks. The question was whether his political support was proportional to the size of the ends he sought. The facts were that Republicans were not monolithic and that Democrats still had enough seats in the Senate to sustain a filibuster. These obstacles, combined with the unsteady situation in Iraq, made Bush's high-stake political gambit even more difficult to achieve.

In line with his own bold approach to leadership, Bush decided to spearhead an effort to reform Social Security. Long known as the "third rail of American politics"—touch it and you die—Social Security loomed (and looms) as a major policy challenge. Demographic trends make it likely that the system will begin operating at a deficit in 2018 and will exhaust its reserves by 2042. As Bush observed in his post-election press conference, he had given many speeches in the campaign on Social Security reform, all of which promoted the general idea of allowing workers to divert some of their payroll tax to private accounts that they would own and control. This plan was part of his broader theme of creating an "ownership society."

Bush thus made Social Security reform the centerpiece of his 2005 State of the Union address. Proclaiming, "Our society has changed in ways the founders of Social Security could not have foreseen," he promised to listen to "anyone who has a good idea to offer." His strategy was to avoid getting locked into any specific proposal, but he insisted on some general principles that included personal accounts and no payroll tax increase. Bush followed up the State of the Union with travels throughout the country to drum up support for the initiative. He succeeded in raising awareness of the issue, and polls showed an increasing percentage of Americans who believed that Social Security was nearing a crisis. But he never got much further.

The obstacles Bush faced were significant.[5] First, Democrats, stung by their 2004 losses and fearful of a major Bush legislative victory, consciously took a page from the Republican playbook in the 1993–1994 health care debate and simply chose to say "no." As Republicans had ultimately formed a unified front against the Clinton health care plan, so Democrats formed a united front in opposition to Bush's Social Security outline. Despite numerous entreaties, Bush was unable to lure Democrats into any significant participation in legislative negotiations. Social Security was the crown jewel of the New Deal, and after four years of losing battles big and small, foreign and domestic, Democrats decided to make their no-compromises stand. Above all, they would not countenance any form of private accounts, a proposal that many prominent Democrats had previously endorsed.[6] Partisan polarization helps explain their sudden revulsion at the idea, and they could hardly fail to note that many Republican viewed private accounts as their way to solidify support among a new generation of voters. With only 55 Republicans in the Senate and 60 votes needed to move anything past the inevitable filibuster, Democratic opposition by itself—whatever its motivation—was enough to doom the plan.[7]

If Democrats did not cause enough trouble for Bush on Social Security, Republicans added to his woes. Having chafed for more than four years under the profligacies of compassionate conservatism, many fiscal conservatives were wary of a proposal that assumed the nation would take on $1 trillion or more of additional debt to pay for the "transition costs" associated with even a modest move to private accounts. These Republicans wanted to know what other domestic spending—in or out of Social Security—would be trimmed to help pay for the costs. That was not a discussion the Bush administration wanted to have. House Republicans, who had the muscle to move a bill, did not want to step out first, only to be left dangling if the Senate did not act; yet the Senate could not act because Democrats were united in their opposition.

Finally, Bush's approach proved questionable on tactical grounds. Although he had discussed it on the campaign trail, he sprung the Social Security proposal on the nation without sufficient preparation, and then never went beyond offering a general outline, rather than proposing a specific plan. This was a calculated approach, but it did not succeed. It gave the impression of something half-baked, and left an open field for opponents to fill in the details in the most negative way possible.

In the fall of 2005, Bush's Social Security offensive ended not with a bang but a whimper. There was never a vote, indeed never even a bill—just an idea, not fully formed, that faded away when it failed to gain traction. Bush touched the third rail of American politics and proved once again that it was the third rail.

The debacle of Social Security reform had the effect of pulling down the second major item on Bush's domestic agenda—tax reform—in the undertow. The general idea here was to simplify the income tax, reducing deductions and rates and encouraging investment. Again, however, the details of so vast an initiative had to be worked out. To move this plan forward, Bush appointed Louisiana's former Democratic Senator John Breaux to head a bipartisan tax reform task force. Breaux suggested that the president tackle taxes first, on the grounds that it was easier or more doable. Success here would help build momentum for the more difficult Social Security effort. Breaux was rebuffed, and by the time his task force completed its work, Congress had no appetite for big projects and Bush had little political capital left to push them.[8]

Social Security and tax reform were already in trouble when a natural catastrophe turned into a political catastrophe for George W. Bush: Hurricane Katrina. When the storm itself largely bypassed New Orleans at the end of August, the nation breathed a sigh of relief. But it was short-lived. Under the pressure of sea swells, the levees broke, flooding New Orleans and producing a humanitarian disaster, as hundred of thousands of people either would not—or could not—be evacuated. There were gross failures at all levels of government. Ray Nagin, the mayor of New Orleans, did not execute the city's evacuation plan. Kathleen Blanco, Louisiana's governor, vacillated for critical hours deciding whether to ask for federal help. But whatever the legal issues on responsibility—and they were enormously important from a constitutional standpoint—the political situation was becoming clearer by the hour. The plight of people in New Orleans, seen clearly on television by the American people, had become a national matter. New Orleans was now the federal government's and George Bush's problem. When federal help was requested, it was disorganized, insufficient, and tardy.

Two immediate images, devastating to President Bush, were burned into the public consciousness during the crisis: one was of the president flying overhead in Air Force One, peering down at the twisted scene below, seemingly detached from the suffering; the other was the President congratulating Michael Brown, the head of the Federal Emergency Management Agency, saying, "Brownie, you're doing a heckuva job." He was not, and Brown resigned days later.

Katrina left a third image, more long-term and complex, that shook up American politics in a profound way. New Orleans became a symbol. To many national and international viewers, it was looked upon as a reminder of the old charge that America was a country of two nations, one black and one white, one poor and one wealthy. Of course George Bush and the Republicans had not made New Orleans into what it was; but the fact that there were so many people who remained in such an impoverished condition raised questions. There were two accounts, one that New Orleans was a great exception that proved the failures of welfare state policies, the other that it was indicative of American politics. The latter tended to win out. Katrina was taken as the cue for questioning the economic and tax policies of the Republican Party. It became a rallying point for Democrats, especially the Left within the Democratic Party. Viewing the sorry conditions of poverty in New Orleans, it was proof that trickle-down economics did not work, that government needed to be doing much more. Katrina was seen as a badge of shame, not just in the response, but even more in the situation that produced it. Had Republicans, had George Bush, done enough—or anything—to help the poor and dispossessed? One certain outcome was that George Bush's political outreach to blacks, which had advanced some distance, was permanently set back.

In the short run, Bush appeared to recover from Katrina. His approval ratings, which were in the mid-40 percent range prior to the hurricane, dipped and then returned to that vicinity by December. Yet it was clear that lasting damage was done beneath the façade. Another and more important part of the Bush image suffered. The Bush administration until then had enjoyed a reputation for competence and decisive action in crisis, acquired in the aftermath of 9-11. Even, or especially, among those who opposed the administration, it was thought to be efficient, albeit unscrupulous. George Bush was loathed, but he was not despised. Katrina altered this image. The new one was of an administration that was bungling and incompetent. It was this sign of weakness that now began to feed Democratic hopes.

The aftermath to Katrina—how to deal with it—continued to reverberate. And Republican fiscal conservatives openly revolted against Bush's proclamation that he would spend whatever it took to fix New Orleans, a price tag estimated at $200 billion. Not least, Katrina gave Republican congressional leaders cover to pull the Social Security issue from consideration, though it was already stalled. It never returned.

Following Katrina, the Bush administration seemed temporarily to lose its bearings. Another matter arose that shook confidence in the administration's judgment—this time initially among Republicans. Over Labor Day weekend, Chief Justice William Rehnquist died, leaving Bush a key appointment to the Supreme Court. Already pending was his nomination of John Roberts, whom Bush had nominated earlier in the summer to fill the seat vacated by the retirement of Sandra Day O'Connor. Before a vote could be taken on Roberts, Bush called for Roberts to be made chief justice, and later announced his pick of White House Counsel Harriet Miers for the second seat. Conservatives were shocked. They saw her as a little-known mediocrity whose credentials as a strict constructionist were unclear; meanwhile, there was a sizable pool of experienced jurists from whom Bush could have chosen. Bush's demand that Republicans should "trust him" on the pick—a demand that echoed his father's disastrous (from a conservative viewpoint) choice of David Souter—seemed especially imperious and provoked open rebellion in the ranks. Columnist Charles Krauthammer spoke for many when he wrote that if Miers "were not a crony of the president of the United States, her nomination to the Supreme Court would be a joke, as it would have occurred to no one else to nominate her." Democrats could afford to stand back and watch the spectacle with some glee, as Republicans went after their own president. Conservative reaction was so strong that Miers withdrew her name from consideration, and Bush finally nominated Samuel Alito, who was well received in conservative circles. But the fiasco further damaged President Bush's image during this pivotal period.

Trying to regain the initiative, Bush began a legislative push in the spring of 2006 for the one remaining big item on his domestic agenda: comprehensive immigration reform. The president had signaled his desire for a major guest-worker program for foreign nationals and a "path to citizenship" for illegal aliens as early as 2001. Politically, the White House was also interested in immigration reform as part of its strategy of expanding the Republican Party by bringing in large numbers of Hispanic voters. But heightened public concerns about border security following the attacks of 9-11 caused

Bush to back off. He renewed the push in 2006, despite strong opposition from many Republicans in Congress and from much of the party's voter base. These opponents insisted on gaining control of the nation's borders and reducing the flow of illegal immigration; administration policies on this count, they argued, had been all talk and very little action. Although it might have been possible to deal with the issue sequentially—first, border security, followed by a guest-worker program—Bush insisted on bundling the package. The Senate passed a bill to Bush's liking, but the House passed only a border security bill, and was not particularly interested in reconciling its version with the Senate's. Bush could never bring enough Republicans along, and the bill died. Interestingly, Bush's approval rating dipped to around 30 percent for the first time during the extended debate over his immigration proposal.[9]

By the spring or summer of 2006, the window of opportunity for passing important legislation began to close. "Politics" took over, and members of Congress began to look to the midterm election. The striking fact about the first eighteen months following Bush's reelection was the ineffectiveness of Republicans' unified control of government. Republicans had their only real majority in more than a half century, and they failed to produce any major accomplishments. Whatever the merits of Bush's plans for Social Security reform, tax reform, or immigration reform, one fact stood out: the Republicans had nothing positive to present to the country. Unified control of government had not allowed Republicans to achieve their aims, but it would allow Democrats to hold Republicans to blame.

MIDTERM DEBACLE

The huge Republican losses in the midterm elections of 2006, in which Democrats regained control of both houses of Congress, were all the more striking for being so unexpected. A year or so before the midterm elections, most political analysts judged that Republicans would likely hold their own, or at the very least retain their majorities. Part of this calculation had to do with what was a friendlier than usual terrain for Republicans in the Senate in 2006 and what was thought to be the character of modern House elections.

In the Senate, where the GOP held a 10-seat advantage, 34 seats were up for election, 22 of which were Democratic and only 12 Republican. Democrats entered the year with far more seats to defend. In the House, Republicans held an advantage of 28 seats, and only about thirty contests in the House were thought likely to be close. Many of these were held by Democrats. Democrats, it seemed, would have to "run the table" to hope to gain even the slimmest of majorities. In addition, some leading experts on American politics advanced the thesis that Republicans held a long-term structural advantage in House elections owing to a more efficient distribution of votes, a large number of safe seats, and lucrative fundraising networks.[10] Charles Cook, a renowned analyst of Congress, held that the odds of Republicans losing even one chamber of Congress were one in five.

But politics is a stronger force than most experts ever acknowledge. As the Republican situation deteriorated and the president's popularity declined, Democratic prospects began to look brighter. Republican seats that once looked safe suddenly appeared vulnerable. Setting the grave situation in Iraq aside for the moment, the problems that Republicans were facing in Congress were not only—perhaps not even primarily—attributable to the president, but were of their own making. Many in the majority appeared content merely with holding power, as if it were theirs by right. They did not think they could lose control; and even if some seats were lost, each faction seemed to think that it would come at the expense of a rival faction, thus strengthening its own role inside the majority. But in truth it was the whole party brand in Congress that was suffering.

A series of major scandals wracked the party during this legislative session. They eventually reached a tipping point and created for the Republicans the public image of a "culture of corruption." House Majority Leader Tom DeLay of Texas was indicted for illegally using corporate money to back Republicans in state elections; he ultimately resigned. Congressmen Randy "Duke" Cunningham (R-CA) and Robert Ney (R-OH) pled guilty to bribery charges. Lobbyist Jack Abramoff, who had close ties with many congressional Republicans, faced big legal troubles. Later on, in the midst of the fall campaign, another scandal broke, which touched on the theme of hypocrisy, a flaw that Americans voters seem to understand best and despise most. It became public knowledge that Florida Republican Mark Foley, a known advocate for tough penalties against child sexual predators, had exchanged sexually explicit emails and instant messages with male congressional pages. No laws were broken, but the symbolism was highly damaging to social conservatism. Just as damaging to the Republicans was the revelation that House Republican leaders had known about Foley's activities for some time and had not taken all the steps they could to put an end to them. Of course, there were Democratic scandals too—like the $90,000 in cash found stuffed in Louisiana Democrat William Jefferson's freezer during an FBI raid for a bribery investigation—but nothing really stuck in the same way. Republicans, in charge of the House now for the last twelve years, were at the center of attention.

For their part, Democrats' fundraising throughout 2006 was strong, with

Democratic campaign committees nearly matching Republicans in the House and surpassing them in the Senate. Democrats also pioneered efforts—for congressional campaign committees—to bring in large quantities of small donations through the Internet, more than doubling their take from small donations.[11] The Democrats were also highly successful at recruiting moderate candidates to run in socially conservative areas such as Indiana, Virginia, and the mountain West. Congressman Rahm Emanuel, who would later become President Obama's chief of staff, was the chief architect of the Democrats' strategy and was notable for his role in forcing more moderate candidates on local parties in order to maximize the Democrats' chance of victory. While he bulldozed more than a few persons, his success won him begrudging respect.

The Democrats' playing field gradually expanded, as Republican opportunities contracted. By Labor Day, it was clear Republicans were in for a rough ride, though just how rough remained to be seen. Unlike the 1994 House Republican campaign, which promoted a detailed programmatic agenda (the "Contract with America"), Democrats in 2006 relied on the more traditional approach of the "out" party in promising midterm election years. They asked, "Had enough?" as Republicans had done in 1946, seeking to turn the election into a negative referendum on congressional corruption, Katrina, and, especially, the continuing morass in Iraq. In this task, they were aided immeasurably by Republican missteps, including George Allen's verbal slander of an Indian ("macaca") that cost him his Senate seat in Virginia, and Conrad Burns's ties with Jack Abramoff, which lost a Senate seat in Montana.

In the last stages of the campaign, analysts debated whether the election was more of a nationalized event with the issue of Iraq its most prominent element, or a series of local elections, which had to be examined seat by seat. When the voting was done, the nationalized model, which predicted much larger gains by the Democrats, proved the more accurate one. Democrats gained thirty-one House seats, winning 52.8 percent of the national House vote. They won their six close Senate races, three of them by 2.3 percentage points or less.[12] At the state level, Democrats added seven governorships, obtaining a majority of states for the first time since 1994.

Interestingly, Republican losses were not traceable to large partisan or ideological shifts in the composition of the electorate. In 2004, Republicans were 38 percent of the national House electorate (to the Democrats' 38 percent); in 2006, they were 36 percent (to the Democrats' 38 percent). In 2006, self-described conservatives led self-described liberals in the electorate by 34–21 percent; in 2006, conservatives led liberals by 32–20 percent. Nor, as some hypothesized, were GOP losses attributable to Republicans coming out but voting for Democrats: in 2004, 93 percent of Republicans voted for

Republican House candidates; in 2006, 91 percent. It was not the composition of the electorate or the loyalty of Republicans that shifted dramatically, but the voting habits of certain key groups. In comparison to 2004, Republican House candidates suffered particularly steep declines among male voters (from 53 percent to 47 percent), independent voters (from 46 percent to 39 percent), and Hispanic voters (from 44 percent to 30 percent). They also lost more among self-described conservatives (minus 3 percent) and white evangelical Christians (minus 4 percent) than they had among Republican identifiers.[13] Taking all of this together, Republicans had big problems with Hispanics and with men who were relatively conservative independents (the Perot voters of yore, who had voted Republican for Congress since 1994).

BUSH'S LAST TWO YEARS: STALEMATE

In the aftermath of the midterm elections, the political climate in Washington changed dramatically. Republicans naturally engaged in recriminations. The Democrats with their new majority had high hopes of stepping in and taking over much of the initiative, if not full control, of the policy agenda in the domestic arena. These hopes were held in check, however, by memories of how President Clinton had thwarted the Republicans in 1995. Democrats were thus prepared for frustration, which is largely what occurred in domestic affairs. In foreign affairs, Democrats would be in for the shock of their lives.

On the home front, Bush and the Democrats circled each other warily as the new Congress began. Democrats quickly passed bills to raise the minimum wage and lower interest rates on student loans, which Bush signed. Bush had one hope for moving at least one issue on his agenda, immigration, on which the new Democrats might prove more tractable than the old Republicans. Consequently, Bush made another push for immigration reform in the spring of 2007. A bipartisan deal sponsored by Edward Kennedy and John McCain fell through, as similar efforts had fallen through the year before, mostly on the strength of opposition by Republicans in Congress and a large part of the public.[14] There were criticisms from both ends of the political spectrum, from conservatives for the bill being a grant of amnesty, from liberals for it being too harsh. George Bush's last chance to achieve a major part of his second-term domestic agenda failed unceremoniously.

Otherwise, Bush struck a combative pose with the Democrats in domestic affairs, confronting the majority over spending issues.[15] The president, who had cast only one veto in his first six years, exercised the veto eleven more times through September 2008, eight of them in protest of excessive domestic spending. Expansion of the State Children's Health Insurance Program

(SCHIP) desired by Democrats was stopped by Bush, among other items. Except for a new energy bill, which was taken up and passed in 2007, the result of the relationship between Bush and Congress remained one of stalemate for most of the rest of the term. Only in the aftermath of the financial crisis that struck in September of 2008 did Bush regain a measure of leadership, acting this time largely in concert with the Democrats.

Foreign affairs and national security were entirely different matters, however. A general assumption took hold in Washington that the election results made it inevitable that Bush would bow to public opinion and begin a withdrawal from Iraq. And it seemed for a moment he was prepared to do so, when he accepted—meaning when he asked for—the resignation of his secretary of defense, Donald Rumsfeld. This step was greeted by many with a sigh of relief and taken as a sign of change of policy in Iraq, which it was. Only it was not the change everyone anticipated. Within weeks of the midterm elections, a commission headed by former Secretary of State James Baker and former chairman of the House Foreign Affairs Committee Lee Hamilton issued a long-awaited report on policy in Iraq. Republican Baker and Democrat Hamilton were widely assumed to be providing bipartisan cover for a withdrawal of U.S. forces. Their recommendation was to initiate a withdrawal coupled with enhanced diplomatic efforts to convince Syria and Iran to stop fomenting trouble in their common neighbor.

Faced with rising public dissatisfaction, an election defeat, a hostile Congress, a near consensus among Beltway elites, and spiraling disorder on the ground in Iraq, Bush set aside the Baker–Hamilton report and looked instead for a way to win. In doing so, he turned to the Army's counterinsurgency manual and its author, General David Petraeus. Bush put Petraeus in command in Iraq, announced that he would be giving him an additional 20,000 troops, and declared, "The situation in Iraq is unacceptable to the American people—and it is unacceptable to me. . . . The consequences of failure are clear . . . Americans will change our strategy to help the Iraqis carry out their campaign to put down sectarian violence and bring security to the people of Baghdad."[16]

Democrats in Congress, believing they had received an electoral mandate to end the war, were as stunned as they were irate. They launched a series of efforts that persisted through 2007 to force a withdrawal deadline, cut off funds, and generally prevent or inhibit execution of what quickly became known as the "Surge." In April 2007, Senate Majority Leader Harry Reid declared, "The war is lost," and most Democrats seemed to agree. Every step of the way, however, they were blocked by Senate Republicans and by Bush, who insisted that Americans had voted against losing, not against fighting. Bush also continued, in this case with limited Democratic help, to get his way in other areas of national security. He succeeded in winning passage of a bill regularizing military commissions for enemy combatants and a foreign surveillance bill codifying the controversial NSA wiretapping program.

The conflict between President Bush and the Democratic Congress represented a classic example of a number of long-standing tensions in American government, and indeed in democratic self-government itself. It highlighted the tensions inherent in America's system of separation of powers and checks and balances. It demonstrated once again how the president holds the high cards where national security is at stake, especially when troops are already committed. And it illustrated the complexities of leadership in a democratic society. Should Bush act as a "delegate," simply following what seemed to be the will of the people as expressed in polls and election results? Or should he act as a "trustee," using his own best judgment even if it conflicted with public opinion at the moment? And what was public opinion, anyway?

The antiwar fever in Congress did not cool until late 2007, after a much-heralded report by Petraeus and U.S. Ambassador Ryan Crocker indicated that progress was being made. The antiwar Left fumed—one MoveOn.org ad called the commander "General Betrayus"—but Democrats largely gave up on trying to force a withdrawal. By the end of the year, there was quietly growing belief—despite consistent underreporting of the new trends by the major media—that a corner had been turned in Iraq. By December 2007, reported Iraqi deaths had fallen by 66 percent compared with December a year before, and U.S. casualties had declined from 112 to 23 in the same months. Nevertheless, ending the war remained a rallying cry for Democrats leading up to the Iowa caucuses, and winning the war remained a rallying cry for Republicans.

The effect of this on the presidential races, at least up until April 2008, was a tale of two perceptions. The perception of defeat that continued to dominate among Democrats helped Barack Obama gain the upper hand as the candidate most opposed to the war. The perception of possible victory that began to dawn among Republicans helped John McCain revive his prospects in the Republican Party as the candidate most favorable to the Surge. What it did not do was change the image of George Bush.

LOOKING OUT AT 2008

As 2007 drew to a close, George W. Bush's approval rating stood at 32 percent in the Gallup poll, and voters were clearly unsettled. There was turmoil in the Republican Party, and Democrats were not free of problems either.

Iraq remained a bitter source of disagreement among Americans. At home, the economy seemed to hum on the surface, but termites were eating away at the heart of the financial district; economists were much later to declare that the economy entered recession in December 2007. At the same time, Americans seemed to have become increasingly disenchanted with George W. Bush's presidential style. The circumstances of his election, the war in Iraq, his combativeness, and his cultural archetype had cemented his place as a highly polarizing president, despite the relative moderation of large parts of his domestic agenda.[17] Democrats, in particular, came to despise Bush, leading to a bigger disparity in partisan appraisals of this president than of any previous executive during the era of polling. Democrats were far more likely than Republicans to disagree with the conduct of the Iraq War and to question the premises behind it.[18] As John Dickerson and Karen Tumulty wrote in *Time*, there was another dimension: "To some, the way that Bush walks and talks and smiles is the body language of courage and self-assurance, and of someone who shares their values. But to others, it is the swagger and smirk that signals the certainty of the stubbornly simpleminded."[19] The nation's major media, never friendly to George Bush, focused on every administration flaw or fault, real or imagined. Overall, in December 2007, only one in five Americans said that they were satisfied with the way things were going in the United States.

Democrats sensed a big opportunity to build on the 2006 gains to win the White House and expand their congressional majorities. The Bush years had left them reorganized, reenergized, and flush with money. After a flashy start, though, the Democratic Congress suffered increasingly poor job-approval ratings, and it was soon polling worse than George Bush. A message of change, from any and everything in Washington, was bound to fall on welcome ears.

For their part, Republicans were on their heels. Even in good times, it is not easy for a party to win a third consecutive presidential term; incumbent parties had tried five times from 1960 through 2000 and succeeded only once, in 1988. The years following 2006 were not good times for Republicans, with an unpopular administration hanging around their necks. More congressional sex scandals plagued them, and Republican fundraising and poll numbers continued falling. Economic conservatives groaned at the growth of government. After passage of the partial-birth abortion ban in Bush's first term, social conservatives found little to cheer, either. Foreign policy conservatives applauded the success of the Surge, but they also had to acknowledge the failures of intelligence and war planning that had preceded it. And they could only wonder why the change in strategy took so long to come. Voters increasingly either did not like or did not know what Republicans stood for. Like Democrats, Republicans were uncertain in which direction to head. Unlike Democrats, they had almost no margin for error in 2008.

NOTES

1. Ryan Lizza, "How Obama Won," *The New Yorker*, November 17, 2008, http://www.newyorker.com/reporting/2008/11/17/081117fa_fact_lizza.

2. October 27, 2008, speech. Cited in Jennifer Marisco, "This Election Has Not Realigned the Country," *Wall Street Journal*, November 12, 2008, http://online.wsj.com/article/SB122645275150719429.html.

3. Michael Gerson, "The Decency of George Bush," November 7, 2008, *Washington Post*, A19.

4. Figures are estimates from Iraqi Body Count, an organization that counts actual news reports and morgue reports of Iraqi deaths, a method which may undercount actual casualties. According to Iraqi Body Count, 14,714 Iraqis died in 2005, compared with 27,577 in 2006, http://www.iraqbodycount.org/database.

5. Christopher H. Foreman, Jr., "The Braking of the President: Shifting Context and the Bush Domestic Agenda," in Colin Campbell, Bert A. Rockman, and Andrew Rudalevige, eds., *The George W. Bush Legacy* (Washington, DC: CQ Press, 2007); Barbara Sinclair, "Living (and Dying?) by the Sword: George W. Bush as Legislative Leader," in Colin Campbell, Bert A. Rockman, and Andrew Rudalevige, eds., *The George W. Bush Legacy* (Washington, DC: CQ Press, 2007); Dan Balz, "Bush's Second-Term Agenda Hits Reality," in John C. Fortier and Norman J. Ornstein, eds., *Second-Term Blues: How George W. Bush Has Governed* (Washington, DC: Brookings Institution and American Enterprise Institute, 2007).

6. These included such highly respected Democrats as Bob Kerrey, Daniel Patrick Moynihan, and Joseph Lieberman.

7. Democrats were also gaining on the social issue, where they felt the president had overreached. A brief episode early in 2005 did more damage to Republicans than was immediately apparent. When Bush and congressional Republicans intervened in the case of Terri Schiavo, a brain-damaged Florida woman whose husband wanted to remove her feeding tube but whose parents protested, there was a broad public reaction against their involvement in what appeared to be a family matter. The case seemed to particularly upset liberals, and contributed to the stiffening of Democratic opposition to Bush's social agenda. As one Democratic congresswoman later recounted, "The Terri Schiavo case was literally the thing that, from that point forward, brought our caucus together and gave us the ability to become more unified." Wes Allison and Anita Kumar, "What Terri's Law Cost the Republicans in Congress," *St. Petersburg Times*, December 18, 2005, A1.

8. Balz, "Bush's Second-Term Agenda Hits Reality," 31–32.

9. The Gallup poll showed Bush's approval rating reaching or falling below the 30 percent level at four points: during the first immigration debate in 2006, during the second immigration debate in 2007, and for extended periods in early and again in late 2008 coinciding with periods of serious economic concern, http://www.gallup.com/poll/1723/Presidential-Job-Approval-Depth.aspx.

10. Jacob S. Hacker and Paul Pierson, "The Center No Longer Holds," *New York Times Magazine*, November 20, 2005.

11. Anthony Corrado and Katie Varney, "The Role of National Party Committees in Financing Congressional Campaigns," Washington, DC: Campaign Finance Institute. Available at http://cfinst.org/books_reports/pdf/Corrado_Party-2006_Final.pdf.

12. Democrat Claire McCaskill defeated incumbent Republican James Talent 49.6 percent to 47.3 percent in Missouri; Democrat Jon Tester defeated incumbent Republican Conrad Burns 49.2 percent to 48.2 percent in Montana; Democrat James Webb defeated incumbent Republican George Allen 49.6 percent to 49.2 percent in Virginia.

13. CNN Exit Polls, national House vote, general election 2004 and general election 2006.

14. Most polls recorded a 2–1 or even 3–1 ratio hostile to the bill and to Bush's approach.

15. Janet Hook, "Bush Boxed in His Congressional Foes," *Los Angeles Times*, December 21, 2007, http://latimes.com/news/nationworld/nation/.la-na-congress21dec21,0, 6679238.story?coll = la-home-center.

16. President George W. Bush, address to the nation, January 10, 2007.

17. See Gary C. Jacobson, *A Divider, Not a Uniter* (New York: Longman, 2006); George C. Edwards III, *Governing by Campaigning: The Politics of the Bush Presidency* (New York: Longman, 2007).

18. Jacobson, *A Divider, Not a Uniter*, 161–62.

19. John F. Dickerson and Karen Tumulty, "The Love Him, Hate Him President," *Time*, December 1, 2003, http://www.time.com/time/magazine/article/0,9171,1006 297-3,00.html.

Chapter Three

The Republican Nomination Contest

Sometimes presidential nominations turn out just the way everyone expected at the beginning. Sometimes there are surprises. And then, on rare occasion, the surprise is that the nomination turns out the way everyone expected at the beginning. The 2008 Republican nomination race was one of those rare occasions.

When eyes turned to the impending nomination races in late 2006, John McCain was widely thought to be the Republican front-runner, the man to beat. On the evening of February 5, 2008, a little more than one month after the Iowa caucuses, it was clear to most observers that McCain had all but wrapped up the Republican nomination. Yet, what transpired in between made the conclusion reached on February 5 seem like an amazing turn of events rather than a coronation.

THE FIELD

The Republican nomination contest intensified over eighteen months in 2007 and 2008, a period characterized by a marked deterioration of GOP prospects. President Bush's approval rating slipped ever downward, public dissatisfaction moved ever higher, and the elections of 2006, which deprived Republicans of their majorities in both the House and the Senate, dispirited partisans and seemed to indicate fragmentation of the potent electoral coalition bequeathed by Ronald Reagan.

The fractured Reagan coalition and philosophical uncertainty within the party led to a scattered field of potential candidates. A number of long-shot contenders threw their proverbial hats into the ring, only to withdraw from the contest before a single vote was cast. These included James Gilmore, former governor of Virginia; Congressman Tom Tancredo of Colorado, who hoped to ride a wave of sentiment against illegal immigration; and former Wisconsin governor and Secretary of Health and Human Services Tommy Thompson. Some long shots entered and remained in the race, including Congressman Duncan Hunter of California, Congressman and one-time Libertarian presidential candidate Ron Paul, and, seeking the Republican nomination for the third time, veteran conservative activist and former ambassador Alan Keyes. A man considered by many Republicans to be their strongest possible contender faced automatic disqualification by virtue of his family ties: Florida Governor Jeb Bush. Widely considered by Republicans to be more talented than his brother in the White House, many believed that if Jeb had won his 1994 gubernatorial run in Florida, it would have been him—not George W.—who would have entered the White House in 2001. Now, the road was closed.

The 2006 midterms also significantly influenced the field. First, they eliminated at least two important potential candidates; Virginia Senator George Allen, who narrowly lost his bid for reelection, and Tennessee Senator Bill Frist, the former majority leader who retired in a cloud of leadership failure, were both punished by anti-Republican sentiment in 2006. Second, the tone of the race changed. Insiders too closely tied to the old Republican Congress or to the Bush administration (such as Secretary of State Condoleezza Rice, whose name had also been mentioned as a potential candidate) were now out. This time, the outsiders were in.

The field of serious contenders, and hence the shape of the contest itself, was defined by a series of preliminary contests within different strands of the Reagan coalition. These contests among candidates emphasizing a particular element of Reaganism or attempting, somewhat mechanically, to hold the coalition together, can be divided into three main groups, three tournament brackets, so to speak. The three brackets included the "compassionate conservatives," stressing the evangelical component of the coalition; the "conventional conservatives," attempting to strike conservative positions across the economic, social, and security spheres; and the national security "hawks" who emphasized national security concerns but relative moderation in other areas. That all the candidates nonetheless claimed to be "Reagan Republicans" may have been as much a sign of the fragmentation of Reaganism as of its enduring rhetorical strength.

The Compassionate Conservatives

Few of the candidates seeking the Republican nomination explicitly identified themselves with George W. Bush's brand of Republicanism. However, two ran with similar messages and enjoyed their greatest strength among social rather than economic conservatives. Former Arkansas governor Mike Huckabee and Kansas Senator Sam Brownback vied for preeminence in this bracket. Neither Huckabee nor Brownback explicitly endorsed Bush's spending habits, but both were clearly competing for the sliver of the Republican electorate that had been least offended by "big government conservatism": that is, socially conservative, economically downscale voters whose politics were most driven by their faith.

Huckabee, born of modest means in Bill Clinton's hometown of Hope, was an ordained Southern Baptist pastor who had been elevated from lieutenant governor of Arkansas in 1996 when Democratic Governor Jim Guy Tucker was convicted in the Whitewater land scandal. He was subsequently elected as governor in his own right in 1998 and 2002. Famous for his crash weight loss program, Huckabee made a strong pitch to evangelical voters as he sought to become only the second ordained minister to occupy the White House (after James Garfield). He was labeled a "big government conservative" by his critics; for example, Pat Toomey of the free market Club for Growth complained that Huckabee had long demonstrated a "tax-and-spend record and hostility toward the free market."[1] Some conservative commentators accused Huckabee of seeking to make the Republicans into European-style Christian Democrats—placing faith, family, and robust government regulation ahead of economic health and limited government.[2] In his own words, "I'm a conservative—but I'm not mad at anybody over it."[3] His populist message touting Main Street rather than Wall Street resonated well among so-called Wal-Mart voters. Huckabee also touted the "fair tax," replacing the federal income tax with a national sales tax. The folksy Huckabee was the youngest man in the Republican field (at fifty-two) and came to be widely acclaimed as the funniest of the Republican contenders, exhibiting the strongest speaking and debating skills.[4] He had the advantage of being an "outsider," but the concomitant disadvantage that hardly anyone outside of Arkansas had heard of him. He also lacked national security credentials at a time when Iraq and the war on terror were front and center on the campaign agenda.

Brownback was first elected to the U.S. House in the Republican tidal wave of 1994 and then won election to the Senate in a 1996 special election and again in 1998 and 2004. A recent convert from evangelical Protestantism to Roman Catholicism, Brownback bridged that gap and appealed most strongly to social conservatives. Like Huckabee, Brownback took the politically risky tack of resisting calls for a crackdown on illegal immigrants, citing the biblical injunction to welcome strangers as support for his position. He expressed doubts about evolution and the death penalty, spoke about social justice and relieving poverty, and took an interest in curbing international sex trafficking and violence in Darfur. He explicitly called himself a "compassionate conservative," thus drawing a closer parallel with Bush (along with calling himself an economic, fiscal, and social conservative) and sought the same voters as Huckabee. However, he was in some sense a mirror image of the Arkansan: neither a national security novice nor an outsider.

The Conventional Conservatives

Two more candidates vied for the title of candidate most faithful to the tenets of what Frank Meyer long ago called "fusionism," a potent mix of libertarianism and traditional conservatism, or what the *National Review* now calls "full spectrum conservatism." These candidates sought to win by appealing to the considerable segment of the Republican electorate that is equally conservative in economics, social and cultural matters, and national security.

Former Massachusetts Governor Mitt Romney was the first to enter this bracket. A successful businessman who had received acclaim for rescuing the 2002 Winter Olympics in Salt Lake City, Romney had run for the Senate against Ted Kennedy in 1994 and had given the liberal lion a run for his money. Romney came back to run successfully for governor of Massachusetts in 2002. As governor, he had worked with the legislature to enact the nation's first statewide universal health care plan. He had also led the fight against the state court's 2003 fiat declaring gay marriage a constitutional right. Romney brought numerous advantages to the nomination contest. He was an outsider as a governor and a businessman conversant in economics. He had great personal wealth and contacts that would assure him of superior resources. He also had a family tradition in politics; his father had served as the popular governor of Michigan and had been an (unsuccessful) contender for the 1968 Republican presidential nomination. And, as many observers noted, the sixty-year-old Romney, blessed with a jut jaw and a perfectly coiffed head of hair, just looked like a president. At the same time, three weaknesses threatened his success. His cool, methodical CEO style induced confidence but not inspiration. His appeal to social conservatives, which had to be an important part of his "paint by the numbers" campaign, ran contrary to a number of pro-abortion and pro-gay statements he had made running for statewide office in Massachusetts in 1994 and 2002. Not least was his adherence to Mormonism, a faith seen by many evangelical Christians as non-Christian at best and cult-like at worst; polls showed as many as 30 percent of Republicans were less likely to vote for Romney because of his religion, though that number had fallen to 18 percent by the end of 2007.[5]

Romney's struggles and the resultant vacuum in this sliver of the Republican field led to the rise of a second candidate within this bracket. Former Tennessee Senator Fred Thompson spent six months in mid-2007 testing the waters before officially joining the fray in September. Thompson's strategy was to position himself as the "real" conservative heir to Reagan's fusionism, overtake Romney, and go into the final stage of the nomination race as the representative of the "conventional conservative" bracket. Thompson had enjoyed a varied career. He had served as Howard Baker's counsel on the Senate Watergate committee, enjoyed a career in acting and lobbying, served in the U.S. Senate from Tennessee from 1995 to 2003, where he compiled a solidly conservative record, and went on to play a major role in the hit television series *Law & Order*. While clearly conservative, Thompson was not entirely predictable, having backed John McCain's campaign finance crusade and voted to acquit Bill Clinton on one of two impeachment charges in 1999. Though he looked and sounded like a president, with commentators waxing lyrical on his "old-school masculinity"[6] and "almost Reaganesque communication skills," he had a limited record of accomplishment in the Senate.[7] His lobbying experience meant he could be painted as a Washington insider, and he developed a reputation for avoiding exertion. Alone among the serious candidates on either side, he intended from the outset to run an effort that would break the conventional rules of presidential campaigns. Not least, Thompson hoped to prove that it was possible to run for president without it being an all-consuming effort.

The Electable National Security Hawks

The final bracket consisted of two candidates who both laid claim to the mantle of the tough, moderately conservative candidate with demonstrated crossover appeal whose primary focus would be national security: Rudy Giuliani and John McCain. Both Giuliani and McCain were outsiders of a sort: Even though he had served as associate attorney general and a federal prosecutor, Giuliani achieved his fame as a mayor far removed from the machinations of Washington, while McCain's long service in the Senate was balanced by his frequent high-profile clashes with his own party's leadership. Both men also emphasized national security and claims of electability, the importance of which grew in the primary contest as Republican fortunes waned elsewhere.

Giuliani served as mayor of New York City from 1993 to 2001. Taking over a city that was spiraling into fiscal and social disaster, Giuliani was widely credited with turning things around by taking on the city's bureaucracy and instituting a "zero tolerance" approach to crime. He briefly challenged Hillary Clinton for the U.S. Senate seat in 2000, but withdrew due to the onset of prostate cancer (since cured) and controversy surrounding his messy divorce. However, Giuliani cemented his reputation on 9-11, acting with calm determination in the face of this unprecedented crisis. He thereby gained instant credibility on the issue of international terrorism, something far beyond the capacity of any other municipal mayor. He would bring his national fame and a sharp wit to the contest, along with the tantalizing promise of reopening the urban northeast to Republican appeals. If Giuliani could make it as a Republican in New York City, he could make it anywhere, and he promised "a revitalized, fifty-state Republican Party."[8] On the downside, Giuliani had a sometimes abrasive personality, a troubled history of marital infidelity, and (like Romney) a record of social liberalism on hot-button cultural issues such as abortion, gay rights, and guns that could hurt him among conservative Republican primary voters. For better or worse, his circle clearly saw themselves as outside the regular Republican establishment, and exuded some measure of resentment. Moreover, his personal history virtually guaranteed that he would face a steep uphill climb among women voters.[9] According to some inside accounts, his wife, Judy, was also a loose cannon. That said, Giuliani believed the nomination calendar gave him an advantage: the Florida primary, with its scads of transplanted New Yorkers, would be relatively early, and Giuliani supporters in a number of early states that were deemed good prospects had arranged for their states to give delegates on a winner-take-all basis, providing much greater potential delegate yields. The balance between his apparent advantages and disadvantages was so difficult to untangle that commentators spent much of 2007 debating whether he could or could not be nominated.[10]

Giuliani's rival in this bracket was John McCain, senator from Arizona since 1986. If elected, McCain would be, as a seventy-two-year-old melanoma survivor, the oldest man to take office as president. McCain was a creature of mixed political provenance, proclaiming his two heroes to be Ronald Reagan and Theodore Roosevelt, and thus drawing from the poles of conservative and progressive Republicanism respectively. Indeed, McCain had baffled and infuriated many Republicans over the years, developing a reputation as a "maverick." In 2000, he had waged a tough race against George W. Bush, during which he had famously accused leaders of the religious right of being "agents of intolerance." In 2004, rumors spread that John Kerry had discussed giving McCain the Democratic vice presidential slot. Over the years, McCain had supported campaign finance reform in the face of overwhelming opposition in his own party—when the legislation was finally enacted in 2002, the final bill even bore his name, united with one of the most liberal Democratic senators, Russell Feingold (D-WI). McCain had further angered his co-partisans by opposing Bush's tax cuts and the federal marriage amendment. He had also acquired a reputation (perhaps exaggerated) for a mercurial temperament. Nevertheless, he had never supported a major tax increase, had voted against the Medicare prescription drug entitlement, and had been beating the drum for spending restraint and more troops in Iraq long before Bush came around to those positions. On balance, he had a generally conservative record, including a strong pro-life record on abortion: his lifetime rating from the American Conservative Union was 82 percent as of 2007.[11] If his support within the party was suspect, he had the advantage of having always enjoyed considerable support among independents, who valued his "maverick" stances; in the 2000 nominating contest, he consistently did best in open primaries that allowed independents and Democrats to vote. Another major component of his appeal was his personal biography, including his service as a naval aviator in the Vietnam War and his harrowing five-and-a-half years as a prisoner of war in Hanoi, though his age was a potential drag. In his 2000 campaign, McCain had enjoyed great fellowship with the press corps, offering open access to reporters and going so far as to call the media "his base." If he could retain that edge, his other strengths would be multiplied. Given his disdain for corn-based ethanol, it was considered unlikely that McCain would do well in the first caucuses in Iowa. However, he had won a big victory against Bush in the first 2000 primary in New Hampshire, and could hope to repeat his performance there.

THE STRUCTURAL ENVIRONMENT: FRONT-LOADING

The 2008 nomination contests in both parties were characterized by extreme front-loading of the primaries and caucuses. Front-loading is the process by which delegate selection contests have been increasingly compressed toward the beginning of the primary and caucus calendar. In 1960, only 2 percent of Democratic and Republican primary delegates had been chosen by the end of the fourth week of primaries; in 2008, that figure was 57 percent of Democratic and 52 percent of Republican primary delegates. A related issue is the ever earlier starting point of the delegate selection system, now beginning at what in the past would have been regarded as an absurdly early point. By tradition, Iowa and New Hampshire hold the first caucus and primary respectively, giving their states apparently disproportionate influence on the dynamics of the nomination contest. Other states have moved up their delegate selection contests so as to remain significant in the nomination process, amid fears that the nominee could be decided long before the state has its vote. Some have rejected Iowa and New Hampshire's claim to priority altogether and sought to leapfrog them, igniting a competitive process of date changes, especially since New Hampshire law requires that its primary be the first in the nation.

In 2008, the national Republican Party stripped five states—New Hampshire, Wyoming, Michigan, South Carolina, and Florida—of half of their delegates because their contests were held before the date allowed by Republican rules. (Democrats also initially deprived Michigan and Florida of all, then half, of their delegates, although the delegates were restored at the Democratic convention.) In 2008, the process would start on January 3 and would allocate a majority of primary delegates by the end of the day on February 5—"Super Tuesday"—when primaries or caucuses were held in around twenty states, including California, Illinois, New Jersey, and New York. Altogether, a larger percentage of primary delegates were chosen by the end of the fourth week in 2008 than in any previous nomination cycle. The assumption of many analysts was that this front-loading would produce an early decision, as the candidate with momentum coming out of the early contests would be able to deliver a knockout blow on February 5. As we will see, the Democratic nomination did not quite turn out this way. The Republican one, however, did.

ROLLER COASTER: THE 2007
INVISIBLE PRIMARY

The early start of the caucus and primary season and the heavy front-loading of those contests meant that the "invisible primary" or "exhibition season" (as political scientists call it) was potentially even more important than before. The first GOP candidates' debate, held at the Reagan Library in Simi Valley, California, took place on May 3, 2007; in the 2000 nomination contest, the first such debate featuring all the major candidates was not held until December 2 of 1999. The candidates—including those who dropped in and out again before the end of the year—fought over fundraising, straw polls, and ground organization. Yet, the intense struggle throughout 2007 did not seem to clarify anything. Instead, the year saw a series of undulations as first one candidate and then another seized a moment of glory, rose above the fray, but then, just as swiftly, receded.

The first major undulation was also the most dramatic; the fall of McCain, who began the year widely assumed to be the front-runner. In preparation for his run, McCain took a number of steps to smooth relations with important constituencies in the Republican Party. In early 2006, he reached out to anti-tax economic conservatives by recanting his original opposition to the Bush tax cuts. Then he tried to repair damage done in 2000 by making amends with Jerry Falwell and speaking at Bob Jones University. This strategy helped ease McCain into the lead position in the race, abetted by the notable tendency of Republicans to prefer giving their nomination to a political "heir apparent," the person whose "turn" seems to be next. At the same time, his embrace of some of his party's orthodoxies strained his relationship with the once-admiring media. For example, E. J. Dionne of the *Washington Post* noted that "McCain seems to have decided that our . . . quarrelsome and unforgiving political environment requires him to be less interesting and more conventional than he used to be."[12] When Bush announced the Iraq Surge in January 2007—essentially following McCain's advice after nearly four years of repetition—it was quickly apparent that McCain's fortunes in the primaries, and perhaps beyond, would be inextricably tied to the success of the Surge.

McCain's frontrunner status lasted only until his interbracket rival Rudy Giuliani announced his intention to run on February 5, 2007. At that point, Giuliani threatened and quickly surpassed McCain in the polls. (Even before his announcement, a Gallup poll showed that Republicans saw Giuliani as more likeable, better in a crisis, and a stronger leader than McCain by margins of two or three to one.[13]) However, the Arizona senator remained close to "America's Mayor" until poor financial management caused the implosion of his own campaign in July, necessitating major staff cutbacks and a rearrangement of key players.[14] Just as importantly, McCain's close association with Bush's 2007 push for immigration reform, which he cosponsored with Ted Kennedy in the Senate, badly hurt his standing among Republican voters, who were strongly opposed to the deal. McCain compounded his problem by suggesting that opponents of the bill were motivated by bigotry.[15] By the end of July 2007, McCain's standing had fallen to around 15 percent in most polls. As the London *Daily Telegraph* informed its readers, "Senior Republicans believe [McCain's] White House bid is doomed and all that remains is for the spoils to be divided. . . . Republican strategists dissecting the carcass of John McCain's presidential campaign concluded yesterday that Rudy Giuliani is likely to be the biggest beneficiary of his friend and rival's demise."[16]

Indeed, McCain's fall overlapped with Giuliani's rise. After appearing on CNN's *Larry King Live*, the mayor reached 40 percent in some polls of Republican voters in the spring. He stumbled on a question about abortion in the first debate, but then sharpened his answer in hopes that he could mitigate its offensiveness to social conservatives without appearing to change his position or pander: He did not like abortion, but would not support a federal ban. He believed *Roe v. Wade* was wrongly decided, and would favor returning the issue to the states where it belonged. Like McCain, Giuliani cultivated leaders of the religious right, and surprised the political world by obtaining the endorsement of televangelist and former presidential candidate Pat Robertson in November. Robertson explained that he believed the most important issue was the threat of radical Islamic terrorism, which he believed Giuliani was best positioned to combat. As would become clear, however, Robertson's clout, always somewhat exaggerated, was now nearly negligible, his Christian Coalition practically defunct as an organizational force.

Giuliani rarely relinquished the lead for the rest of 2007. By midyear, former George W. Bush speechwriter Michael Gerson warned that "many social conservatives remain in denial about Rudy Giuliani's chances . . . Giuliani's political strength cannot be dismissed as a fad or a fluke."[17] Those not in denial worried aloud that the influence of social conservatives in the party was gravely threatened by Giuliani's rise.[18] Despite retaining the nominal lead, however, Giuliani was in fact suffering a slow bleed throughout the year. Excerpts of an internal vulnerability study on Giuliani produced for his first New York mayoral run were published on the Smoking Gun blog in early 2007, and provided considerable ammunition for opponents and journalists alike.[19] Shots about his excessive liberalism gradually took their toll. The candidate also displayed off-putting quirks, such as taking cell phone calls from his wife in the middle of a speech. In early December a mini-scandal erupted when it became known that while serving as mayor, he had used a New York City Police Department detail to transport his then mistress, who later became his wife, around town.

Added to Giuliani's difficulties, it became increasingly apparent that his strategic position in the race did not match up well with the primary and caucus calendar after all. He was never a good fit with Iowa, a rural state dominated by socially conservative caucus-goers. Though he made some effort there, visiting the state twenty times throughout 2007, he ultimately concentrated his resources elsewhere.[20] His campaign hoped to make a breakthrough in New Hampshire, and he actually led some polls there in 2007, but McCain and Romney both had a head start in the Granite State—McCain due to his 2000 investment and Romney as former governor of neighboring Massachusetts (and a homeowner in New Hampshire). After running a heavy advertising campaign, Giuliani saw by December that he was getting little traction in New Hampshire and he scaled back his campaign there, too. The next major contest, South Carolina, was, like Iowa, not natural territory for successful cultivation by Giuliani. Against expectations, he briefly led in polls there, but by December his alien New York persona had caught up with him and he trailed. This left Florida, in the fourth week of voting, as the chief Giuliani firewall. As 2008 drew near, Giuliani pointed out somewhat plaintively that "You're not going to win in the first inning or the second inning"; a lot of good teams come back in the middle innings.[21] His hopes for such a comeback, though, seemed to be rapidly dimming.

Another key story—perhaps the key story of 2007—was the non-rise of Mitt Romney. Romney was highly successful at fundraising, having raised $53 million and lent himself another $30 million (at least) by the end of December. He built a strong organization in most early states, was an impressive presence in many of the debates, and insisted on a methodical and businesslike campaign. His early rhetoric was also forceful and effective: in September, he gave a major speech in which he said, "We Republicans have to put our own house in order. . . . When Republicans act like Democrats, America loses. We have to start acting like Republicans, not earmarking Republicans, not big-spending Republicans, not big government Republicans, but like Reagan Republicans." These strengths enabled him to lead for some time in both Iowa and New Hampshire. But he never led in national polls, where he was stalled below 15 percent for most of the year. Analysts differed about the key factor holding Romney back, and many advanced his Mormonism as an explanation. A December 2007 Pew survey provided some supportive evidence for such an explanation: it showed that only 52 percent believed Mormons were Christians, only 53 percent had a favorable view of Mormons, 25 percent of Americans (and 36 percent of white Republican evangelicals) said Mormonism would make them less likely to vote for a candidate, and the word most often volunteered by respondents to describe their impressions of Mormonism was "polygamy" or "bigamy."[22] Others pointed to Romney's inconsistent record on social issues, a particular problem in the YouTube era, where the candidate's varying statements on an issue are easily accessible and can thus be readily lampooned. For some, Romney's privileged background or his demeanor were key. He seemed a bit too perfect, a bit too programmed, and a bit too passionless. At one debate in October, Romney drew ridicule for suggesting that he would decide after sitting down with his attorneys whether to take military action against Iran's nuclear program. As one pundit observed, Romney "could never shake the odor of inauthenticity."[23] Or, as a Republican activist put it, "I don't want to end up in a knife fight with Hillary [Clinton] armed with nothing but Romney's hair."[24] Whatever the explanation, he failed to meet the expectations generated by his impressive resume, and was forced to pin his hopes on early wins creating unstoppable momentum toward the nomination.

The decline of McCain and the inability of Giuliani or Romney to capitalize decisively led to a vacuum that invited the entrance of new candidates. By mid-2007, two potential newcomers had emerged: Newt Gingrich and Fred Thompson. Gingrich, the former House Speaker who had led House Republicans to victory in 1994, tested the waters, waited to see what Thompson would do, and backed away. For his part, Thompson enjoyed a meteoric rise as Republicans unimpressed with their existing choices flocked to him. One prominent Republican consultant held that Thompson was "filling this tremendous void in the conservatives' eyes."[25] Another critical observer noted that "the candidate has a touch of the blank-slate phenomenon working for him, allowing savior-hungry Republicans to project onto him whichever personal and ideological traits they most desire."[26] The beginning of the Thompson boomlet can be traced to March 11, when Thompson acknowledged to Chris Wallace on *Fox Sunday Morning* that he was "seriously considering" a White House run. Thompson clearly aimed to be the "full spectrum" conservative, and emphasized a Reagan-like appeal to first principles (such as federalism and limited government) in a way most of the other candidates in the GOP field had avoided. However, he hoped to succeed with an unconventional, low-key campaign emphasizing new technologies. For example, he contributed to a conservative blog and made a big splash with two low-cost YouTube videos, one lampooning Michael Moore's views on health care in Cuba and the other taking on Hillary Clinton's revamped health care proposal. He shadowed the field without being an official part of it. In early May, as Republicans geared up for their first debate at the Reagan Library in California, Thompson conveniently arranged to give a major address to the Lincoln Club of Orange County. At that point, many of his supporters thought that he was on the verge of entering the race.[27]

However, rather than announce his candidacy in late spring or summer when interest was at its peak, he let the moment, and the momentum, slide by. Despite originally touting the end of May as an entry date, Thompson only established an exploratory organization. Then the beginning of July was touted for a launch, and then the end of July. By this point, he was in second place in most national polls of Republicans, and was leading the Rasmussen and Zogby polls with about a quarter of the vote. "We're testing the waters," Thompson repeated, "and the waters are feeling pretty warm." As late as the Wednesday after Labor Day, Thompson skipped a key New Hampshire candidates' debate, appearing on the *Tonight Show with Jay Leno* instead. When he finally announced on the show and began his campaign in earnest the next day, the waters were not quite as warm. He was still widely considered one of the big three candidates alongside Giuliani and Romney, and even continued to lead some polls for awhile, but much of the energy surrounding his candidacy had dissipated. Some conservative Christians such as James Dobson began to question his credentials, he proved an uneven performer on the campaign trail, raised less money than he hoped, and had to shake up his staff in late July amid suggestions his wife, Jeri, was really running the campaign.[28] There were moments when he seemed poised to retake the initiative, such as when he took control of a debate in Iowa by confronting the moderator; asked to give a yes-or-no answer to a question on global warming,

Thompson boomed, "You want a show of hands, and I'm not giving it to you."[29] And he clearly hurt Romney.[30] By the end of December, though, Thompson's actual campaign was in a weaker position than his noncampaign had been six months earlier. National polling that month showed he had receded to somewhere between 7 and 13 percent. He was fighting to merely stay alive in Iowa and New Hampshire, with increasingly distant hopes that he might break through in South Carolina. And if Romney never dominated his bracket, as some might have expected, let alone the race as a whole, he also never wilted away under pressure from Thompson.

Only the "Compassionate Conservative" bracket gained any clarity by the end of the year, thanks to the rise of Mike Huckabee. As late as October 2007, Huckabee was still stuck under 10 percent in national polls. Among the major contenders who would survive to January 1, Huckabee was by far the weakest fundraiser. Yet the last half of 2007 saw a strong close by the former Arkansas governor. He began making his move in August when he came in a surprising second in the Iowa straw poll, with 18 percent to Romney's 32 percent. Within three days, his campaign had attracted one thousand online donations.[31] Actor and martial arts expert Chuck Norris served as Huckabee's celebrity spokesman, a less imposing but still potent version of Barack Obama's champion, Oprah Winfrey. Norris appeared with the candidate, cut ads for him, and stirred support among key constituencies. Huckabee was also credited with two strong debate performances in October, and his growing strength could be seen at the Values Voter Summit in late October, a confab of social conservatives where he nearly tied Romney in the total straw votes cast over two months and won big among the votes cast by those who had heard the candidates' speeches in person.[32] The withdrawal of Sam Brownback from the race on October 19 was both the cause and effect of Huckabee's rise; Brownback's exit meant that Huckabee was the first major candidate to clear out his bracket. The "Compassionate Conservative" sliver was now all his, while candidates in the other areas were still fighting it out.

Huckabee had long recognized that Iowa was his kind of state. Having won the showdown with Brownback, he was free to fully engage any other candidate who showed strength in Iowa.[33] That other candidate was Mitt Romney, who was spending gigantic sums in Iowa and leading in the polls there. Romney was, however, vulnerable to an attack from his right on social issues and from the populist front on economic issues—Huckabee's fortes. Huckabee proceeded to press those attacks, both in Iowa and nationally. Though lacking Romney's resources, he built a campaign around word-of-mouth "viral" advertising, homeschooling networks, a YouTube video featuring Norris, and possession of an impressive email list of Iowa Christians.[34] Romney's Mormonism also came to the fore, as Huckabee refused to clarify whether he thought Mormons were Christians amid signs that Romney's faith was hurting him in Iowa.[35] By the end of October, Huckabee was already closing in on second place in Iowa polls; by the end of November, he was challenging Romney for first, bolstered by evangelical Christians who saw Huckabee as more trustworthy than Romney and more likely to understand their concerns.[36] Huckabee's supporters also seemed to have an enthusiasm advantage. As one Iowa politico reported about campaign workers in his state, "[F]or many, Romney is purely a job. Huckabee is a cause."[37]

In early December, Romney felt compelled—driven by Huckabee—to deliver an address on religion that he had long resisted making. Marketed as a parallel to John F. Kennedy's famed 1960 speech to the Houston Ministerial Conference, in which he pledged foremost fealty to the Constitution rather than to Rome, Romney's speech received mixed reviews and left unanswered questions about his own particular faith, focusing instead on his view of the general place of religion in politics. At any rate, the speech failed to stem the losses toward Huckabee, who not only led in Iowa but gained the national lead for a short time in some polls. Then, in mid-December, Huckabee built a bridge to the Republican establishment by appointing longtime GOP operative Ed Rollins as his national campaign chairman. (Rollins was Catholic, suggesting that his appointment was also an attempt by Huckabee to broaden his religious appeal.) Yet Huckabee's own weaknesses began to appear as he became better known. His lightly veiled attack on Romney's Mormonism brought its own backlash, and he was forced to apologize for anti-Mormon comments he made in a *Time* magazine interview.[38] His harsh attack on George W. Bush's foreign policy in an article in *Foreign Affairs* magazine, where he accused the administration of an "arrogant bunker mentality," left many Republicans puzzled. Huckabee also faced his own Willie Horton problem, as it became widely known that as governor he had promoted parole for a man, Wayne DuMond, who went on to assault and murder a woman after his release.[39] In late December Huckabee became embroiled in an ongoing skirmish with Rush Limbaugh, who accused him of engaging in "identity politics" by running as a self-proclaimed "Christian leader." It seemed possible that, as with previous candidates such as Pat Robertson and Pat Buchanan whose core support lay among social conservatives, Huckabee might face a real ceiling on his potential.

Amidst all of this campaign chaos—the rise and fall of Giuliani, the non-candidacy of Gingrich, the rise and fall of Thompson, the arrested rise of Huckabee, and the non-rise of Romney—slowly, almost imperceptibly, one more key ingredient to the 2007 invisible primary was added: the resurrection of John McCain. Though widely viewed as politically dead in July 2007, by December McCain had clawed his way back into the race. He was able to do so because no one else had yet succeeded in filling the vacuum, but his return to the forefront was not inevitable.

McCain cut back costs and returned to a successful tactic of his 2000 nomination campaign, the "Straight Talk Express" bus tour. This time labeled the "No Surrender Tour," capitalizing on McCain's (as the campaign portrayed it) politically courageous refusal to accept defeat in Iraq as the Democrats seemed willing to do. As signs of the Surge's success began to accumulate through the fall, McCain's message began to resonate. By September, news reports pointed out that "McCain's stabilization presents a problem for Giuliani, as both appeal to many of the same voters."[40] In December, McCain gained the endorsement of Joe Lieberman, the hawkish 2000 Democratic vice presidential nominee (Lieberman had lost his 2006 Senate primary to antiwar candidate Ned Lamont, only to retain his seat by beating Lamont as an independent). As analysts pondered why Republican voters had failed to coalesce behind a candidate, many hit upon an explanation that identified McCain as the only contender to really possess the stature to be president. As one pundit argued, "All of the others look inexperienced next to McCain."[41] Helping McCain as well were national polls showing that he was doing much better than Giuliani, and much better than the other Republican candidates, in head-to-head matchups against Hillary Clinton—at that point, the presumptive Democratic nominee.[42] And then, in late December, Pakistan's Prime Minister Benazir Bhutto was assassinated by terrorists, thrusting national security and terrorism—McCain's strengths—once again to the front of the nation's attention.

Indeed, though it was not widely recognized at the time, by mid-December McCain appeared to be in a position not unlike that held by John Kerry at an equivalent point in the 2004 Democratic nomination race. Like Kerry, McCain had once been the front-runner but had fallen out of favor to the point of being considered nonviable. Nevertheless, no clear alternative front-runner had subsequently emerged. Like Kerry, McCain was highly dependent on biography and claims of electability, and stood to gain from the fratricide of those who had leapfrogged him. Also like Kerry, McCain was in a position to get a strong second look from voters who had still not settled on a candidate; he was acceptable to nearly everyone, though few were enthusiastic. He was at least as attractive to independents as Giuliani, but with a record much more acceptable to social conservatives; he had the national security credentials lacked by Romney and Huckabee; and he had a record on spending (including his crusade against earmarks and his 2003 vote against the Medicare prescription drug entitlement) that gave him credibility among fiscal conservatives. Finally, he had a personal story that no one in the field could match. In retrospect, he had found a political sweet spot.

McCain's quiet but growing strength aside, no candidate had really consolidated support among conservatives as the voting was about to begin. McCain had the support of the *Weekly Standard*, while Romney won the endorsement of the *National Review*. Romney also had the support of conservative radio talk show hosts Hugh Hewitt and Rush Limbaugh, while McCain enjoyed the support of Michael Medved. Giuliani was endorsed by Pat Robertson, Huckabee by James Dobson, and Fred Thompson by the National Right to Life Committee. The fragmentation of conservatism obvious in the character of the field itself was replicated in the endorsement lists. It would not be sorted out until the Republican primary electorate did the sorting, and the electorate itself was far from settled. The last national poll released in 2007, Rasmussen Reports from December 27 to 30, said it all: McCain 17, Huckabee 16, Romney 16, Giuliani 15, Thompson 12. It was still anybody's game.

THE REAL VOTING BEGINS: IOWA (JANUARY 3)

The first contest in the nation—the Iowa caucuses—were not finally scheduled until mid-October, when Iowa Republicans set them for January 3 and efforts to leapfrog the state's position ceased. There were two candidates for whom a win in Iowa, by strategic design, had become essential: Romney, who had long led there, and Huckabee, who by December was hard on his heels. Having failed to develop a national consensus, Romney needed Iowa and New Hampshire to start an avalanche. Huckabee was the classic Jimmy Carter–style long shot. He needed to win Iowa just to prove he was a plausible contender, but he also thought that he had a good chance of doing so, given Iowa's demographics and voting proclivities. Iowa also loomed large for Thompson, who saw it "as his best chance to get back in the game," and scheduled two bus tours of the state taking a total of sixteen days before and after Christmas.[43] Giuliani had forsaken Iowa long before; weighed down by his opposition to ethanol, McCain did not run a full-scale campaign there either. He and also-rans such as Duncan Hunter and Ron Paul hoped to finish in the top three to gain some momentum before New Hampshire.

Because of the closeness of the race and the centrality of Iowa to their strategies, Romney and Huckabee spent the last six weeks of the campaign in Iowa engaged in a rapid-fire slugfest reminiscent of the 2004 duel between Howard Dean and Richard Gephardt, which left neither victorious and both nursing wounds. Although the attacks and counterattacks did not preclude the victory of either, they left an opening for others to improve their position. Once again the Iowa caucuses provided a testing ground for the proposition that one wins Iowa with passion and organization, or with passion, organization, and money, but never with money alone. Like Steve Forbes in 1996, who spent an estimated $4 million in Iowa and finished in fourth place, Romney's $7 million expenditure on television ads in Iowa was not enough to compensate for the lack of passion behind him.[44]

When the caucus vote was counted on January 3, Huckabee had upended Romney by the healthy margin of 34 percent to 25 percent. Thompson and McCain finished in a virtual tie for third place, with Thompson slightly ahead with 13.37 percent as compared to McCain's 13.13 percent. Entrance polls pointed to several important trends. First, events in Pakistan (where violence had erupted in the wake of former Prime Minister Benazir Bhutto's assassination) and the increased salience of national security worked in McCain's favor; McCain did his best among the 44 percent who said events in Pakistan were "very important," while Huckabee and Romney both did their best among the 11 percent who said those events were "not too important." Second, Huckabee did four times better than Romney among the voters identifying themselves as born-again or evangelical Christians. In Iowa, they were a whopping 60 percent of the voters; in other states, that figure would be far smaller. Third, McCain did twice as well among independents as among Republicans; to win future contests, he would have to do better in the GOP. And, while Huckabee and Romney did best among voters who were "enthusiastic" or "satisfied" about George W. Bush, McCain did best among voters who described themselves as "dissatisfied" or "angry" about Bush.[45]

At the time, Iowa seemed like the precursor to a long and confused nominating season, but in retrospect, the strategic winner was McCain. He placed well enough in Iowa, despite having run a minimal campaign, that he could move to friendlier territory in New Hampshire with some wind to his back. And Romney, who was trying hard to consolidate a conservative base, and possessed the resources to run a national campaign with the potential to bury McCain, was in trouble. His one-two punch didn't get to one. In a broader sense, Huckabee's rise may have seriously undercut Romney's efforts beyond Iowa, especially in the South, though Huckabee himself almost certainly could not have gained the nomination. As McCain's campaign manager Rick Davis saw shortly before the Iowa caucuses, "Mike Huckabee gives us a new deck of cards to play with. And anything that gives us a new deck of cards is a good thing."[46] However, McCain was far from forging a winning coalition.

McCAIN SEIZES THE POLE POSITION: NEW HAMPSHIRE (JANUARY 8)

In New Hampshire, voting on January 8, the contest had already boiled down to McCain or Romney, and Iowa meant that McCain would get a boost. (The irony, of course, is that Romney finished well ahead of McCain in Iowa. But he performed worse than expected, and McCain the reverse, thus illustrating the importance of expectations in establishing primary campaign momentum.) Huckabee naturally got a bit of a boost from Iowa, as well, but was never really competitive, and there was still some residual support for Giuliani, although he had already downplayed the state.

In one sense, the campaign for New Hampshire had been going on for two years or more, since the major candidates and minor candidates alike encamped there. Romney had long expected to do well in New Hampshire, as had previous statewide officeholders from neighboring Massachusetts such as John F. Kennedy, Henry Cabot Lodge, Michael Dukakis, Paul Tsongas, and John Kerry. Indeed, Romney led the RealClearPolitics polling average in New Hampshire from roughly mid-May 2007 until January 2, 2008; on December 4, one month before the primary, he led McCain 34–16 percent. For just as long, McCain had pinned his hopes on the Granite State, whose hardy independent streak had given him a big win against George W. Bush in 2000. Even before Iowa, McCain had made his move, passing Giuliani in second place in mid-December and winning the endorsement of the *Manchester Union-Leader*, the largest newspaper in the state. And though the *Concord Monitor* stopped short of endorsing McCain, it attacked Romney nonetheless. In another sense, though, it was perhaps the shortest whirlwind of a primary campaign in American history—the New Hampshire vote took place on the fifth day after Iowa. The candidates frenetically crisscrossed the state. Romney was headed down, McCain was headed up, and the only question was whether they would cross paths by the fifth day. They did.

McCain ended with 38 percent of the primary vote, Romney with 32 percent. Others followed far behind: Huckabee (11 percent), suggesting the limitations of his appeal, Giuliani (9 percent), Paul (8 percent), and Thompson (1 percent). As in 2000, McCain won with independents, who supported him by a 40–27 percent ratio. He also got 34 percent of Republican voters, a shade behind Romney's 35 percent. Romney won self-described "very conservative" voters by a 43–18 percent margin, but McCain put together a coalition of "somewhat conservative" and "moderate" voters (he also won among the 15 percent who called themselves "somewhat liberal"). McCain beat Romney among every age group but those sixty-five and older; did a bit better among female voters than male voters; beat Romney soundly on Iraq, terrorism, and the economy, losing only on immigration; and dealt him a particular blow as the candidate who "says what he believes." As in Iowa, Romney took the voters who were satisfied with Bush, McCain those who were not.

Several signs emerged of McCain's broadening appeal. McCain, Romney, and Huckabee won an even three-way split among those who described themselves as evangelical or born-again Christians. McCain won both among those who thought abortion should be legal in all or most cases and those who believed it should be illegal in all or most cases. He also won among all categories of church attendance—once a week, a few times a month, a few times a year, and never—except for the 9 percent who attend more than once a week (Huckabee won there). And he won decisively among gun owners.[47] Within three days, a CNN poll showed McCain leading the pack with 34 percent nationally, up from 13 percent one month before.[48] In light of his New Hampshire win, McCain chose to opt out of public financing for the nomination phase, joining all other major candidates in both parties.

ROMNEY HANGS ON: MICHIGAN (JANUARY 15)

The race then traveled to Michigan, which was already suffering economic travails—foreshadowing the severe economic crisis that would hit in September. As in New Hampshire, two and a half campaigns ran strongly—McCain, Romney, and Huckabee (the half). McCain was coming off his win in New Hampshire, and had won Michigan soundly in 2000. But Romney, as the son of a former governor, had deep roots in Michigan. Moreover, his strategy of winning the earliest contests having come unglued, he had to win Michigan. Huckabee's middle-class economic populism had the potential to play well in Michigan, but as in New Hampshire he lacked the resources to fully exploit his Iowa win, so he chose to focus on upcoming South Carolina.

Romney turned the tables on McCain, emphasizing his economic expertise and the theme of change (already appropriated on the Democratic side by Barack Obama), while McCain continued to emphasize character, experience, and national security. Engaging in his legendary "straight talk," McCain declared that "There are some jobs that aren't coming back to Michigan," an opinion that Romney immediately capitalized on.[49] McCain, for his part, attacked Romney on taxes. The liberal blog the Daily Kos urged like-minded individuals in Michigan to cross over and vote for Romney in the Republican primary, on the grounds that it would be better for Democrats if the Republican race remained in turmoil.[50] (Later, Rush Limbaugh would return the favor by urging his listeners to vote for Hillary Clinton in open Democratic primaries.)

The race in Michigan illustrated the great difficulty with the front-loaded primary schedule, where important contests are fought without a clear sense of the other party's nominee, or whether the current issues of debate will still be critical in the fall. Both parties faced this challenge, but—because they ultimately completed their nomination for all practical purposes long before the Democrats did—it hit Republicans harder. Because there was no incumbent or (by mid-January) even a dominating front-runner in either party, both parties were shooting at a moving target. In 2008, Republican primary voters had to pick a nominee by making their best guess about the match-up in the opposite party and the issues that would be most important come the general election campaign.

In Michigan, the difficulties in making such assessments first became apparent. Romney's emphasis on the economy raised the question for Republican voters: would the economy or national security be the most salient issue in November? Which candidate would best push forward on that front? And would the GOP contestants match up differently against Hillary Clinton than against Barack Obama? Some commentators (though not Romney himself) suggested that McCain might do well against the polarizing Clinton but not so well against the youthful vigor of Obama.

In Michigan, Romney succeeded in cashing in on his economic theme and his pedigree, while McCain failed to repeat his 2000 victory. Romney's 39–30 percent win kept him alive as the race moved south. Huckabee finished a distant third with 16 percent. No one else finished in double digits. Unlike in New Hampshire, Romney consolidated the conservative vote and beat McCain on the economic issue (42–29 percent) and on having the right experience (52–40 percent), a question which for the first time revolved around his business experience. These successes were potentially transferable to other states, but other advantages he enjoyed in Michigan were not—Romney's margin was made by the 44 percent who thought his Michigan ties were important, among whom he beat McCain by a 58–13 percent margin.[51] McCain retained his advantage among independents, and polling showed Republicans nationwide coalescing around McCain, who was the only GOP candidate with rising numbers across all states.[52] This suggested that the result in Michigan might be a blip rather than the start of a trend.

HUCKABEE'S DEAD END: SOUTH CAROLINA (JANUARY 19)

Since 1980, South Carolina has served as a relatively early gateway primary for Republicans. Many a GOP campaign has run aground in the Palmetto State, from John Connally in 1980 to Pat Buchanan in 1996. Most recently, it was John McCain who had seen his presidential hopes sidetracked there. After McCain's impressive win over George W. Bush in New Hampshire in 2000, Bush retooled his message (becoming "a reformer with results") and ran a tough negative campaign aimed squarely at McCain. McCain was smeared by outside groups, and when he lost in South Carolina, his campaign never fully recovered its momentum. In 2008 McCain would have another chance, and there were indications he might benefit from buyer's remorse in the GOP primary electorate. McCain fought hard for the large military vote and hoped to benefit from South Carolina's open primary rule. Romney and Huckabee fought it out for the considerable evangelical vote (though Romney directed most of his attention to the Nevada caucuses held the same day), and Thompson, who had once led South Carolina in some polls, determined to make a last stand. Giuliani had long before dropped out of South Carolina when polls turned against him.

Huckabee led the RealClearPolitics polling average in South Carolina from December 8 until January 16, three days before the primary; as recently as January 8, he led McCain by a 32–20 percent margin, suggesting the importance of religious and cultural issues in the state. However, McCain succeeded in establishing his own pro-life credentials by pointing to his congressional record and to the adoption of his daughter Bridget.[53] In the end, McCain savored a hard-won victory, as both a crucial strategic win and a vindication for 2000. The Arizona senator won 33 percent to Huckabee's 30 percent. Thompson, with 15.6 percent, beat out Romney's 15.3 percent for third place, an ill omen for Romney's standing in the South. As part of a familiar pattern, McCain lost 18–44-year-olds and won those over 45; put together a coalition of the moderate and somewhat conservative voters while losing "very conservative" voters (this time to Huckabee); won all income levels over $50,000 (Huckabee won those below that level); did best among those who were dissatisfied or angry with the Bush administration; won among those who most wanted a candidate who says what he believes and has the right experience (Huckabee won those who said that a candidate who "shares my values" was most important); and won by 17 percentage points among independents. By the time South Carolina's primary rolled around, electability was also a more crucial issue: More than twice as many voters thought McCain had the best chance of winning in November as thought the same of Huckabee, and 69 percent of those voted for McCain.[54]

On the same day as the South Carolina primary, Romney decisively won the Nevada caucuses with the help of the state's large Mormon population, which constituted about half of the voters. Indeed, Romney won nearly as many delegates in Nevada as McCain had won in South Carolina. However, his win was devalued because he was the only major candidate who had mounted a serious effort there, and it was South Carolina that had long ago attained a reputation as a Republican gatekeeper. This again points to the importance of perceptions and expectations in the dynamics of the nomination contest.

Consequently, despite Nevada, South Carolina meant that whatever boost Romney had gained from Michigan was gone. McCain regained the status of clear front-runner; now he had bested both Romney and Huckabee in big showdowns on neutral ground. Huckabee, running in the first southern primary, was shown to face an upper ceiling that was too low to allow him to win the nomination. Romney, who was now one for four in the first big contests, was dealt another blow, though at long last he succeeded in clearing out his bracket when Thompson, having not achieved his South Carolina breakthrough, withdrew from the race on January 23. Thompson's experiment in running for president as a normal human being, not utterly consumed by desire for the office, had failed. To what degree this was a poor reflection on Thompson's motivation and to what degree a poor reflection on the character of the modern presidential selection system was an open question. Thompson's failure could be interpreted as further confirmation, if any were needed, of the breakdown of the Founders' aim of controlling ambition through the presidential selection system.[55]

GIULIANI'S LAST STAND: FLORIDA (FEBRUARY 29)

Florida was the last major stop on the road to Super Tuesday, the February 5 mega-primary day that featured twenty-one state primaries and caucuses and would provide more than a thousand delegates to the Republican convention. It was also a large state with a winner-take-all primary, meaning that whichever candidate eked out a plurality would get the full slate of Florida's delegates. Though it was the first in which Giuliani would be a factor, the contest ultimately centered on McCain and Romney, with Huckabee nipping at Romney's heels among evangelicals. Indeed, some Romney supporters suggested that Huckabee and McCain had formed a quiet alliance; McCain's motivation was to drain Romney's vote, while Huckabee's motivation, some speculated, was a shot at the vice presidential nomination under McCain—or perhaps it was just a deep dislike of Romney.

McCain hoped to do well among relatively moderate northern transplants, the large military presence in Florida, and Cubans, who made Florida the first Republican primary with a significant Hispanic vote. Sensing that he had the upper hand and that this was Romney's last chance to regain momentum before Super Tuesday, McCain took the offensive, accusing Romney of politically driven indecisiveness and calculation about the Surge. While Romney vehemently denied the charge and accused McCain of unfairness, McCain's criticism fed into an emerging narrative of Romney as a "flip-flopper," to use

George W. Bush's 2004 characterization of John Kerry, an image that had gained traction due to Romney's previous reversals on social issues. Romney himself ratcheted up his rhetoric on immigration, trying to make hay out of McCain's support for the 2007 immigration bill. However, Romney's credibility on the issue had been damaged when Giuliani, in the November 2007 CNN/YouTube debate, had scorched him for maintaining a "sanctuary mansion" when it turned out that landscapers working on his Belmont, Massachusetts, home were illegal aliens. McCain's age became an issue when Chuck Norris commented that McCain would be too old to withstand the rigors of the presidency, though Florida's demographic was not inclined to hold his years against him.[56]

McCain had the advantage of renewed momentum flowing from his narrow but important victory in the gateway primary in South Carolina, a fact that his ninety-six-year-old mother, Roberta, sensed when she told an interviewer that although Republicans might be "holding their nose," they were "going to have to take him."[57] He also faced a new challenge in the person of Rudy Giuliani. Giuliani's absence from the fray in Iowa, New Hampshire, Michigan, and South Carolina had allowed McCain to consolidate the vote in his bracket, but Giuliani had chosen to take his stand in Florida and would be targeting many of the voters McCain needed to win. However, it soon became clear that Giuliani had miscalculated, waiting too long to join the battle. By Florida, McCain had established dominance over their common sector of the electorate and indeed had gained the front-running position in the field as a whole. Giuliani relinquished his average lead in the state around January 15. Days before the primary, Florida's Republican Senator Mel Martinez and Governor Charlie Crist endorsed McCain. America's Mayor found that there was not very much oxygen remaining. In contrast to the rough exchanges between McCain and Romney, though, McCain and Giuliani remained friendly throughout, always emphasizing their mutual respect.

On Election Night, McCain pulled out to a small but steady lead over Romney. In the end, he won by a 36–31 percent margin. Giuliani placed a distant third with 15 percent, a death knell for his campaign. Huckabee finished fourth, just behind Giuliani with 13 percent, having notable success only in the conservative Panhandle. If Thompson's experiment in running as a normal person had failed, so too had Giuliani's experiment in running a campaign that ignored the crucial first primaries and caucuses. In retrospect, he might not have had much choice. His campaign did not originally intend to cede the early states, but was driven to that decision piecemeal as his poll numbers in those states took a dive. In the end, the decision not to fight until Florida reflected Giuliani's shortcomings as a candidate in interaction with the primary and caucus calendar. The next day, Giuliani left the race and endorsed McCain, appearing with him at the Reagan Library. Giuliani's exit allowed McCain to solidify his hold on his bracket, and brought a stream of major endorsements: California Governor Arnold Schwarzenegger, who had previously been neutral, endorsed McCain; Governor Rick Perry of Texas, a Giuliani supporter, shifted to McCain; and the GOP apparatus in New York and New Jersey likewise fell in behind the Arizonan.

The exit polls showed again that McCain was judged most likely to win in November over Romney by a 43–33 percent plurality, and seven out of ten of those in the plurality wound up voting for McCain. McCain again won independents by nearly a 2–1 margin over Romney, won the voters who were most dissatisfied with the Bush administration, and held together his coalition of the moderate and the somewhat conservative. For the first time, however, he also won a bare victory among born-again or evangelical Christians. Not least, Florida was the first primary state with a substantial Hispanic population—12 percent of the GOP electorate—and among those voters McCain won by a whopping 54–14 percent gap against Romney. Among the subset of Cuban voters, his margin was 54–9 percent. Romney actually won the white vote, 34–33.[58]

McCAIN'S COUP DE GRACE:
SUPER TUESDAY (FEBRUARY 5)

On Tuesday, February 5, twenty-one states across the nation held Republican primaries and caucuses. Only two candidates could meaningfully compete across that swath. McCain, with his position as front-runner solidified, was assured of favorable free media, while Romney retained the personal resources to run everywhere. Indeed, up through the eve of the Florida primary, Romney had spent more money on television advertising than all the other Republican candidates combined—a total of $29 million on 34,821 ads.[59] The two ran a spirited national campaign, as McCain pressed his advantage and Romney accused his rival of using Nixon-like tactics by unfairly attacking his stance (or, as McCain put it, stances) on Iraq.[60] Huckabee concentrated his meager resources on selected targets of opportunity in the South. In Romney's original plan, February 5 was to be the day when, flush from a string of early victories, he would finish off his competition. In reality, it became the day when his own hopes for the 2008 nomination were buried.

On Super Tuesday, McCain won nine primaries or caucuses, Romney seven, and Huckabee five. On the face of it, this result represented a relatively even three-way split. But this amounted to a decisive strategic victory for

McCain. He won all of the biggest states, including California, New York, New Jersey, Illinois, and Missouri, most by wide margins. In several key states, Giuliani's endorsement seems to have been an important factor.[61] Furthermore, most of the states that McCain won were either winner-take-all statewide or winner-take-all by congressional district, allowing him to rack up a huge delegate advantage. McCain won 100 percent of the delegates from New York (87), Missouri (58), New Jersey (52), Arizona (50), and Delaware (18); 95 percent of Illinois' delegates (54 of 57); 90 percent of the delegates from Connecticut (27 of 30); and 84 percent from Oklahoma (32 of 38). The biggest blow came in California, where McCain won 158 of 170 delegates. Romney placed first in only four of California's 53 congressional districts. For his part, Romney won primaries in Alaska, Massachusetts, and Utah, and caucuses in Colorado, Minnesota, Montana, and North Dakota. Huckabee won his home state of Arkansas, plus Alabama, Georgia, Tennessee, and West Virginia. Altogether, McCain won 608 delegates on February 5 to Romney's 197 and Huckabee's 160. At the end of the day, he possessed more than 60 percent of the delegates needed to secure the Republican nomination.[62]

Although McCain was far from the consensus choice (he received 50 percent or more of the vote in only three contests), he clearly had the broadest support. Of the three major candidates, he had not only the most wins but also the most second-place finishes (see table 3.1). McCain, alone among the candidates, also won at least one primary in the Northeast, Southern or border states, Midwest, and West (see table 3.2). Romney's strength was concentrated in the West, and he won no southern or border states. Huckabee won only southern or border states, had the most third place finishes of any candidate, and was the only candidate of the top three to actually have some fourth place finishes (behind Ron Paul).

McCain's victory was also interesting in another respect. Only three of his nine wins came in states George Bush had won in 2000 or 2004; the other six were in states Al Gore and John Kerry carried. In contrast, five of Romney's seven wins, and all five of Huckabee's wins, came in Bush states. As McCain's supporters would have it, the result was a demonstration of McCain's appeal in Democratic-leaning states, and of his potential to shake

Table 3.1.   First, Second, Third, and Fourth Place Finishes by the Major Candidates

	First	Second	Third	Fourth
McCain	9	9	3	0
Romney	7	8	6	0
Huckabee	5	3	10	3

Table 3.2.   Wins by Region by the Major Candidates

	Northeast	South/Border	Midwest	West
McCain	4	2	1	2
Romney	1	0	2	4
Huckabee	0	5	0	0

up the electoral map. McCain's critics countered that his showing merely demonstrated his ongoing estrangement from the Republican Party. (During the Democratic primaries, a parallel debate took place over whether Obama's success in "red states" was a manifestation of his strengths as a potential Democratic nominee or his weaknesses.)

Romney partisans bitterly complained that Huckabee, who had been out of real contention since at least South Carolina, had blasted Romney's chances by staying in the race. If Romney had received the Huckabee vote on February 5, he—not McCain—would have won the day. This contention was mathematically correct and politically plausible, but far from self-evident, assuming an affinity between Romney voters and Huckabee voters that cannot be taken for granted. Huckabee's down-home populism was at best an uneasy fit with Romney's Wall Street demeanor and privileged pedigree, and Huckabee's evangelical base was demonstrably uncomfortable with Romney's Mormonism. It was Huckabee and McCain, not Huckabee and Romney, who seemed to achieve some symbiosis on the campaign trail. During late 2007, Huckabee's November national surge seemed to come at the expense of the "full spectrum conservatives"; his bigger December surge seemed to come at the expense of the national security conservatives (and undecideds). When Huckabee receded at the end of the month, most of his losses moved back to the national security conservatives, not to the full spectrum conservatives.[63] Not least, McCain finished second in four of Huckabee's five Super Tuesday wins, Romney in only one. Even had Romney been able to inherit a plurality of Huckabee's vote, his win would not have been automatic; he would still have had to leapfrog McCain. McCain's standing among key voting groups did not change dramatically on Super Tuesday. Rather, he had the good fortune to be running in a large number of states where the groups that were his strongest supporters were disproportionately numerous.

Once analysts probed past the superficial closeness of the Super Tuesday results and focused on the depth and breadth of McCain's victory, it became apparent that the nomination was his in all but name. On February 7, speaking before the Conservative Political Action Committee, Romney made a surprise announcement: He was stepping aside from the race. If he carried on, he said,

"I'd forestall the launch of a national campaign and, frankly, I'd be making it easier for Senator Clinton or Obama to win. Frankly, in this time of war, I simply cannot let my campaign be a part of aiding a surrender to terror." An hour later, McCain addressed CPAC, calling himself a "foot soldier in the Reagan Revolution" and making the case for his conservative credentials.

CLEANUP

Although he had dispatched his most dangerous opponent and built a seemingly insurmountable delegate lead, McCain still had to finish the race. Mike Huckabee remained. He was no longer a viable contestant for the nomination—if he had ever been one—but he simply refused to depart from the stage. Hence, while Super Tuesday was the decisive moment in McCain's quest for the nomination, he still had to mop up the opposition.

This occurred in three stages. In the first stage, Huckabee proved that he could not simply be taken for granted. A mere four days after McCain's triumph, and only two days after Romney's exit seemingly cleared the way for McCain, Huckabee won convincingly in Kansas (with 60 percent of the vote), won narrowly in Louisiana (with 43 percent to 42 percent for McCain), and lost narrowly in Washington State (25 percent for McCain to 23 percent for Huckabee). All three were caucus states that favored Huckabee's intense and well-organized evangelicals. For a brief moment, questions surfaced about whether McCain's nomination was as secure as it seemed, and indeed Huckabee's wins did point out the probable nominee's ongoing weaknesses with social conservatives, and the ongoing strength of outsiderism in 2008. Yet Huckabee was not able to compete in primaries, where the electorate was much larger and intensity was less crucial to success.

In the rapid-fire environment of 2008, another set of primaries—the so-called Potomac Primary—gave McCain a chance to quickly answer those questions. On February 12, McCain beat Huckabee 68–16 percent in the District of Columbia and 55–29 percent in Maryland. In the crucial state of Virginia, which presented Huckabee with his best opportunity to extend his winning streak, McCain beat the upstart by a 50–41 percent margin. Here, three quarters of primary voters believed that McCain was the candidate most likely to beat the Democratic nominee, and nearly two-thirds of them voted for him.[64] By sweeping the three-state Potomac Primary (and all 113 of the delegates at stake), McCain put the lid on the speculation of his vulnerability. On February 14, Romney formally endorsed McCain and called on his delegates to vote for the Arizonan. However, Huckabee continued to poll well, holding McCain to just over 50 percent of the vote in the smattering of primaries throughout February (particularly in Washington State, which held both caucuses and a primary, and Wisconsin). Nonetheless, preliminary skirmishing in the general election campaign had begun, with McCain picking fights with Barack Obama over terrorism and Iraq.

Finally, on March 4, McCain broke through and secured the nomination not only practically but mathematically. Two large states and two small states were contested that day, and McCain swept them all. He won Ohio handily (60–31 percent) and Texas, where demographics were more favorable to Huckabee, a little less handily (51–38 percent). McCain also blew Huckabee out in two New England states, Vermont and Rhode Island, with 65 and 72 percent of the vote respectively. As on Super Tuesday, McCain demonstrated the breadth of his appeal, winning in the Northeast, Midwest, and South (or Southwest, depending on how one classifies Texas). A campaign by Rush Limbaugh to try to stop the McCain nomination met its final failure. In Ohio, just over one-third of voters said that radio talk show hosts had an important effect on their vote, while two-thirds said they did not; both groups voted about 60 percent for McCain.[65]

When the dust had settled, McCain had accumulated enough delegates to mathematically assure him of the Republican nomination. Huckabee withdrew and endorsed McCain, leaving McCain to finish the primary season without serious opposition. What eight months before would have been considered fantastical—John McCain's decimated candidacy recovering to win the Republican nomination—was now a reality.

THE RON PAUL PHENOMENON

No discussion of the 2008 Republican primaries would be complete, however, without consideration of the Ron Paul phenomenon. Paul was no part of the play-off brackets; he was a one-of-a-kind candidate who transcended categorization. And there was never a realistic possibility that he could compete successfully for the nomination. Yet he endured longer than any other also-ran, raised considerably more money than Huckabee, and elicited more raw enthusiasm per supporter than most of the field, including some of the top competitors. In the fourth quarter of 2007, Paul raised almost $20 million, more than any other Republican contender.

Paul was a longtime Republican congressman from Texas who had run in 1988 as the Libertarian Party's nominee for president. He argued for a strict interpretation of the Constitution, limited foreign involvements, and big tax and spending cuts; his nickname in Congress was "Dr. No." In short, he sought to supply what many in and out of the Republican Party had concluded were George W. Bush's shortcomings. He was also pro-life on abortion, and favored overturning *Roe v. Wade* and returning the issue to the jurisdiction of the states, facts that many of his supporters probably did not know. But he went far beyond that. He also seemed to advocate a new isolationism, lent support to a number of conspiracy theories, harshly criticized Bush's homeland security measures, seemed to blame Islamist terrorism on American intervention in the world, and even declared that the Civil War was Abraham Lincoln's fault. Paul filled large auditoriums, and did reasonably well in a variety of settings. At the same time, his views on terrorism severely restricted the upper limit of his support; Giuliani's best debate moments throughout the campaign season came when he skewered Paul on that subject.

Paul never won a primary or caucus, but he did place ahead of bigger name candidates in several states (on Super Tuesday, he finished in third place ahead of Huckabee in three states). He broke into double-digit support in Iowa, Maine, Minnesota, Montana, North Dakota, Pennsylvania, Nebraska, Oregon, and Idaho. He did his best after Huckabee left the race, when he was left as the only visible opponent to McCain in several states. Paul ran to the very end of the primary season, netted twenty-one delegates, and then withdrew. He refused to endorse McCain, instead forming an organization called the "Campaign for Liberty" to advance his views.

Who were the Ron Paul voters? Men more than women, young more than old, independents (in open primaries and caucuses), and people who described themselves as "very angry" about the Bush administration. In this respect, his voters were a microcosm of one key segment of the electorate that had shifted away from Republicans in the 2006 midterms. His voters were also consistently more secular and more supportive of abortion than not. His ongoing success implied two things: There was a niche market for a relatively libertarian approach within the Republican Party, and McCain could not take for granted that limited-government Republicans or independents angry at Bush would coalesce behind him.

John McCain began the invisible primary season as the Republican front-runner. He ended as the de facto Republican nominee. In between, his campaign nearly collapsed amid financial mismanagement and political miscalculation. Though Rudy Giuliani temporarily filled the vacuum, he could not sustain the effort; Mitt Romney had the resources to take control of the race, but never caught fire among voters; Fred Thompson appeared briefly viable, but arrived too late and with too little drive; and while Mike Huckabee won the intramural contest for supremacy within his bracket before anyone else, his appeal was too narrow for a real shot at the nomination. Thus the vacuum left by McCain's demise was ultimately filled again by McCain himself.

In the end, the race came back around to McCain, partly because he doggedly clawed his way back into the mix and partly because none of his competitors was able to capitalize on his opportunity. Although he had irritated many Republicans, McCain was perhaps the most broadly acceptable of the candidates, and by the time voting began he seemed to be the one Republican who might be able to salvage a tough year. It was also, as many Republicans remembered, his turn. In 2000, George W. Bush had beaten McCain by forging a coalition of self-described "very conservative" and "somewhat conservative" voters; in 2008, McCain won by building a coalition of self-described "somewhat conservative" and "moderate" voters. He consistently won older voters, voters who were dissatisfied or angry with Bush, independents in open primaries, voters who thought terrorism and the war in Iraq were the most important issues, and voters who valued character, leadership, and experience over specific issues. Despite Huckabee's special appeal to evangelicals, McCain routinely held his own among those voters, and despite Romney's purported strength on economic issues, McCain frequently bested his rival among those who listed the economy as the top issue. He also won because quirks of the primary calendar, including winner-take-all rules in a number of moderate Republican states (many of which had been engineered to aid Rudy Giuliani), came to favor him. Political scientist Larry Bartels' study of presidential primary momentum held that, in 1984, Gary Hart enjoyed about three weeks of momentum after his win in New Hampshire against Walter Mondale. Because the primary calendar was much more spread out in 1984, Hart's momentum faded long before he could secure the nomination.[66] In 2008, Super Tuesday was only four weeks after New Hampshire.

In the end, luck also favored McCain. As noted political analyst Michael Barone pointed out, McCain won the Republican nomination largely because his rivals' strategies failed, rather than his own winning out. After his campaign fell apart in mid-2007, McCain's strategy was to "keep the candidate in the field and hope that other candidates would screw up and that external events would strengthen McCain's appeal. . . . He was like the safecracker who must tackle an unfamiliar safe and must get one tumbler after another to fall into place." For McCain, who benefited from his opponents' failures, the success of the Surge, and the reemergence of national security at the end of December, "all the tumblers fell into place."[67] John McCain was literally the "last man standing."[68]

What McCain's nomination meant for the Republican Party was more difficult to say. On one hand, McCain's coalition was less dependent on conservatives and more reliant on independents and moderates than Bush's had been. On the other hand, McCain could be seen as a move back toward a more traditional Republican commitment favoring spending restraint. Likewise, he was not the first choice of evangelical leaders, but his nomination hardly represented the defeat of the pro-life position in the GOP; quite the contrary. Much would depend on the campaign he would run, and the vice presidential nominee he would pick, to begin defining the post-Bush Republicans.

While the Democratic nomination race would call into question many of the assumptions made by political scientists on the workings of the front-loaded primary system, the Republican race seemed to confirm those assumptions. The front-loaded race made it a prerequisite for candidates to raise a large "entry fee" before voting; of the three candidates still somewhat viable on February 5, two had raised at least $37 million in 2007. As predicted by political scientists, the high financial and organizational cost of running led to a serious thinning of the field before the voting even began, and a further thinning shortly after it started; of eleven GOP candidates, seven had dropped out by January 30. And the race was effectively wrapped up by February 5, only a month after the voting began. McCain seized the momentum in New Hampshire, as John Kerry had done in Iowa in 2004, and rode it to the nomination in fairly short order. Predictions by some analysts that the multicandidate race would remain fragmented, leading to a stalemate and a brokered convention, came to naught, as did the ruminations of others that McCain's intraparty critics might coalesce to stop him after South Carolina.[69]

Insofar as McCain came back from the political graveyard, and insofar as his win represented broad success across the country, his win was impressive. Insofar as he won the crucial states of New Hampshire, South Carolina, and Florida with 38, 33, and 36 percent of the vote respectively, his win was closely run, hardly representing a consensus among Republicans and heavily dependent on contingency. On Super Tuesday, which cemented his nomination for all practical purposes, he won only nine of twenty-one primaries and caucuses. If Republicans had used Democratic proportional representation rules for delegate allocation in all states, the race would have been far from over. Even after Super Tuesday, McCain was unable to put down Huckabee for a month.

McCain clearly benefited from the swell of media coverage he received as he was securing the nomination; he actually led Democratic candidates for some time in the polls in March, one of the few times he did so during the entire campaign.[70] On the other hand, the success of the Surge in Iraq, which had helped propel him to the nomination, was becoming a nonstory to much of the media.[71] Likewise, the relatively early conclusion to the nominating race was a mixed blessing. It was an asset in that McCain could rest, prepare for the general election, and avoid intraparty attacks. However, it was a liability in that it took him out of the news for months while Democrats settled their exciting race.

McCain had won the prize that had eluded him in 2000. He had emerged victorious in his own party and was ready to take on the Democrat. The only question was, which Democrat?

NOTES

1. Stephen Dinan and Eric Pfeiffer, "Straw Poll Revives Huckabee's Bid," *Washington Times*, August 17, 2007, A1.

2. Henry Olsen, "The GOP's Time for Choosing," *Wall Street Journal*, January 5, 2008, A9.

3. Adam Nagourney, "Dark Horse Rode Humor to Second Place in Iowa; Straw Poll Rewards Arkansas Underdog," *International Herald Tribune*, August 14, 2007, 4.

4. To cite one widely noted example, in the November 28 CNN/YouTube debate, Huckabee was pressed on his support for the death penalty. Asked whether Jesus might be said to support such a position, Huckabee replied, "Jesus was too smart to ever run for public office," drawing laughter and cleverly sidestepping an awkward question.

5. Dan Balz and Jon Cohen, "Clinton, Giuliani Maintain Leads, but GOP Shows Signs of Shifting," *Washington Post*, June 3, 2007, A4, http://www.gallup.com/poll/103150/Percentage-Unwilling-Vote-Mormon-Holds-Steady.aspx#2.

6. Michelle Cottle, "Who's Your Daddy? The Masculine Mystique of Fred Thompson," in Franklin Foer, ed., *A Voter's Guide: Election 2008* (New Haven: Yale University Press, 2007), 159.

7. Carl Hulse and Patrick Healy, "Stir in GOP As Ex-Senator Moves to Run," *New York Times*, May 31, 2007, A1.

8. Donald Lambro and Stephen Dinan, "In Florida, Giuliani Seeks to Brake Fall; The State Initially Seen as His Firewall against Early Losses Is Now a Must-win," *Washington Times*, December 16, 2007, A1.

9. Helen Kennedy, "Rudy Has a Woman Problem, Poll Finds," *New York Daily News*, December 16, 2007, 6.

10. For example, see Thomas M. DeFrank, "Why Rudy Can't Win," *New York Daily News*, August 12, 2007, 15; David Saltonstall, "Why Rudy Can't Lose," *New York Daily News*, August 12, 2007, 15.

11. See http://www.acuratings.org/2007all.htm#AZ.

12. E. J. Dionne, Jr., "A Maverick No More?" *Washington Post*, March 28, 2006, A23.

13. Sarah Baxter, "Giuliani Gains a Glow as Republican Savior in Waiting," *The Sunday Times*, February 4, 2007, 27.

14. For a detailed examination of the disarray on McCain's staff from January through mid-July, see Michael D. Shear, Dan Balz, and Chris Cillizza, "Rivalries Split McCain's Team; After Months of Staff Fights, Rick Davis Emerges as the Leader of a Diminished Campaign," *Washington Post*, July 14, 2007, A1. See also Alex MacGillis and Dan Balz, "McCain again Falls Short of Cash Goals; He Slashes Staff, Narrows Strategy," *Washing-*

ton Post, July 3, 2007, A1; Carl Hulse and Adam Nagourney, "Short on Money, McCain Campaign Dismisses Dozens," *New York Times*, July 3, 2007, A1.

15. Michael D. Shear, "Immigration Stance Is Costly for McCain," *Washington Post*, June 28, 2007, A1.

16. Toby Harnden, "Giuliani Set to Benefit as McCain's Campaign Lies in Ruins," *The Daily Telegraph*, July 12, 2007, 19.

17. Michael Gerson, "R. Milhaus Giuliani; A Front-Runner's Political Baggage," *Washington Post*, July 18, 2007, A19.

18. See Marc Santora and Adam Nagourney, "Giuliani Takes on GOP Orthodoxy on Social Issues," *New York Times*, May 12, 2007, A1; Jill Lawrence, "GOP's Commitment on Social Issues Tested; Some Republicans Believe the Clout of Christian Conservatives Is Waning," *USA Today*, May 21, 2007, 6A; Robin Toner, "Anti-Abortion Leaders Size Up GOP Candidates," *New York Times*, July 30, 2007, A13.

19. Among other things, the story in the Smoking Gun highlighted what the vulnerability report called Giuliani's "weirdness factor." "Rudy Giuliani's Vulnerabilities," The Smoking Gun, February 12, 2007, http://www.thesmokinggun.com/archive/years/2007/0212072giuliani1.html.

20. See Celeste Katz, "Rudy Swoops In and Zooms Out," *New York Daily News*, December 30, 2007, 31.

21. David Jackson, "Plans to Make Move in Middle Innings," *USA Today*, December 31, 2007, 6A.

22. Scott Keeter and Gregory Smith, "How the Public Perceives Romney, Mormons," December 4, 2007, http://pewforum.org/docs/?DocID=267.

23. "Mitt Takes a Swipe at Own Party," *New York Post*, September 23, 2007, 7; Joel Achenback, "John McCain's Perfect Ride," The Trail, http://blog.washingtonpost.com/the-trail/2008/02/07/john_mccains_perfect_ride_1.html.

24. Baxter, "Giuliani Gains a Glow."

25. Scott Helman, "Thompson Set to Run, in Jolt to GOP Field; Late Entry Poses Challenges," *Boston Globe*, May 31, 2007, A1.

26. Cottle, "Who's Your Daddy?" 160.

27. See Carl Hulse, "Ex-Senator Seen as Rehearsing for Prime Time," *New York Times*, April 30, 2007, 1; Marc Santora, "Potential GOP Contender Tries Out Lines," *New York Times*, May 4, 2007, 34.

28. Thompson's admitted poor church attendance record led Dobson to opine that he didn't think Thompson was a Christian. Thompson also had to fend off charges that he had lobbied for a pro-choice group in 1991. See Jo Becker and David D. Kirkpatrick, "Group Says It Hired Fred Thompson in Abortion Rights Bid," *New York Times*, July 7, 2008, A9. See also Susan Saulny, "Thompson's Race Hasn't Quite Begun, but Turmoil Has," *New York Times*, July 28, 2007, A13.

29. The campaign turned the episode into a YouTube ad ("Thompson's defining moment") comparing Thompson's response to Ronald Reagan's confrontation with a moderator at the Nashua, New Hampshire, debate in 1980.

30. A study of Thompson's initial fundraising report, detailing $3.46 million of donations, showed that Thompson took more money from previous Romney donors than from prior donors to any other candidate. Michael Cooper and Aron Pilhofer, "A Look at the Fund-Raising of a GOP Non-candidate," *New York Times*, August 3, 2007, A16.

31. Sridhar Pappu, "Music to His Ears; Mike Huckabee Hits a Chord in Iowa and Is Off and Running," *Washington Post*, August 31, 2007, C1; Dinan and Pfeiffer, "Straw Poll Revives Huckabee's Bid"; Nagourney, "Dark Horse Rode Humor to Second Place in Iowa."

32. Ralph Z. Hallow and Stephen Dinan, "Values Voters Back Mike, Mitt; Romney Wins Overall, but Summit Attendees Turn Out Big for Huckabee," *Washington Times*, October 21, 2007, A1. Of all votes, Romney beat Huckabee by a bare 27.6 to 27.1 percent margin; among those at the Summit, Huckabee beat Romney 51.3 to 10.4 percent.

33. There were numerous signs that Brownback's fall directly aided Huckabee in Iowa. For instance, Chuck Hurley, a former state legislator and president of the Iowa Family Policy Center, had supported Brownback but endorsed Huckabee after the senator dropped out. Polling also indicated that Huckabee picked up most of Brownback's support. Stephen Dinan, "Rise a Surprise to All but Huckabee; Simple Conservative Pitch Draws Fervent Faction," *Washington Times*, December 6, 2007, A1; Dan Balz and Jon Cohen, "Huckabee Gaining Ground in Iowa," *Washington Post*, November 21, 2007, A1.

34. Chris Cillizza and Shailagh Murray, "The Man Who Helped Start Huckabee's Roll," *Washington Post*, December 2, 2007, A2; Peter Slevin and Perry Bacon Jr., "Home-School Ties Aided Huckabee's Rise; Early Backers Rallied Conservative Network," *Washington Post*, December 17, 2007, A1; Dinan, "Rise a Surprise to All but Huckabee."

35. Michael Luo, "In Iowa, Mormon Issue Is Helping Huckabee," *New York Times*, November 28, 2007, 26.

36. Michael Luo, "From Back of the GOP Pack, Huckabee Is Stirring," *New York Times*, November 9, 2007, 20; Balz and Cohen, "Huckabee Gaining Ground in Iowa."

37. Ralph Z. Hallow, "Word of Mouth Boosts 'Huck' in Iowa Polls," *Washington Times*, November 22, 2007, A1.

38. In the interview, Huckabee asked, "Don't Mormons believe Jesus and the devil are brothers?" "Huckabee Apologizes for Comments on Mormons," CNN.com, December 12, 2007, http://www.cnn.com/2007/POLITICS/12/12/huckabee.mormons/index.html.

39. Michael Luo and Kathleen Q. Seelye, "Parole Case Haunting Campaign of Ex-Governor; Huckabee's Decisions Draw Fresh Scrutiny," *International Herald Tribune*, December 10, 2007, 6.

40. Dan Balz and Jon Cohen, "Giuliani's GOP Lead Shrinks in New Poll; Ex-Mayor's Numbers at a Low for the Year," *Washington Post*, September 12, 2007, A6.

41. James Joyner, "2008 Election Prediction: McCain Over Clinton," *Outside the Beltway*, https://www.outsidethebeltway.com/archives/2008_election_prediction_mccain_over_clinton. See also Andrew Sullivan, "Only One Republican Can End This War with Honour," *Times Online*, November 18, 2007, http://www.timesonline.co.uk/tol/comment/columnists/andrew_sullivan/article2889302.ece; "John McCain for President," December 21, 2007, http://www.sicsemper.com/node/157.

42. The averages of December head-to-head polls versus Hillary Clinton were McCain +5, Giuliani −4, Romney −5, Huckabee −5, and Thompson −6.

43. Michael Cooper, "GOP Candidates Scrambling to Cope with Rise of Huckabee," *New York Times*, December 17, 2007, A1.

44. Michael Levenson, "Romney Waits for Iowa's Verdict," *Boston Globe*, January 3, 2008, http://www.bostoncomnews.com/politics/politicalintelligence/2008/01/romney_waits_for.html.

45. "Entrance Polls: Iowa," http://www.cnn.com/ELECTION/2008/primaries/results/epolls.

46. Cooper, "GOP Candidates Scrambling to Cope with Rise of Huckabee."

47. "Profile of the New Hampshire Primary Voters: The Republicans," http://politics/nytimes.com/election-guide/2008/results/vote-polls/NH.html; "New Hampshire Exit Poll," *Los Angeles Times*, http://www.latimes.com/news/custom/timespoll/la-exitpoll-nh-graphic,1,6151676.htmlstory.

48. Paul Steinhauser, "Poll: New Hampshire Win Rockets McCain to Frontrunner Status," CNN.com, January 11, 2008.

49. Jonathan Weisman, "Romney Took McCain's Words for a Spin," *Washington Post*, January 16, 2008.

50. See http://www.dailykos.com/storyonly/2008/1/10/2713/87225/55/434206.

51. In contrast, the 56 percent who felt that Romney's Michigan ties were unimportant voted for McCain by a 39–23 percent margin. See "Exit Polls: New Hampshire," http://www.cnn.com/ELECTION/2008/primaries/results/epolls; also "Profile of the Michigan Primary Voters: The Republicans," http:politics/nytimes.com/election-guide/2008/results/vote-polls/MI.html.

52. Charles Franklin, "An Emerging Republican Consensus? Can It Be?" January 17, 2008, http://pollster.com/blogs/an_emerging_Republican_consens.php.

53. Marc Ambinder, "McCain's South Carolina Pro-Life Mailer," *The Atlantic Monthly*, January 11, 2008, http://marcambinder.theatlantic.com/archives/2008/01/mccains_south_carolina_prolife.php.

54. "Exit Polls: South Carolina," http://www.cnn.com/ELECTION/2008/primaries/results/epolls/; also "Profile of the South Carolina Primary Voters: The Republicans," http://politics/nytimes.com/election-guide/2008/results/vote-polls/SC.html.

55. As advisor Rich Galen said, Thompson showed a sense of decency and honor that proved a handicap in the race, http://www.mullings.com/01-23-08.

56. Huckabee, when asked in a Florida debate whether he agreed with his surrogate Norris's assessment, said, "I was standing with him, and I didn't disagree with him at the time, because I was standing next to him. It is as simple as that. This is a guy that can put this foot on that side of my face, and there's nothing I can do about it. . . ."

57. Teddy Davis and Talal al-Khatib, "Sneak Peek: McMom: 'Hold Nose' and Vote," ABC News, January 24, 2008, http://abcnews.go.com/print?id = 4187172.

58. "Exit Polls: Florida," http://www.cnn.com/ELECTION/2008/primaries/results/epolls; also "Profile of the Florida Primary Voters: The Republicans," http://politics/nytimes.com/election-guide/2008/results/vote-polls/FL.html.

59. By contrast, McCain had spent $8 million on 10,830 ads. See Alexander Bolton, "Romney Spends More on TV Ads Than All Other GOP Candidates Combined," *The Hill*, February 2, 2008, http://thehill.com/index2.php?option = com_content&task = view&id = 71131&pop = 1&page.

60. Elisabeth Bumiller and Michael Luo, "McCain Wins Schwarzenegger Endorsement, and Romney Delivers Barb," *New York Times*, February 1, 2008.

61. In New York, for instance, 53 percent of voters said the endorsement was important, and 68 percent of those voted for McCain; in New Jersey, 48 percent said it was important, 71 percent of whom voted for McCain; even in Missouri, 36 percent said the endorsement was important, and McCain beat Huckabee by 20 percent (and Romney by 25 percent)

among those voters. The final results in Missouri were McCain 33 percent, Huckabee 32 percent, and Romney 29 percent. "Exit Polls: New York," "Exit Polls: New Jersey," and "Exit Polls: Missouri," http://www.cnn.com/ELECTION/2008/primaries/results/epolls.

62. For a good summary of the Republican contests on Super Tuesday, see Russ Buettner, Kareem Fahim, Jennifer Medina, and William Neuman, "Super Tuesday: Republican Races," *New York Times*, http://politics.nytimes.com/election-guide/2008/supertuesday/republicanpreview/?scp = 13.

63. The table below shows the aggregation of polling results for each of the brackets at varying points in September through December 2007:

	National Security	Full Spectrum	Compassionate
Sept. 2–9	35%	37%	8%
Sept. 16–23	36%	38%	6%
Nov. 7–10	38%	26%	9%
Nov. 28–Dec. 1	37%	24%	15%
Dec. 14–17	29%	28%	23%
Dec. 27–30	32%	28%	16%

Source: Rasmussen Reports.
Notes: National security = Giuliani + McCain; full spectrum = Romney + Thompson + Gingrich; compassionate = Huckabee + Brownback (estimated at one-half of "other" category in September polls).

64. See http://www.cnn.com/ELECTION/2008/primaries/results/epolls.

65. See http://www.cnn.com/ELECTION/2008/primaries/results/epolls.

66. Larry M. Bartels, *Presidential Primaries and the Dynamics of Public Choice* (Princeton, NJ: Princeton University Press, 1988).

67. Michael Barone, "Republicans Unite; Democrats Divide," January 30, 2008, http://www.usnews.com/blogs/barone/2008/1/30/republicans-unite-democrats-divide.html.

68. Charles W. Dunn, "John McCain: The Last Man Standing," *The Chuck Dunn Report*, April 7, 2008, http://thechuckdunnreport.blogspot.com/search?updated-max = 2008-07-09T14%3A34%3A00-07%3A00&max-results = 7.

69. For an example of the former, see Charles W. Dunn, "Cherry Picking and Leveraging in a Civil War," *The Chuck Dunn Report*, January 22, 2008, http://thechuckdunnreport.blogspot.com/search?updated-max = 2008-02-18T11%3A56%3A00-08%3A00&max-results = 7. For an example of the latter, see Jay Cost, "Is McCain Inevitable?" *RealClearPolitics HorseRaceBlog*, January 23, 2008, http://www.realclearpolitics.com/horseraceblog/2008/01/is_mccain_inevitable.html.

70. "McCain Wins the Coverage Battle as Media Move to Anoint Him," Pew Research Center, Journalism.org, http://www.journalism.org/node/9610.

71. "Iraq War Coverage Plunges," Pew Research Center, Journalism.org, http://www.journalism.org/node/10345.

Chapter Four

The Democratic Nomination Contest

While the Republican race was unfolding, Democrats gave the country another surprise. At the start of 2004, Barack Obama was an obscure Illinois state senator, barely known outside political circles in Springfield and Chicago. The next few months would change everything. Obama was running for the U.S. Senate, and the gods of politics had already shown that they held him in special favor. He had been a legislator since 1996, enduring for most of that time the frustrations of being in the state senate's minority party. In 2002 Democrats gained control, and Obama sensed an opportunity. "You know, you have a lot of power," he said to Emil Jones, Jr., the new senate president. "You can make the next U.S. senator."[1] Jones then began giving Obama prominent bills to pilot through the chamber, allowing him to portray himself as a highly productive lawmaker.

The door to Obama's campaign to the U.S. Senate opened when former Senator Carol Moseley Braun, who would have been a favorite of many African Americans, chose not to run. Obama's prospects profited even more from a speech he had delivered two years before, one that would later also help launch his presidential campaign. In October 2002, a Chicago activist asked him to address a rally against the Iraq War. National security had never been Obama's top concern, but after some hesitation, he accepted. The speech put him on record as an early opponent of the war, a status that would appeal to Chicago's affluent "lakefront liberals" and allow Obama to raise the funds to compete against his principal rival, millionaire Blair Hull.[2]

Obama was more than lucky. His campaign excelled at fundraising and organizing. His rhetorical skills enabled him to connect with diverse audiences. And despite his Ivy League degrees, Chicago had taught him the art of political warfare. Just before the 2004 primary, damaging court files about Hull's messy divorce became public. According to the reporter who broke the story, the Obama camp "worked aggressively behind the scenes to fuel controversy about Hull's filings."[3] After winning the Senate primary, Obama enjoyed another stroke of good fortune. The Republican nominee, facing a messy divorce of his own, withdrew from the race. Unable to find a prominent Illinois Republican to replace him, the state GOP recruited Alan Keyes of Maryland, a brilliant but controversial African American conservative. He never had a chance. Obama was now sure to win the general election.

Democratic presidential candidate John Kerry campaigned with Obama. Taken by Obama's charisma, Kerry picked him to deliver the keynote address at the Democratic national convention. In the speech, he focused on national unity, saying that "there is not a liberal America and a conservative America—there is the United States of America."[4] The oration enthralled thousands at the convention and many more who watched it on cable. Soon there was talk that Obama might run for president—someday.

After the November election, Obama told the *Chicago Sun-Times*: "I have never set foot in the U.S. Senate . . . the notion that somehow I'm immediately going to start running for higher office just doesn't make sense. So look, I can unequivocally say I will not be running for national office in four years. . . ."[5] There were good reasons, of course, why Obama may have doubted that he could be a plausible presidential candidate in 2008. By presidential standards, he was very green—and not just in the ecological sense. As a legislator, he had represented about two hundred thousand constituents, roughly one-third the size of a typical U.S. House district, and his record, while respectable, was not spectacular. Whereas every presidential nominee of the nuclear age had served in the armed forces or run a government organization, Obama had done neither.

The same was also true of the presumptive front-runners for the Democratic nomination, Senator Hillary Clinton (D-NY) and former Senator John Edwards (D-NC). But both had other advantages. As a former first lady, Clinton enjoyed high name recognition and a vast network of contacts. Edwards had sought the 2004 Democratic nomination and served as John Kerry's running mate. Clinton and Edwards had won their Senate seats against serious Republican opponents, so they could say that they knew how to beat the GOP. By contrast, Obama came from a heavily Democratic district and had never had a real fight in a general election. He was no slayer of Republican dragons.

Candidates have sometimes risen to the top tier by championing an ideological cause or a party faction. In 1972, George McGovern rallied the Vietnam peace movement. In 2004, before he flamed out, Howard Dean burned bright as the voice of opposition to the Iraq War and "the Democratic wing of the Democratic Party." But as Obama entered the Senate, it was hard to see how he could set himself apart from Senator Clinton and former Senator

Edwards. There were no major philosophical differences among the three: all cast themselves as progressive problem-solvers.

But then there was the question of their life stories or "personal narratives." Both Clinton and Edwards had or devised compelling narratives of their own. Clinton stood to be the first female president. Many Democratic women could identify with her challenges balancing motherhood with a professional career. John Edwards could point to working-class roots. As he never tired of saying, his father had worked in a textile mill (though he seldom added that Wallace Edwards became a manager).[6] He was also a Southerner, and one who could lay the accent on pretty thickly when he chose to. (No non-southern Democrat had become president since John F. Kennedy in 1960—and JFK squeaked in with less than a majority of the popular vote.)

Obama had an even more dramatic narrative, and he was already an author who had proven skillful in relating it. If he won in 2008, he would be the first African American president. And as he said in his 2004 keynote, there was more. Calling himself a "skinny kid with a funny name who believes that America has a place for him, too," he spoke eloquently of his background. "[M]y presence on this stage is pretty unlikely. My father was a foreign student, born and raised in a small village in Kenya." His mother's parents "studied on the GI Bill, bought a house through FHA, and later moved west all the way to Hawaii in search of opportunity." Together his parents "shared not only an improbable love, they shared an abiding faith in the possibilities of this nation. They would give me an African name, Barack, or 'blessed,' believing that in a tolerant America your name is no barrier to success."[7]

Within the narrative lurked some dangers. The United States had just fought a war against Saddam Hussein, and "Hussein" was Obama's middle name. (Imagine that the GOP nominee in 1944 and 1948 had been Thomas Hitler Dewey.) "Obama" came from Swahili, not Arabic, but it rhymed with the first name of Osama bin Laden. People sometimes mixed up the names, as Senator Edward Kennedy did at a 2005 National Press Club appearance: "Why don't we just ask Osama bin—Osama Obama—Obama what—since he won by such a big amount."[8] Obama's grandfather, the source of his middle name, was a Muslim, and his name sometimes led people to mistake him for a Muslim, a potential handicap at any time, but especially after 9-11.[9]

Other potential stumbling blocks stemmed from Obama's racial identity. Few Americans admitted that they would be unwilling to vote for a black presidential candidate, yet 40 percent thought that the country was unready to elect one.[10] (Hillary Clinton had a problem here, too, since 38 percent said the same of a woman president.) Obama would thus have to confront the belief that the White House was closed to blacks. And not just from white Americans. African Americans were even more likely than whites to doubt that an African American could win. But Obama had another problem. Because he had a white mother and Kenyan father, some cast doubts on his racial authenticity. "Obama isn't black," wrote African American essayist Debra J. Dickerson. "'Black,' in our political and social reality, means those descended from West African slaves. Voluntary immigrants of African descent (even those descended from West Indian slaves) are just that, voluntary immigrants of African descent with markedly different outlooks on the role of race in their lives and in politics."[11] If Obama won, the first black president would be the descendent not of slaves, but (on his mother's side) of slave owners.[12]

Despite these obstacles, Obama sensed a possibility. For the first time in eighty years, neither an incumbent president nor vice president was seeking a major-party nomination. President Bush's 2004 victory was narrow, and his plunging approval ratings gave Democrats an edge in the next election. Democrats would welcome someone who was as unlike Bush as possible. As an African American liberal, a former president of the *Harvard Law Review*, and a gifted rhetorician, Obama fit the description. In this climate, his inexperience might actually be an asset at the polls. As a newcomer to Washington politics, he could run as a change agent not bound to the mistakes of the past. Obama strategist David Axelrod later said: "[V]ery few candidates suffer for having run too soon. Many suffer from running too late and waiting. This was the year that matched up with what he was."[13] From countless poker hands, Obama understood the roles of skill, luck, opportunity, and the rules of the game. And he learned that aspects of the nomination process could work for a skinny kid with a funny name.

THE NOMINATION SYSTEM AND
THE DEMOCRATIC RULES

In late August 1968, Barack Obama was seven years old and living in Indonesia. In most states at the time, party leaders—not the voters—chose convention delegates. Candidates sought party nominations by courting the leaders' support, and the winners tended to be men with deep experience, longstanding fame, or great personal wealth.

That era was about to end.

Nearly ten thousand miles away from young Obama, the Democratic National Convention was taking place in his future hometown of Chicago. Amid disorder inside and outside the hall, party leaders helped Vice President Hubert Humphrey win the nomination even though he had not entered a single primary. Antiwar candidates had done so, and their supporters seethed. To quell the discontent, the convention set up a commission to draft procedural reforms. As a result of the commission's work, the nomination system would thereafter rest on the principle that voters should determine the results through primaries and caucuses.

Senator George McGovern of South Dakota chaired the reform commission. In 1972, he was also the first candidate to win nomination under the new system. Running against President Richard Nixon in the fall, he suffered the worst defeat in his party's history, carrying only Massachusetts and the District of Columbia. Some Democrats began to long for the old system.

In 1976, a former Georgia governor named Jimmy Carter surprisingly took first place in the Iowa caucuses. He parlayed that upset into greater support in subsequent primaries, eventually winning the nomination. His victory in the general election suggested that the new system might work after all. But Carter ran as an outsider, a posture that helped him gain votes but made it hard for him to govern. Despite large Democratic majorities, he had a rocky relationship with Congress. During the 1980 campaign, he beat back a nomination challenge from Senator Edward Kennedy. But by the time of the Democratic convention, many Democratic leaders worried that Carter would lose the general election to Ronald Reagan—which he did.

After the election, another commission devised further changes. Future conventions would include delegates unpledged to any candidate. These "superdelegates" would consist mainly of party leaders and elected officials. Though voters would continue to choose most delegates, the superdelegates would make the nominee more accountable to party organizations and the party in government. Said commission chairman James Hunt: "We must also give our convention more flexibility to respond to changing circumstances and, in cases where the voters' mandate is less than clear, to make a reasoned choice."[14]

In 1984, superdelegates helped put former Vice President Walter Mondale ahead of insurgent Senator Gary Hart. In 1988, *New York Times* reporter Richard Berke explained that superdelegates "are intended to represent the party establishment, particularly if no candidate wins the 2,082 delegates needed for the nomination and there is a brokered convention."[15] But no brokered conventions lay ahead. Between 1988 and 2004, one candidate would always secure the nomination well before the convention, and superdelegates would play a secondary role.

Many superdelegates held elected office. If they displeased their party's voters, future primary challengers might try to deny them renomination. If those voters intensely preferred one presidential candidate over the other, these superdelegates would feel pressure to go along—even when the candidate was an "outsider." But until 2008, this scenario would remain hypothetical.

Meanwhile, the nomination process evolved in other ways. During his 1988 campaign against Michael Dukakis, Jesse Jackson was frustrated that his share of delegates was smaller than his share of the vote. He complained about winner-take-all primaries, in which the candidate with the most votes in a congressional district got all the delegates for that district. He favored mandating a return to a system of proportional representation, used in 1976 and 1980, that allocated each district's delegates according to the candidates' vote shares. After Dukakis clinched the nomination, he agreed to this change in return for Jackson's support. In the talks that led to the agreement, one of Jackson's representatives was longtime Democratic activist Harold Ickes, whom we shall meet again shortly.

Proportional representation had two important potential effects. First, whereas cash-strapped candidates had to focus on states that they could win outright, well-financed candidates could campaign in states where they were unlikely to finish first. After all, there was a prize for second place. They could "lose" a statewide vote and yet take a fair number of delegates. The second effect was the flip side of the first. Once one candidate built a sizable lead in delegates, it would be hard for rivals to catch up.[16]

As with superdelegates, however, proportional representation played only a minor part in the next several elections. One reason was the calendar. States took part in front-loading in hopes of getting more attention and influence. The first-in-the-nation Iowa caucuses and New Hampshire primary had been getting a large portion of candidate time and media coverage. Individual states moved up their dates in order to share in this bounty. But as more and more states did so, they canceled out one another.

Front-loading changed campaign strategy. In 1976, Carter started small and gathered momentum over several months. By the 1990s, with so many primaries and caucuses coming so early, the Carter approach was obsolete. Even if a long-shot candidate won Iowa or New Hampshire, there was now little time to gather resources for later contests. Serious contenders would need a pile of money in advance, leading to a widespread assumption, generally confirmed in practice, that front-loading gave a prohibitive advantage to the front-runner. Officials in both parties disliked the trend, believing that it would make the nomination contest less deliberative. National party committees tried to discourage front-loading, but since each state's party leaders or legislators set the voting date, these efforts had only limited effect.

After the 2004 campaign, the Democratic National Committee formed yet another commission, this time to modify the schedule. It recommended maintaining the first caucuses in Iowa and the first primary in New Hampshire.

There was little choice, as the two states would have fought attempts to move them from the top of the schedule. The commission did, however, propose allowing one or two sets of caucuses between Iowa and New Hampshire, and one or two primaries between New Hampshire and February 5, 2008. Under existing rules, other states could have primaries and caucuses between that date and June 10, a period known as "the window."

The idea behind "pre-window" events was to add greater geographic and ethnic diversity. Western and southern states had long resented the influence of Iowa and New Hampshire. African Americans and Latinos had also noted that both states were mainly white. Accordingly, the Democratic National Committee decided in 2006 to add the Nevada caucuses and the South Carolina primary to the "pre-window" period. Nevada was a western state with a growing Latino population. South Carolina had a large number of African Americans. No evidence indicates the committee chose these states to help any candidate, though there was speculation that Nevada might lean to Governor Bill Richardson of New Mexico, a Hispanic westerner. As for South Carolina, complaints came from DNC member Harold Ickes, who had negotiated for Jesse Jackson in 1988 and was now advising Hillary Clinton.[17] His argument, which did not prevail, was that South Carolina would be an easy win for state native John Edwards. (Ickes will turn up yet again in our story.)

In the first part of 2007, a number of states moved up the dates of their 2008 primaries or caucuses. In the end, twenty-two states and American Samoa held Democratic contests on the first day of the window, February 5. Reporters and political activists came to refer to the date as "Super Tuesday" or "Mega Tuesday." Without approval from the DNC, two states scheduled primaries before that day: Michigan (January 15) and Florida (January 29). Party rules empowered the Democratic National Committee to strip all delegates from states that violated the window. The committee applied this penalty to both states, so a pair of January primaries would now have no delegates at stake.

Even so, the moves started a game of primary leapfrog. The South Carolina primary was originally to take place on January 29. When Florida made its unauthorized move, South Carolina Democrats kept their "first in the South" status by advancing their primary date to Saturday, January 26. A New Hampshire law requires the state to vote at least a week before any other primary. So when Michigan moved to January 15, New Hampshire's secretary of state rescheduled his state's primary to January 8. To maintain its customary position ahead of New Hampshire, Iowa Democrats moved their caucuses to January 3. So despite all the efforts to curb front-loading, the 2008 nomination season had the earliest start in history.

The *New York Times* expressed disapproval: "[T]he two nominees could be settled as early as the first week of February. The longest general election in modern history would follow—a Sahara of hustings boilerplate, venomous Swift-boating, and deepening cynicism from disengaged Americans."[18] Events would not play out that way.

As front-loading continued apace, the need for early fundraising was greater than ever. Candidates' strategic calculations had to include not only the shifting schedule, but the rules and practices of campaign finance. In the early 1970s, Congress created a system of partial public financing of presidential nomination campaigns. Eligible candidates could then get federal funds to match individual contributions, up to $250 per individual. Between 1976 and 2000, most serious candidates took part in this system. Only three candidates, all Republicans, opted out.

By the new century, the matching-fund system was becoming inconvenient. Participants had to abide by national and state spending caps. While the national caps included an inflation adjustment, they did not account for lengthening campaigns, now starting a year before the Iowa caucuses. The state spending caps depended on voting-age populations and made no allowance for states with the greatest significance (i.e., Iowa and New Hampshire). Moreover, the system did not provide for payments until January 1 of the election year.[19] Candidates facing a competitive nomination race feared that they would tap out their treasuries just getting the nomination, leaving themselves vulnerable to opposition attacks during the months' long "interregnum" before their party convention.

Just as public funds became more problematic, two developments made it easier to do without them. The first was Internet fundraising. In his 2000 race for the Republican nomination, John McCain learned that a "hot" candidate could gather millions online. Four years later, Howard Dean went further, reaping more than $20 million through the Web.[20] Dean decided to forgo federal matching funds—the first Democrat ever to do so—and rival John Kerry soon followed. After winning in Iowa and New Hampshire, Kerry was awash in money. Like Dean, he got much of it through the Internet.

The second boost to private financing came from a new law. Under a 1974 statute, individuals could give presidential candidates no more than $1,000 for the primary season. The law did not peg the ceiling to inflation, so it had lost much of its value a quarter-century later. The Bipartisan Campaign Reform Act of 2002 (BCRA) raised the limit to $2,000 with an inflation adjustment. (By 2008, the cap was $2,300.) War chests could now get much bigger.

Higher limits encouraged reliance on "bundlers," people who could harvest large numbers of maximum contributions from well-off individuals. In the 2004 primary season, President Bush opted out of the matching-fund system, as he had four years earlier. He raised $262 million—more than triple his 2000 take—with between 29 and 40 percent coming through a few hundred bundlers.[21] Kerry did nearly as well, raising $248 million, with at least 17 percent through bundlers. His performance showed that bundling and Internet fundraising could be a powerful combination.

During this time, the Internet itself underwent rapid change. Blogging was having an impact as early as 2004, when bloggers showed that a CBS news story about President Bush's military service had apparently relied on forged documents. By 2008, there were thousands of minor political blogs and dozens of major ones, some drawing millions of visitors per month. Online liberal activists acquired the title of "the netroots."[22]

Facebook launched in 2004. The social-networking website served only students at first, but after two years of fast growth, it opened to everyone over thirteen with an email address. The year 2005 saw the debut of YouTube, a video hosting website enabling users to view, upload, and share video clips. At their birth, Facebook and YouTube seemed like playthings, but they would soon become tools in presidential politics. Some feared that the Federal Election Commission might clamp strict rules on cyberspace. In 2006, the Commission allayed these concerns with a unanimous vote not to regulate Internet political activity except for paid advertisements.

One last aspect of the nomination process stirred no major fights during the run-up to 2008. Thirteen states chose delegates through caucus systems. (Texas used a hybrid caucus–primary system.) In caucus states, delegate selection began with many small meetings of Democratic voters. Whereas primaries only involved a brief stop at a polling place (or a few moments filling out a mail ballot), caucus voters had to give up hours of free time. Winning caucuses thus required organization and enthusiasm. In years past, the Iowa caucuses played out in the media spotlight, while the other caucuses (mainly in small states) took place far from the cameras. In theory, caucuses fostered community and civic deliberation. In practice they prevented participation by those who had little time to spare. In 2004, caucuses drew no more than 6 percent of eligible voters.[23] Because the post-Iowa caucuses had seldom mattered, criticisms were barely audible in the din of campaign coverage.

When Barack Obama was a youngster, the nomination system generally produced established or privileged candidates such as Franklin Roosevelt and John Kennedy. By the time he was a senator, it favored candidates who could raise huge sums via websites and bundlers. Money alone would not be enough. After spectacular fundraising in 2003, Howard Dean collapsed in 2004 in part because of disorganization and wasteful spending. The system smiled on well-financed candidates who could spend resources wisely, prepare for the pileup of early contests, exploit the opportunities of proportional representation, understand the uses of new technology, and mount sophisticated efforts to court superdelegates and get rank-and-file supporters to caucuses. These "technical" requirements opened the way for someone just like Obama, who could also excite Democrats at the grassroots and netroots. It might just be Barack Obama's time after all.

THE DEMOCRATIC PARTY

When Barack Obama was born in 1961, the Democratic Party was still a coalition of southerners and blue-collar workers, along with smaller numbers of African American and Jewish voters. A different Democratic Party would nominate him forty-seven years later.

Until the mid-1960s, most southern Democrats were whites who opposed civil rights laws. As late as 1952, this wing was strong enough to secure a vice presidential nomination for Senator John Sparkman of Alabama, a supporter of segregation. Literacy tests and other devices had kept blacks from voting in much of the South. In 1964, only 38 percent of voting-age southern blacks were registered. The 1965 Voting Rights Act cracked the obstacles, and by 1970, black registration was 67 percent.[24]

Nearly all of these voters were Democrats. In states where segregationists had recently held sway, the black vote soon became pivotal in Democratic primaries. Andrew Young, the first African American House member from Georgia since Reconstruction, said that southern white politicians freely used racial slurs as long as blacks could not vote. "Then you registered 10 percent to 15 percent in the community, and folks would start saying 'Nigra,'" Young observed. "Later you got 34 percent to 40 percent registered, and it was amazing how quick they learned how to say 'Nee-grow.' And now that we've got 50 percent, 60 percent, 70 percent of the black votes registered in the South, everybody's proud to be associated with their black brothers and sisters."[25]

By the 1980s, blacks were a crucial part of the Democratic coalition, with about one-fifth of Democratic voters nationwide, and greater shares in the South. In 1988, Jesse Jackson won presidential primaries in Alabama, Georgia, Louisiana, Mississippi, and Virginia. Jackson had only limited appeal to white voters, however, so his support had a low ceiling. While no other major black candidates emerged over the next several elections, white Democratic candidates seriously courted black voters.

Another demographic trend was changing the party's makeup. Between 1970 and 2008, the Hispanic share of the population more than tripled—from just under 5 percent to just more than 15 percent.[26] Because many Hispanics were minors or noncitizens, their share of the electorate lagged behind. By 2008, however, they accounted for about 11 percent of Democrats nationwide, with larger percentages in California, Texas, and Florida.[27]

Women tend to live longer than men, so they have long held a slight majority of the population. Since the 1970s, Democrats have had an advantage among women, especially the unmarried. Because of their larger numbers and stronger Democratic leanings, women made up 59 percent of Democrats at the time of Obama's run, compared with 50 percent of Republicans.[28] "A gender gap is not a big factor in Democratic Party politics," said one expert on gender politics in 2004. "Women and men Democratic voters are much more alike politically than Republican voters."[29] Up to that point, all major candidates had been men. Hillary Clinton's candidacy would test whether a female contender would open a gender gap within the Democratic Party.

As the party's demography was changing, so was its economic base. Unions had long supplied Democrats with money and volunteer work. At organized labor's peak in the 1950s, about 32 percent of workers belonged to unions. By 2007, that figure had fallen to 12 percent. Only a small portion of union members still labored in old smokestack industries, while nearly half now worked in the public sector.[30]

White collar jobs had proliferated, and their occupants were increasingly identifying as Democrats. Professional and managerial workers went from 29 percent of white Democratic voters in the 1960s to 51 percent in the first decade of the twenty-first century.[31] Of Democratic voters, 53 percent had at least some college, and 14 percent had a postgraduate degree.[32] Referring to stereotypes about beverage tastes, commentators came to refer to the college-educated white-collar Democrats as the "wine track" and the blue-collar Democrats as the "beer track."

The new Democratic Party had greater social and economic diversity, but when it came to ideology, it had turned more homogeneous. In the middle of the twentieth century, the party had a strong conservative wing, both in the electorate and among public officials. Conversely, the Republican Party included a clutch of liberals. By the start of the twenty-first century, the voters and politicians had sorted themselves out, with the liberals going to the Democratic side, the conservatives to the GOP.[33] Democrats still differed in their degree of liberalism, and in their approach to political strategy, but the party lacked profound rifts on policy.

In the first years of the new century, most Democrats opposed President George W. Bush. Right after the 2004 election, Gallup found that only 16 percent of Democrats approved of his job performance, compared with 92 percent of Republicans. The seventy-six-point gap was the largest ever recorded for a president who had just won a second term.[34] Some Democrats merely disagreed with his policies, while others loathed him on a deep personal level. One poll even found that 35 percent of Democrats thought that he knew about the 9-11 attacks in advance.[35]

Antagonism toward President Bush and his policies inspired a new generation of Democratic activists. They posted on blogs such as Daily Kos and MyDD, and gave money to groups such as MoveOn.org and Act Blue. The netroots disdained compromise, seeking to smite Republicans and anyone who collaborated with them. "Vichy Democrat" was the slur that some netroots activists applied to any member of their party who backed Bush's Iraq policy.

Senator Joseph Lieberman was the chief target of such disdain. Though he was a loyal Democrat on most issues, he sided with Bush on Iraq and antiterrorism policy. During 2006, the netroots got behind Ned Lamont, who challenged Lieberman in the Connecticut senatorial primary. Lamont won, prompting Lieberman to run as an independent. In the fall campaign, most national Democratic leaders backed Lamont. With support from Republicans and independents, Lieberman won another term in the Senate, where he would remember the Democrats who had abandoned him.

In all, a number of dividing lines crisscrossed the Democratic landscape: wine track and beer track; white, black, and Hispanic; female majority and male minority; hate-Bush and dislike-Bush. To win the nomination, a candidate would have to gather multiple pieces of this mosaic. Anyone reading this book knows that Barack Obama did it. But *how* did he do it? This chapter will shortly address this fascinating question. Right now, we shall consider another: who else tried to do it?

THE FIELD

The 2008 cast of characters falls into three categories: those who did not run, those who ran but had little chance, and those who counted.

Many Democrats thought that the courts had cheated Al Gore out of victory in 2000, and there was some speculation that he might try to redeem himself in 2008. He eventually opted out. He had grown comfortable in private life, and he could console himself with significant honors: an Emmy for his interactive television network, an Oscar for a documentary on climate change, and most of all, the Nobel Peace Prize, which he shared with the UN Intergovernmental Panel on Climate Change.

John Kerry had narrowly lost to Bush in 2004, and in hindsight, a number of Democrats saw him as a flawed candidate. He reacted slowly when the

Swift Boat Veterans for Truth attacked his war record, and he made damaging gaffes. During the 2006 midterm campaign, he made another. "You know education, if you make the most of it, you study hard, you do your homework and you make an effort to be smart, you can do well," he told students at Pasadena City College. "And if you don't, you get stuck in Iraq."[36] Kerry meant it as a swipe at President Bush, but it sounded like an insult to the troops. It snuffed out his chances, and he soon announced that he would not run again in 2008.

Three Democrats made abortive runs. Tom Vilsack, the outgoing governor of Iowa, declared his candidacy in 2006 and withdrew in 2007, with few voters noticing either announcement. Former Governor Mark Warner of Virginia and Senator Evan Bayh of Indiana were moderate, accomplished leaders who had won Republican states: if electability had been the main criterion, they would have been contenders. But Democrats wanted to beat Bush's party, not meet it halfway. Warner tried to compensate by hiring netroots guru Jerome Armstrong, but when no cyber-groundswell materialized, he bowed out. Bayh formed an exploratory committee, only to close it after two weeks.

Representative Dennis Kucinich of Ohio and former Senator Mike Gravel of Alaska ran low-probability, low-budget campaigns. (To reach the National Press Club for his announcement, Gravel took the Washington subway.) In televised debates, they both raged against the war in Iraq, but with no impact.

Senators Christopher Dodd of Connecticut and Joseph Biden of Delaware were more serious candidates. Both were white males with long service in high office and extensive records on national issues—exactly the kind of figures who once dominated presidential politics. In the 2008 election cycle, they ended up as also-rans. And in his own way, each served as a cautionary example for Barack Obama.

Dodd was a reminder that opportunities may come too late. The youngest winner was John Kennedy at forty-three, and the oldest was Ronald Reagan at sixty-nine, so we can say roughly that candidacy is practical between the ages forty and seventy. A thirty-year period may sound lengthy, but it only covers eight presidential elections. There is no guarantee that any will offer a clear shot—as Dodd's career showed. He won his Senate seat in 1980 at the age of thirty-six. In 1984, Walter Mondale seemed a heavy favorite for the nomination, and his main challenger was Dodd's friend Gary Hart. Three other times, another New England liberal got into the race (Michael Dukakis in 1988, Paul Tsongas in 1992, and Kerry in 2004). Bill Clinton had a lock on the nomination in 1996, and Al Gore had a near-lock in 2000. Any Democrat who won in 2008 would be the presumptive nominee four years later. Despite Hillary Clinton's advantages, 2008 was Dodd's last chance. By this time, he was an old, jowly member of the Washington establishment with no natural constituency. The political gods had barred Dodd from the White House. The lesson was simple: if fate offers you a handhold, grab on. It may never come back.

Biden's lesson was different. He did seize an early opportunity, running for president in 1988. He botched it by plagiarizing from a British politician and wildly distorting his own academic record. With some help from other candidates' opposition researchers, the media scorched him, and he withdrew. By the 2008 campaign, his reputation as a gaffe machine had faded. He promptly revived it, joking that Indian Americans ran all the convenience stores in Delaware and referring to Obama as "clean" and "articulate"— words that many African Americans took as condescending. Biden's slips reminded Obama—already a disciplined politician—never to let down his guard.

On paper, the best-qualified candidate was Governor Bill Richardson of New Mexico, who had previously served as a House member, UN ambassador, and Secretary of Energy. With his Hispanic heritage and Spanish fluency, he could appeal to a fast-growing demographic group. In a general election, his pro-business record could win Republican votes.[37] Two problems held him back. First, he had made many of his political contacts in the Clinton administration, and Hillary Clinton had first call on their money and expertise. Second, he was sloppy in preparing for media appearances and public events. Journalist Margaret Carlson said that watching Richardson's mid-2007 interview on *Meet the Press* was to see a candidate "get rattled, come undone, and finally condense into a puddle on the studio floor."[38]

The top tier started with John Edwards. Before joining the Kerry ticket, he had been Kerry's longest-surviving rival for the nomination. During that campaign, he had shifted from the center to the left, moving toward Howard Dean on the war and protectionist Richard Gephardt on trade. His migration continued after the general election. "He has worked very hard over the past four years to figure out what every constituency wants," said a leading progressive activist.[39] In 2005, he made a dramatic statement on Iraq: "I was wrong. . . . It was a mistake to vote for this war in 2002. I take responsibility for that mistake."[40] He proposed a bold health care plan, which he suggested could lead to a single-payer system. He also pledged a new war on poverty and trade policies that "put workers first."

As mentioned earlier, he had youthful good looks and an appealing working-class background. He also had several weaknesses that would become more and more evident. With no executive experience, he proved unwise in choosing subordinates. He tried to cultivate the netroots by hiring two prominent bloggers. The move backfired when conservatives attacked them for posting anti-Catholic statements on other sites. Edwards initially declined to fire them, but they soon quit. Thus he incurred conservative wrath for hiring them and liberal wrath for letting them go. His political action committee spent more than $100,000 for a videographer with whom he was having an affair. News of the liaison would hit the tabloids by the end of 2007.

His physical appearance was a liability as well as an asset. YouTube videos showed him fussing with his hair (some versions included the song "I Feel Pretty") and campaign finance reports included bills for $400 haircuts. More seriously, a set of disclosures scratched up his "man of the people" image. He had made millions as a trial attorney, and used some of the money to buy a 28,200-square-foot home on a 102-acre estate.[41] After the 2004 election, he set up a nonprofit organization to fight poverty, but press reports later revealed that most of its funds went to his travel and other activities to keep him in the news.[42] One trip took him to the University of California at Davis, where he gave a speech on poverty—for which he charged $55,000.[43]

Edwards arguably had special ties to white southerners and blue-collar workers. Decades before, they were the party's bulwarks, but now they were just two shrinking pieces of the Democratic Party's mosaic. Amid questions about his authenticity, it was not certain that he could even hold on to these pieces.

In all of American history, being a white male had been a virtual prerequisite for the presidency. In 2008, it put Edwards at something of a disadvantage. One blogger said: "Edwards is so great on the issues young people care about. But I think the possibility of having the first female or African American president embodies change in a way that Edwards can't."[44]

For years, it seemed likely that a female president would come before an African American president. Whereas Geraldine Ferraro had been the Democratic vice presidential nominee in 1984, no African American had ever been on a major party national ticket. In the 1992 campaign, Hillary Clinton had half-jokingly suggested that she would be a copresident: "If you vote for my husband, you get me; it's a two-for-one, blue-plate special." After her 2000 election to the Senate, thoughts about a Hillary Clinton presidency became more serious. Even as she was seeking reelection to the Senate in 2006, she was gathering staff for a national campaign.

In addition to her near-universal name recognition and support from women, Clinton had gained other advantages. As a senator, she had burnished her national security credentials with a seat on the Armed Services Committee. After the 9-11 attacks, she helped secure federal aid for New York's recovery, so she could now claim experience in crisis management. She could say that she had proved her electability in her reelection race. She carried fifty-eight of New York's sixty-two counties, including Republican strongholds.

There was a reason for doubt, however. Her 2006 showing said little of her national chances, since she had faced a weak opponent in a great year for her party. She remained a polarizing figure, with 39–44 percent of the electorate saying that they would not vote for her.[45] After losing two close presidential elections, many Democrats worried that she might cost them a third. Moreover, there was opposition from within. "She's part of the Clinton machine that decimated the national Democratic Party," wrote Markos Moulitsas of the Daily Kos. "And she remains surrounded by many of the old consultants who counsel meekness and caution."[46]

A 2008 Hillary Clinton victory would be another "two-for-one, blue-plate special," with the former president joining her both in living quarters and the public mind. He was the ultimate mixed blessing. His administration was a time of peace and prosperity, political scandal and policy frustration. He outmaneuvered Republicans and compromised with them. He secured his own reelection and presided over the first GOP takeover of both chambers of Congress since 1952. Poll respondents gave him high marks for performance and low marks for character. His presidency had made her candidacy possible, but it also rendered it risky.

Perhaps her biggest problem was her vote to authorize the Iraq War. While changing her position, she refused to apologize or say that her initial stand had been a mistake. That refusal angered the netroots. Biden, Dodd, and Edwards had voted for the war too, but all eventually made acts of contrition.

Clinton's troubles ensured that many Democrats would want an alternative. But who would it be? A 2007 survey asked Democrats which was more important to their candidate choice: experience or the ability to bring about change. Only 26 percent chose experience while 73 percent wanted change.[47] If Democrats valued freshness over familiarity, Obama was the one. Edwards was relatively young, but he was already a two-time loser (first the presidential nomination in 2004, then the vice presidency). The others belonged to an older generation: Biden and Dodd were both in Congress before Obama graduated from high school, and Clinton was born only five years later than Obama's mother, who died in 1995 at age fifty-three.

Despite his 2004 promise not to run for national office in 2008, he started positioning himself for a future race soon after entering the Senate. "The Plan," as his aides called it, meant establishing his national security credentials through international travel and raising his profile with a new book.[48] *The Audacity of Hope*—a title that came from a sermon by his pastor, Jeremiah Wright—was part memoir, part manifesto. It topped best-seller lists, and the book tour got press attention in dozens of cities. During the 2006 midterm campaign, he appeared at many Democratic events, including Senator Tom Harkin's Steak Fry in the critical caucus state of Iowa.

Obama's stock went up as approval for the Iraq War went down. Thanks to his 2002 Iraq speech, he could say that he had opposed the war right from the start—a claim that no other major candidate could make. By itself, credibility on Iraq would not be enough. In 2004, Howard Dean ran on his antiwar position, only to lose early and big. Dean's stridency, which attracted antiwar activists, put off voters who disliked polarization. When he addressed followers after his loss in the Iowa caucuses, television captured the "Dean Scream," an exuberant cheer that sounded on television like a crazy rant. Unlike Dean, Obama could fire up supporters while keeping cool. There was never an "Obama Scream," and it is hard even to imagine one.

Obama had the rare gift of satisfying audiences who wanted contradictory things. He voted against John Roberts as chief justice, but perplexed some liberals when he refused to condemn Democratic colleagues who voted for him. Blogging at the Daily Kos, he argued against the "with us or against us" attitude: "I think this perspective misreads the American people. From traveling throughout Illinois and more recently around the country, I can tell you that Americans are suspicious of labels and suspicious of jargon." Yet even as he was coming across as a unifying, post-partisan figure, he reassured progressives by attacking a "sharply partisan, radically conservative, take-no-prisoners Republican Party" that supported "homophobia and Halliburton," sought to "dismantle government safety nets," and embraced "a theological absolutism."[49] He would reach across the aisle with one hand and make a fist with the other.

Obama deftly adapted his language and accent to his listeners. With college students, he slipped in pop-culture references. With groups of professionals, he adopted a professorial tone. With urban African American audiences, he spoke in a street accent. Such "code switching" is hard to pull off, and politicians can embarrass themselves when they do it poorly. In early 2007, Hillary Clinton spoke at a church in Selma, Alabama, and used dialect to quote a hymn: "Ah don't feel noways tahred!"[50] She sounded silly, and the line soon became an object of ridicule.

As the campaign drew near, it was clear that Obama was nimbler than Clinton. It was also clear that she had daunting strengths. The Clintons had been working together on political campaigns since 1974, when Obama was thirteen years old. While their "machine" may have irritated liberal bloggers, this network of supporters reached across the country and could raise huge sums of money. Obama needed black voters, but early polls showed that they favored Clinton.[51] Bill Clinton's support among African Americans had apparently transferred to his wife. Despite his success in Illinois and his promise on the national stage, Obama could claim nothing comparable. She had boots on the ground. He had the audacity of hope.

STRATEGY AND TACTICS IN 2007

Two days after Christmas 2006, John Edwards announced his candidacy with an Internet video.[52] Clinton and Obama did the same a few weeks later. Obama followed his online message with a more traditional announcement speech in Springfield, Illinois. In the speech, he invoked Abraham Lincoln, implicitly likening himself to the "tall, gangly Springfield lawyer" who "called on a divided house to stand together."[53]

Early on, Clinton and Obama both decided to decline federal matching funds and thus avoid the restrictions that came with them. (Obama also promised that if he won the nomination, he would pursue an agreement with the Republican nominee to preserve public financing of the general election campaign.[54]) On April 1, Clinton announced that she had raised $26 million in the first quarter of 2007. Clinton aides were happy not only that she had set a record for that stage of a campaign, but that she had so strongly outpaced Edwards, who had raised only $14 million.

On April 4 came word of Obama's total: $25 million. That figure surprised the political world and instantly established Obama as Clinton's main competitor. How did he raise so much?

Most came from people who gave $1,000 or more.[55] Obama profited from the Democratic Party's new economic and demographic profile. Despite polls showing black support for Clinton, areas with concentrations of affluent African Americans gave much more to Obama.[56] Other groups were fertile sources as well. With his youth, innovative approach to politics, and tech savvy (he kept a Blackberry with him at all times), Obama was a natural fit for Silicon Valley. It was his for the taking. During the Clintons' last national campaign, in 1996, the Internet was just getting started, so she did not have the same ties to tech entrepreneurs as to other business leaders. Her campaign failed to make a serious approach, thus leaving Obama with a huge pool of money all to himself.[57] Seeing that Clinton drew from "old money" types such as bankers, "new money" types such as hedge-fund managers gravitated to Obama. It was a matter of access, or as one hedge-fund manager put it: "To be in Hillary's inner circle, you had to be giving a decade ago, when Bill was president."[58] Obama also made inroads in Hollywood, due in part to talent agent Ari Emanuel, brother of Representative Rahm Emanuel (D-IL).

In the name of reform, Obama refused money from lobbyists and political action committees. His refusal gained him favorable publicity and set up a contrast with Clinton, who accepted such contributions. "It's a politically smart position for him to take. It sounds profound," said Massie Ritsch, communications director for the Center for Responsive Politics. "But in fact neither PACs nor lobbyists give a lot to presidential campaigns. He's not leaving a whole lot of money on the table by eschewing PACs and lobbyists."[59] Like Clinton and Edwards, he relied on "bundlers" to gather most of his contributions over $1,000. Also like them, he recruited a large portion of his bundlers from the ranks of lawyers and law-firm employees.[60]

Obama had one hundred thousand contributors in all, twice Clinton's number. A majority gave through the Internet, and their contributions amounted to nearly $7 million, compared with just over $4 million for Clinton. Less than half had "maxed out" at the $2,300 contribution cap, while two-thirds of Clinton's donors had done so. Because so many of Obama's donors gave small sums at first, he could tap them again during the campaign.[61] Clinton would have to prospect for additional money.

Obama's message was firing up large numbers of people. His campaign staged huge fundraising events with low-priced tickets. "Those rallies drove huge interest from the community, and these people went right home to their computers to donate," said a member of his finance committee. "These, for the most part, were people who had never been involved before."[62] Obama supporter Steven Westly, former California controller and eBay founder, said that "he's got an extraordinary thing going on in the cyberworld of politics . . . a lot of sophisticated social networking tools, blogging teams and stuff that no one has been coming close to."[63]

Obama's social networking site, MyBarackObama.com, invited supporters to create their own profiles, blog about their campaign work, identify recruits, organize events, and raise money.[64] The campaign also used Facebook, MySpace, Twitter, Flickr, Digg, and BlackPlanet, among others. Much of the pro-Obama cyber-activity was spontaneous. On the day that Obama announced in January, a University of Missouri staffer started a Facebook group called "One Million Strong for Barack." Within a month, it had more than a quarter-million members. Only 3,700 signed up for "One Million Strong for Hillary."

YouTube enabled anyone to see Obama speeches at will, including his famous 2004 keynote address. Some freelancers got into the act. An Obama supporter made a video mashup of Clinton clips and the famous *1984* Macintosh ad. It depicted the Clinton campaign as a model of mindless, "Big Brother" conformity and ended with a graphic showing the Obama campaign's Web address. Aspiring model Amber Ettinger, a.k.a. "Obama Girl," appeared in "I Got a Crush . . . On Obama." The campaign did not approve of its suggestive visuals and lyrics, but its millions of views did Obama no harm. The video was a sign of "Obamamania," the celebrity appeal that Republicans would later lampoon. And in an odd way, it showed how far race relations had progressed. A 1968 television musical caused national controversy when singer Petula Clark merely touched Harry Belafonte's arm. Forty years later, a white woman sang about her "crush" on an African American presidential candidate. Critics panned the video's raciness, but hardly anyone noted a racial angle.

The mainstream media remained important. Candidates ran broadcast ads and sought "free" or "earned" media by way of news coverage. And they had debates—seventeen in 2007 (including one on National Public Radio), and nine more in 2008. With eight candidates on stage, the early debates did not allow for lengthy, thoughtful discussion, but they did influence the campaign in several ways.

During the debates, John Edwards forcefully presented liberal arguments on Iraq, health care, poverty, and other issues. Although Clinton and Obama already had liberal records, Edwards tugged them a bit farther to the left: in May, for instance, both voted against a funding bill for the wars in Iraq and Afghanistan. "He's a serious candidate and he's not to be discounted just because he lags in the national polls," said Democratic pollster Mark Mellman, who was neutral in the contest. "It's a smart strategy for the front-runners to follow him."[65]

Clinton showed that she was a formidable debater, able to parry tough questions such as why she did not read the National Intelligence Estimate before voting for the Iraq War. She did hit one rough patch. In October, she bobbled a question about New York Governor Eliot Spitzer's plan to give driver's licenses to illegal aliens. "I did not say that it should be done, but I certainly recognize why Governor Spitzer is trying to do it." Dodd cut in: "Wait a minute. No, no, no. You said yes, you thought it made sense to do it." She replied: "No I didn't, Chris." But after a follow-up question, she said: "It makes a lot of sense. What is the governor supposed to do?" And then: "Do I think this is the best thing for any governor to do? No."[66] This showing did not immediately dent her national poll numbers, but it did supply ammunition to her opponents. In hindsight, the October debate, which came shortly after the much-publicized release of her health care plan and a seemingly significant breakthrough over the 50 percent mark in polls, may have marked the beginning of her fall.

Obama's most controversial debate moment came during the YouTube debate in July 2007. A viewer video asked if candidates would meet with hostile foreign leaders "without precondition." Obama said that he would, and Clinton later declared his stand to be naïve. Noting that presidents had met with the likes of Stalin and Mao, Obama told his staff not to back down. Obama communications director Dan Pfeiffer said: "Instead of writing a memo explaining away our position to reporters, we changed our memo and wrote an aggressive defense of our position and went on the offense. . . . It was like we had taken our first punch and kept on going."[67] And as the months wore on, Obama got sharper in debate. His early performances were sometimes stiff and professorial, but by the end he was regularly able to redirect the discussion to his basic themes of change, hope, and a "new kind of politics."[68]

On November 12, six of the candidates spoke at the Iowa Democratic Party's Jefferson Jackson Dinner in Des Moines. Obama was the star, giving an impassioned speech with tough jabs at Bush and implicit digs at Clinton: "When I am this party's nominee, my opponent will not be able to say that I voted for the war in Iraq; or that I gave George Bush the benefit of the doubt on Iran; or that I supported Bush-Cheney policies of not talking to leaders that we don't like."[69] The speech drew ovations from the crowd and praise from the netroots. "The Iowa Jefferson Jackson Dinner ended up being a tipping point in the election," said Pfeiffer. "That's when we took the lead in our internal polling in Iowa for the first time."[70] Obama campaign manager David Plouffe explained why the speech was so crucial. Clinton, he said "had a lot of different ways to win and we only had one. We had to win Iowa, and then obviously we had to win this delegate battle, when it turned into a long race."[71] Obama needed Iowa in order to destroy Clinton's air of "inevitability" and reinforce his own credibility.

As Plouffe's remarks suggest, Obama's post-Iowa strategy was all about delegate arithmetic. Instead of trying to run up his total popular vote in big primaries, the campaign would exploit proportional representation and target districts from which it could win delegates.[72] It would work the small-state caucuses, where organization mattered more than costly media buys. This plan was efficient: after all, a Wyoming delegate counted just as much as a California delegate, and would cost far less to win. And early in 2007, the Obama campaign was already calling superdelegates. By the end of the year, Clinton had a big lead among superdelegates who had announced a preference, but most remained undecided. Though Obama had not yet won their votes, he had gained their ear.

The Clinton campaign's strategy was different. A staff member told journalist Roger Simon: "They thought it was all about winning states and not delegates."[73] Clinton would win Iowa or New Hampshire (preferably both), sweep the Super Tuesday primaries, and that would be that. Democratic voters and politicians would swing massively in her favor, forcing Obama out of the race, and making the subsequent primaries and caucuses irrelevant. In mid-2008, a Clinton strategist looked back with regret: "We just thought we'd win the primaries, and the caucuses would follow along. It's on the top of the list of changes we'd like to do over."[74]

In hindsight, the Clinton approach seems disastrous. But it is easy to see how it could have made sense at the time. As front-loading had advanced, so had the date at which candidates sewed up the nomination. In 2004, Kerry won the Super Tuesday primaries on March 2, and Bush called to wish him a good general-election campaign. In 2008, Super Tuesday included even more states and came even earlier, so it was reasonable to think that the contest would end in February.

The early-knockout scenario overlooked differences between 2008 and past campaigns. When previous insurgents upset front-runners in early contests, they usually could not raise money and muster troops fast enough to compete in the big, expensive later contests. Front-runners could recover from setbacks by falling back on their superior resources and organization. This time, the outsider had equivalent resources—both candidates raised about $100 million in primary money during 2007—and a better organization. Whereas the Clinton campaign suffered from internal warfare and tangled lines of authority, the Obama team was unified and disciplined. And his staff had stronger motivation. Working for Obama was a cause, while working for Clinton was a career move. As one staffer put it: "We were a DC-based, bloated campaign with people who were with her because she was the safest bet and we paid the most and hired the most and she was the most likely nominee. And at headquarters, we were all just worried about getting shivved in the shower."[75]

An Iowa victory would enable Obama to keep the campaign going to the point where delegate arithmetic would start to trump front-runner psychology. Only one major Clinton advisor grasped this possibility: Harold Ickes, who had helped shape the proportional-representation system twenty years earlier. Twelve days before the Iowa caucuses, he wrote in a memo: "Assuming that after Iowa and New Hampshire the presidential nominating contest narrows to two competitive candidates who remain locked in a highly contested election through 5 February, the focus of the campaign and press will shift to the delegate count." He concluded that the Clinton campaign would then have to shift resources accordingly.[76] Ickes finally got the campaign's attention at the start of the year, but by that time it was very late for the necessary planning.

If Clinton aides lacked a strategy for hunting delegates, they did know the voters they were targeting. In March 2007, Clinton strategist Mark Penn wrote: "Our winning strategy builds from a base of women, builds on top of that a lower and middle class constituency, and seeks to minimize [Obama's] advantages with the high class Democrats."[77] Hillary Clinton, Wellesley College '69, Yale Law '73, may seem an improbable champion of the working class. But she had also been first lady of the "beer track" state of Arkansas and a senator from New York, an industrial state with the nation's highest rate of union membership.

The Clinton team also had good reason to count on the Hispanic vote. Her connections stretched back to 1972, when she helped register voters in San Antonio. Her husband had always been popular among Hispanics, and her New York constituency included a large Hispanic population. In some places, moreover, political friction between black and Hispanic communities seemed likely to disadvantage Obama. Clinton seemed ready to bridge that divide, as a December Gallup poll showed that black Democrats preferred her by a margin of 53–39 percent.[78] She had the endorsement of leading black Democrats such as Representatives John Lewis (Georgia) and Charles Rangel (New York) as well as former Atlanta mayor Andrew Young.

Late in 2007, Obama got his own high-profile endorsement, from Oprah Winfrey. Although it generated news stories and campaign contributions, it did not solve a basic problem: many black voters worried that prejudice rendered him unelectable. His campaign needed to prove that white voters would go for a black candidate, and the best place to do so was in a mostly white state. "We have to do well in Iowa and New Hampshire, and if we do, we will win South Carolina," said his campaign's national political director. Black support hinged on white support.[79]

There was a generation gap among both blacks and whites. Older voters leaned toward Clinton—the older, more experienced, and more familiar candidate. Younger voters, especially students, were more likely than their elders to support Obama—the younger, more exciting, and fresher candidate.[80] Obama already had an energetic cadre of young volunteers. Because of lower participation rates in the past, however, turning out large numbers of young voters would take work.

Former law school lecturer Obama did well among upper-income professionals, as Penn's memo suggested. And while progressives and netroots activists liked Edwards, they preferred outsider Obama to insider Clinton. At the 2007 Yearly Kos, an annual netroots meeting, Obama and Clinton argued about special interests. Clinton defended her acceptance of lobbyist contributions: "A lot of those lobbyists, whether you like it or not, represent real Americans. They represent nurses, social workers and yes, they represent corporations and they employ a lot of people." The remark drew boos and hisses. Obama got applause for attacking the influence of special interests such as insurance and drug companies.[81]

Although Clinton and Obama had similar *positions*, the Yearly Kos story stands as a vivid reminder that they had different *messages*. One way to analyze these messages is to lay out what each campaign said about itself and what it said about its opponent. The two kinds of messages were linked, as each side used its strengths to highlight the opposition's weaknesses, and vice versa.

Obama on Obama: "The fundamental idea behind this race from the start has been that this is a 'change' election, and that has proven out," said an Obama strategy memo in October 2007.[82] The word "change" was useful because people could interpret it as they liked: it could mean change from Bush policies, from party polarization, or from policy gridlock. Obama embraced his outsider status and framed his inexperience as independence. In his Springfield announcement address, he said: "I know I haven't spent a lot of time learning the ways of Washington. But I've been there long enough to know that the ways of Washington must change."[83] He would stand up to the Republicans, and at the same time unify the country by rising above partisan politics. And he would also be the candidate of authenticity, willing to take risky positions (e.g., meeting hostile foreign leaders) and not relying on poll-tested slogans.

Obama on Clinton: "We cannot let Clinton especially blur the lines on who is the genuine agent of change in this election," the Obama strategy memo said. Clinton "embodies trench warfare vs. Republicans, and is consumed with beating them rather than unifying the country . . . [S]he prides herself on working the system, not changing it." Obama had to be careful about attacking Clinton too directly. Not only would frontal assaults clash with his "new kind of politics," but they touched on another sensitivity. Representative Jesse Jackson, Jr., put it bluntly: "The natural reminder here is O. J. [Simpson]—how does an African American candidate attack a white woman?"[84] Allusion was one way around this problem. Obama would speak of "calculation" and "conviction," knowing that listeners would understand which word applied to which candidate. The campaign also worked through surrogates and leaks. In August 2007, it helped place a newspaper story that Clinton contributor Norman Hsu was a fugitive from justice. Clinton then had to return $850,000 that Hsu had bundled for her.[85]

Clinton on Clinton: "Experience" was her label. "Change, change is just a word if you do not have the strength and experience to make it happen," she said at the Iowa Jefferson Jackson Dinner. "We must nominate a nominee who has been tested, and elect a president who is ready to lead on day one."[86] "Caring" was another Clinton theme. It emphasized her nurturing side as a mother and her concern for the less fortunate. "We are the candidate of people with needs," said Penn's memo. "Caring" is not just an emotion, but an activity, and she often used the term in the context of health and family issues.

Clinton on Obama: Just as she stressed her own experience, Clinton pounded Obama's inexperience: one variation on the theme was her accusation that he was "naïve" about hostile foreign leaders. She also tried to knock down his image of "authenticity" by suggesting that he was phony, calculat-

Table 4.1.   Obama vs. Clinton

	Obama's Message	Clinton's Message
About Obama	Change agent/outsider Unifying Authentic	Inexperienced Phony Calculating
About Clinton	Insider/status quo Polarizing Calculating	Experienced Tested Caring

ing, or shifty. In the fall of 2007, she criticized his practice of voting "present" in the Illinois State Senate, saying that he had dodged tough issues. One attack backfired. To disprove his claim that he had only recently decided to run for president, the Clinton campaign issued a press release noting that he had written an essay titled "I Want to Become President"—in kindergarten. The release made Clinton look petty. One can sum up these themes in a "message grid" (see table 4.1).

By the end of 2007, Clinton still led in most national polls of Democratic voters. But Obama's message seemed to be getting through, and he had pulled ahead in some surveys of the Iowa caucuses and New Hampshire primary. Commentators who had earlier predicted a Clinton victory were starting to hedge their forecasts.

THE LONG CAMPAIGN SEASON OF 2008

The Iowa caucuses consisted of 1,781 meetings in local precincts. Participants would choose delegates to county conventions, which would pick delegates to conventions at the congressional district and state levels, which in turn would select delegates to the national convention. Such a process required intense involvement by the candidates, and intricate ground-level organization by their supporters. In this campaign, seven contenders (Gravel stayed out) made 199 visits totaling 533 days.[87] Edwards had twenty-five Iowa field offices, Clinton thirty-four, and Obama thirty-seven.

The number of offices did not tell the whole story: the Obama campaign simply out-hustled the slow-moving Clinton campaign. Obama had other advantages in the state. One was geography: Illinois lay just across the Mississippi River, so for months hundreds of Obama's home-state supporters crossed bridges to ring Iowa doorbells.[88] The second was timing. With the extremely early date of January 3, the caucuses took place when nearly all

American colleges and universities—a hotbed of Obama support—were on winter break. Students from Iowa were able to caucus for Obama in their home precincts. Those from other states had time to travel to Iowa for a week or two of campaign work. "We were the army of people that went out and made sure that people voted," said an Obama supporter from UCLA.[89]

In order to get any delegates from a precinct, a candidate needed 15 percent of its caucus-goers. Supporters of candidates who fell below this threshold had to switch to another candidate in a second round of voting. Minor candidates could thus tip some crucial support to major candidates. On January 1, Kucinich did so with a statement: "[I]n those caucus locations where my support doesn't reach the necessary threshold, I strongly encourage all of my supporters to make Barack Obama their second choice. Sen. Obama and I have one thing in common: Change."[90]

With the "change" message, Obama also sought to expand the universe of caucus-goers to include nontraditional targets such as young people, Republicans, and independents. (Only registered Democrats could caucus, but eligible voters could register at the caucus site, or instantly change their registration if they were Republicans or independents.) As Iowans poured into classrooms, church basements, and other caucus sites on the evening of January 3, it was evident that the universe had indeed expanded. Democrats reported a record 239,000 caucus-goers, nearly double the 2004 figure.

Obama won 37.6 percent of the precinct delegates to 29.7 percent for Edwards. Clinton was third with 29.5 percent. The entrance poll showed Edwards ahead among those who had attended caucuses before, but most caucus-goers were first-timers, and they gave Obama a big plurality.[91] "We all understood Edwards would be in our lane as a 'change' candidate," said Obama strategist David Axelrod. "Had the [voting] universe been the same, Edwards would have won. Edwards was good in the prescribed universe of existing caucus-goers, but he didn't go outside the lines."[92] Moderates split between Clinton and Obama, but they only made up 40 percent of those who attended. Most were liberals, and they flocked to Obama. Clinton won senior citizens, but there were just as many caucus-goers under thirty, and they favored Obama. When the poll asked which candidate quality mattered most, half said, "can bring about needed change." Obama beat Clinton in this group, 51 percent to 19 percent. He even led among women.

Iowa had immediate consequences. Biden and Dodd got only a handful of precinct delegates and dropped out at once. For Edwards, second place was not good enough. He might have won some delegates, but failed to get the psychological boost that he needed. For Clinton, third place was a disaster, and there was talk that a New Hampshire defeat would force her from the race. As for Obama, he had scored the victory that everything else would depend upon.

New polls showed Obama vaulting ahead in New Hampshire, but Clinton came back hard. In a Manchester debate, she displayed poise and toughness when Edwards and Obama seemed to gang up on her. She merged the "change" and "experience" themes with an effort to shed the "special interest" tag. "I'm not just running on a promise of change. I'm running on thirty-five years of change. I'm running on having taken on the drug companies and the health insurance companies, taking on the oil companies."[93] Obama did not help himself when he seemed condescending, consoling his rival with, "You're likable enough, Hillary."[94] On the trail, both Clintons hit Obama as a phony activist, suggesting that the 2002 speech was the sum total of his involvement in the early Iraq debate. Bill Clinton called Obama's claim that he had better judgment on Iraq "the biggest fairy tale I've ever seen."[95]

The morning before the primary, a friendly voter asked Hillary Clinton how she held up under adversity. "You know, this is very personal for me," she said as her eyes misted and her voice broke. "It's not just political. It's not just public. I see what's happening, and we have to reverse it. Some people think elections are a game, lots of who's up or who's down. It's about our country."[96] Some reporters thought that the "cry" might doom her. They recalled that Edmund Muskie lost the 1972 primary after apparently weeping during an outburst against a newspaper publisher. But Clinton was expressing compassion instead of anger, and intense coverage of the incident dramatized the "caring" image that she had been trying to convey.

Although she was behind in every published poll, she won a narrow victory over Obama. Did the debate or the "cry" make the difference? The evidence is mixed. On the one hand, the exit poll showed that she did best among voters who had decided a month earlier, long before either event.[97] On the other hand, she won voters who said that the debates were important and those who put "caring" as the top candidate quality. In contrast to Iowa, she won strongly among women. How did she regain this part of her base? Some columnists cited sympathy for her difficulties or Obama's condescending tone. A Democratic pollster had a more hard-headed conjecture: "Maybe a long-standing Clinton infrastructure in New Hampshire grounded her base with lower socioeconomic folks, who happen to be more likely to be women."[98] Whatever the cause, the return of women to Hillary meant that a keystone of her strategy was still viable for the long haul.

Obama took college graduates, while she won those without a degree. He won modestly among the two-thirds making more than $50,000 a year while she won big among those making less.[99] "Put another way," wrote Republican strategist Karl Rove, "Mrs. Clinton won the beer drinkers, Mr. Obama the white wine crowd."[100] New Hampshire kept Clinton in the race and brought Obama back to earth. A third-place finish pushed Edwards closer to the exit, and a fourth-place finish sent Richardson home to New Mexico.

For Clinton, new trouble accompanied renewed hope. Many African Americans interpreted Bill Clinton's "fairy tale" remark as referring to Obama's candidacy itself, not only the Iraq issue. Hillary Clinton said that while the civil rights movement needed the oratory of Martin Luther King, it also needed the experienced leadership of Lyndon Johnson. Her comment was hard to dispute as a matter of history, but to some it seemed to belittle King. "There's a groundswell of reaction to these comments—and not just these latest comments but really a pattern, or a series of comments that we've heard for several months," said a spokesperson for Obama. "Folks are beginning to wonder: Is this really an isolated situation, or is there something bigger behind all of this?"[101] The implication was that the Clintons were subtly appealing to racism.

A few weeks earlier, black voters had supported Clinton, 53 percent to 39 percent for Obama. But the controversial comments hurt Clinton. More important, Obama's victory in Iowa and close second-place finish in New Hampshire proved that a black presidential candidate could win white votes. Those showings removed a major barrier to an Obama breakthrough among African Americans. The upshot was a stunning reversal: a mid-January Gallup survey showed black Democrats backing *Obama* by 57–32 percent.[102] That shift was a turning point in the campaign. In the months to come, black votes would tilt key contests in Obama's direction.

Clinton won the popular vote in the Nevada caucuses eleven days after New Hampshire, a noteworthy result given that the powerful Culinary Workers Union had backed Obama. Poll results held encouraging signs for Clinton, who won by large margins among women and Hispanics. Even so, Obama ended up with more convention delegates. This result stemmed from a bit of procedure that the Obama team understood and the Clinton camp was slow to grasp. Clinton won places with an even number of delegates that split between her and Obama. Obama won places with an odd number of delegates, meaning that he often took two delegates to Clinton's one. As with the shift in the black vote, Obama's delegate victory was a portent of things to come.

Meanwhile, attention swiftly moved to South Carolina. A debate in Myrtle Beach cosponsored by the Congressional Black Caucus featured a nasty exchange. Obama denied any sympathy for Republican ideas, and used the occasion to link Clinton to an object of Democratic disdain: "Because while I was working on those streets watching those folks see their jobs shift overseas, you were a corporate lawyer sitting on the board at Wal-Mart." Clinton struck back by noting Obama's ties to a shady businessman: "I was fighting against those ideas when you were practicing law and representing your contributor, [Tony] Rezko, in his slum landlord business in inner-city Chicago."[103]

Obama won South Carolina by a twenty-eight-point margin that disappointed Clinton forces and finally prompted Edwards to withdraw. While the harsh words about Wal-Mart and Rezko got national attention, demography likely determined the results. African Americans cast most of the vote, and about 80 percent of them went for Obama. Bill Clinton tried to dismiss the result: "Jesse Jackson won South Carolina in '84 and '88. Jackson ran a good campaign. And Obama ran a good campaign here." ABC correspondent Jake Tapper blogged sarcastically: "Boy, I can't understand why anyone would think the Clintons are running a race-baiting campaign to paint Obama as 'the black candidate.'"[104]

Clinton won the Florida primary, as she had earlier won Michigan. The victories did not add to her delegate count, since the Democratic National Committee had stripped them of delegates for violating the "window." Clinton nevertheless counted both primaries as victories, and even held a rally outside Fort Lauderdale shortly after the Florida polls closed. Obama managed to overshadow Clinton's quasi-victory with key endorsements. Senator Edward Kennedy joined his son, Representative Patrick Kennedy, and his niece, Caroline Kennedy, in endorsing Obama at an American University rally. All three compared Obama to President John F. Kennedy.

On Super Tuesday, Clinton had the satisfaction of winning the Massachusetts primary even though Obama had the support of Governor Deval Patrick as well as the Kennedys. She also got a morale boost from California. Several polls had given the lead to Obama, and his supporters hoped that California might deal a fatal blow to Clinton. But demographics worked to Clinton's advantage. Hispanics accounted for 30 percent of the vote—a state record—and went for Clinton by a two-to-one margin. African Americans backed Obama three to one, but made up only 7 percent of the vote.[105]

Early in the process, Clinton strategist Mark Penn actually thought that winning California would give her *all* of the state's 370 delegates. "How can it possibly be," asked Harold Ickes in horror, "that the much vaunted chief strategist doesn't understand proportional allocation?"[106] With 52 percent of the popular vote, she got 203 delegates, or 55 percent of the total—a good score, but hardly a game-ender.

Overall, on Super Tuesday, Obama won thirteen contests to Clinton's ten. "But Clinton won the biggest states, and six of Obama's thirteen wins were in caucus states," wrote journalist Thomas Edsall. "A caucus state victory is generally considered less significant than taking first place in a primary, although there is no difference between caucuses and primaries in terms of the number of delegates to be won." [107] There *was* a big difference in cost, however. Caucuses generally took place in smaller states, had much lower turnout, and did not require the enormous media buys that went into primary states. It was thus more efficient to rack up delegate margins in caucuses than in primaries. In the New Jersey primary, Clinton got 112,000 more votes than Obama and got eleven more delegates. In the Idaho caucuses, Obama got 13,000 more votes than Clinton and twelve more delegates. [108]

So even though Clinton won a slight plurality of popular votes on Super Tuesday, Obama came out with more of the delegates at stake that night. With Michigan and Florida out of the tally, it would take 2,025 delegates to win the nomination, and at this point he had a total of 1,006 pledged delegates to Clinton's 965. [109]

In the week after Super Tuesday, Obama scored a string of victories. His ground operation enabled him to sweep the Nebraska, Maine, and Washington State caucuses, while the near-unanimous support of African Americans helped him take the Louisiana primary, as well as the "Potomac primaries" of Virginia, Maryland, and the District of Columbia. He now had a lead of at least one hundred delegates, and because of proportional representation, it would be very difficult for Clinton to overtake him. "We don't think our lead will drop below one hundred delegates," Obama campaign manager David Plouffe told the *New York Times*. "The math is the math." [110]

From this point on, Obama would also outpace Clinton in most national polls. The Obama campaign argued that he was clearly the choice of the Democratic electorate, and that the superdelegates should follow suit. Many of the undecided superdelegates may have actually favored Clinton, but a growing number found that their constituents were voting for Obama. Undecideds started to break toward Obama, and even some of Clinton's superdelegates switched sides. The most prominent was Representative John Lewis of Georgia, who came from a pro-Obama district and who had recently drawn a primary challenger who criticized his support for Clinton. "I think the candidacy of Senator Obama represents the beginning of a new movement in American political history that began in the hearts and minds of the people of this nation," said Lewis. "And I want to be on the side of the people, on the side of the spirit of history." [111]

Meanwhile, the Clinton campaign was in disarray. Overspending in 2007 had left it short on cash by January, and Clinton had to lend the campaign $5 million of her own money just to compete on Super Tuesday. Staff shake-ups were worsening her already dismal press coverage. Because of tight money, the internal disorganization and the absence of a detailed post–Super Tuesday plan, the Clinton campaign allowed Obama to capture the Wisconsin primary. With a large blue-collar vote and a relatively small black electorate, the state should have been in her column.

She still had hopes for the big primaries on March 4. Texas had a large Hispanic population and Ohio was Rust Belt, union territory. Both had large numbers of socially conservative white voters, and the Clinton campaign went after Obama from the right. It provided journalists with news clips about Obama's ties to William Ayers, a former fugitive and a founding member of the radical Weather Underground. In an email to the media, a Clinton spokesman suggested that the issue would hand the other party a lethal weapon if Obama were the nominee: "Wonder what the Republicans will do with this issue."[112] In Texas, it ran a television ad suggesting that she would be a safer custodian of national security. "It's 3 a.m., and your children are safe and asleep," a narrator said over images of sleeping boys and girls. "But there's a phone in the White House, and it's ringing." The narrator reminded viewers that their vote could decide whether a tested and experienced leader would respond. "Who do you want answering the phone?"

Help for Clinton came from an unlikely corner. Conservative radio host Rush Limbaugh announced "Operation Chaos," an effort to get Republicans to cross into Democratic primaries to vote for Clinton. The point was not to elect her president but to damage the Democratic Party by prolonging a divisive primary battle.

On March 4, Clinton won by a healthy margin in Ohio and a narrower one in Texas. Operation Chaos may have brought some additional votes to Clinton, though exit polls showed that crossover voters split evenly in Ohio and slightly favored Obama in Texas. As on Super Tuesday, there was a welcome boost to Clinton morale. But also as on Super Tuesday, the delegate numbers were disheartening. Because of its complex hybrid caucus–primary system, Texas actually gave a majority of its delegates to *Obama*. From Ohio, Clinton got only nine more delegates than Obama, and Obama countered a week later with a seven-delegate edge in the Mississippi primary.

Turbulence then hit the Obama campaign. Television and radio news programs featured excerpts of sermons by Obama's pastor, Jeremiah Wright. "'God bless America.' No, no, no, God damn America, that's in the Bible for killing innocent people," went Wright's most incendiary comment, from a 2003 sermon. "God damn America for treating our citizens as less than human. God damn America for as long as she acts like she is God and she is supreme."[113] Amid questions as to why he had associated with such a pastor for two decades, Obama gave a well-received speech in Philadelphia. He said that Wright's comments "were not only wrong but divisive, divisive at a time when we need unity; racially charged at a time when we need to come together to solve a set of monumental problems."[114] Obama's speech limited the damage, but the Wright clips remained available on YouTube.

Clinton soon learned that YouTube giveth and YouTube taketh away. In a recent speech, she told a story that was supposed to confirm her battle-tested experience. During a 1996 visit to war-torn Bosnia, she said, sniper fire had forced her to skip an airport greeting ceremony and run to a vehicle. "Problem is," said a CBS News story, "that's not how it happened at all. And we should know. CBS News accompanied the First Lady and daughter Chelsea on that Bosnia trip." The report then showed video of Clinton cheerfully talking to a child at the greeting ceremony.[115] The story went viral, and the resulting ridicule harmed her credibility.

The next major contest would be the Pennsylvania primary on April 22. It was good ground for Clinton: an aging, working-class electorate that was mainly white except for Philadelphia. Shortly before the primary, the *Huffington Post* put up a full audio recording of Obama's comments at a recent high-end fundraising event in San Francisco. Obama seemed to be disparaging the state he was courting: "You go into some of these small towns in Pennsylvania, and like a lot of small towns in the Midwest, the jobs have been gone now for twenty-five years and nothing's replaced them. . . . And it's not surprising then they get bitter, they cling to guns or religion or antipathy to people who aren't like them or anti-immigrant sentiment or anti-trade sentiment as a way to explain their frustrations."[116] Here was the ultimate "wine track" versus "beer track" moment, and Clinton pounced. "I think his comments were elitist and divisive," she said. "I think it's very critical that the Democrats really focus in on this and make it clear that we are not [elitist]. We are going to stand up and fight for all Americans."[117]

Clinton won Pennsylvania by a double-digit margin, but proportional representation struck again. She emerged with eighty-five delegates to Obama's seventy-three—a net advantage of just twelve. Obama kept gaining superdelegates, and by early May, he had more than Clinton. Still, she fought on: during April, she lent her campaign another $6.4 million from her own pocket.

Her dwindling hopes focused on Indiana and North Carolina. In many respects, Indiana was like Ohio and Pennsylvania: a largely white, industrial state. North Carolina would be much more difficult. Not only did it have a large African American population, but the Raleigh–Durham area comprised major universities and was full of wine-track professionals. On the evening of May 6, the news was grim. She won Indiana by only a narrow margin, while Obama easily took North Carolina. Shortly after midnight Eastern time, Tim Russert of NBC News said: "We now know who the Democratic nominee's going to be, and no one's going to dispute it. . . . Those closest to her will give her a hardheaded analysis, and if they lay it all out, they'll say: 'What is the rationale? What do we say to the undeclared superdelegates tomorrow? Why do we tell them you're staying in the race?' And tonight, there's no good answer for that."[118]

Clinton remained in the race, but the rest of May had the air of a simulation rather than a real battle. Though Clinton won West Virginia and Kentucky, her delegate gains were modest, and Obama more than compensated through a lengthening roster of superdelegate endorsements. On May 20, a victory in the Oregon primary gave him a majority of the pledged delegates. Clinton's last chance was an appeal to the Democratic National Committee to seat the Michigan and Florida delegations. The members said no, though they tried to appease the states by giving them half-votes—too little to jeopardize Obama's lead.

On June 3, Clinton won the South Dakota primary, nothing more than a consolation prize. Between a win in Montana, and a flood of new superdelegate endorsements, Obama claimed victory: "I can stand before you and say that I will be the Democratic nominee for President of the United States." A few days later, Clinton withdrew. Three months after he mathematically clinched the Republican nomination, John McCain knew with certainty which Democrat he would face in November.

WHAT IF?

The campaign was closer than one might think. Table 4.2 shows how the race stood at the time that Obama clinched the nomination.[119] Clinton actually won a plurality of the delegates chosen in primaries.[120] Obama prevailed because of his nearly two-to-one advantage from the caucus states, which helped him build an early and persistent lead among pledged delegates. And in turn, this lead helped persuade many of the superdelegates that he was the inevitable nominee.

In any event, it is ironic that Barack Obama did best with superdelegates

Table 4.2. Delegate Count at Time Obama Clinched Nomination

	Obama	Clinton
Superdelegates	463.0	257.0
Caucus Delegates	327.0	175.0
Primary Delegates	1418.5	1464.5
Totals	2208.5	1896.5

Source: As recorded by RealClearPolitics.

and caucuses—the *least* democratic aspects of the nomination process. The numbers also raise some fascinating political questions:

- If Clinton had focused earlier and more carefully on the caucuses, might she have erased Obama's lead among pledged delegates?
- If she had erased that lead, would the superdelegates still have flocked to Obama?
- If she had won in Iowa, would Obama have gotten the surge in black support that enabled him to win South Carolina and other states?
- If he did not get that surge, would he have even survived Super Tuesday?

At least until fairly late in the contest, there was nothing inevitable about the outcome. In a broader sense, there was surely nothing inevitable about the journey that brought Obama to the presidential contest in the first place. As Malcolm Gladwell explained in his 2008 book *Outliers*, even the most talented and hardworking people depend on chance and circumstance for their success. Seemingly small things can make the difference between a moderately successful technology administrator and Bill Gates. One can apply this perspective to Obama. Consider:

- Could he have become a senator if Carol Moseley Braun had run in 2004? Or if Blair Hull and Jack Ryan had not undergone spectacularly bad divorces? Or if the BCRA "millionaire's amendment" had not been in place, allowing him to raise more money against Hull?
- Could he have come to national prominence if John Kerry had picked somebody else to keynote the 2004 Democratic convention?
- Could he have become the antiwar alternative to Hillary Clinton if he had not received or accepted a speaking invitation in 2002?

Obama was lucky that these events broke his way. And despite all the unpleasant moments of the primary campaign, one can argue that its length worked to his advantage. Months of national campaigning honed his skills, sharpened his message, and seasoned his organization. The contest with Clinton put him at the center of national attention through June, when the vice presidential selection and preparations for the national convention kept him in the news. For him, it was much better that the names of Wright, Rezko, and Ayers all came up in the spring. By autumn, they were old news, and could not do him much harm. Intentionally or not, Obama was speaking the truth when he accepted Clinton's concession and said: "I'm a better candidate for having had the privilege of competing with her."

NOTES

1. David Mendell, *Obama: From Promise to Power* (New York: HarperCollins/Amistad, 2007), 180.

2. Normally, drawing such a foe would have been bad news, but the 2002 Bipartisan Campaign Finance Act included the "millionaire's amendment," raising contribution limits for candidates with self-financing opponents. Obama could now raise much more from the lakefront liberals. His timing was fortunate: four years later, the U.S. Supreme Court would strike down the millionaire's amendment.

3. David Mendell, "Obama Lets Opponent Do Talking," *Chicago Tribune*, June 24, 2004, http://www.chicagotribune.com/news/local/chi-0406240383jun24,0,5972661.story.

4. Barack Obama, "The Audacity of Hope: 2004 Democratic National Convention Keynote Address," July 27, 2004, http://www.americanrhetoric.com/speeches/convention2004/barackobama2004dnc.htm.

5. Scott Fornek, "Obama for President? That's 'Silly,'" *Chicago Sun-Times*, November 4, 2004, 17.

6. Patrick Healy, "From Mill Town to the National Stage," *Boston Globe*, October 5, 2003, http://www.boston.com/news/nation/articles/2003/10/05/from_mill_town_to_the_national_stage_boston_globe.

7. Obama, "The Audacity of Hope."

8. "Text: Sen. Kennedy on the Future of the Democratic Party," National Press Club, Washington, DC, January 12, 2005, http://www.washingtonpost.com/ac2/wp-dyn/A4354-2005Jan12.

9. During his first haircut after moving to Chicago, the barber asked his name. When he responded, the barber said: "Barack, huh. You a Muslim?" Barack Obama, *Dreams from My Father: A Story of Race and Inheritance* (New York: Three Rivers Press, 2004), 149. In 2006, a national survey asked: "Would you say you have a generally favorable or unfavorable opinion of Islam?" By a 46–43 percent margin, respondents had an unfavorable opinion, *Washington Post*/ABC News Poll, March 6, 2006, http://www.washingtonpost.com/wp-srv/politics/polls/postpoll_iraqwar_030606.htm.

10. Jeffrey M. Jones, "Six in 10 Americans Think U.S. Ready for a Female President," Gallup Poll, October 3, 2006, http://www.gallup.com/poll/24832/Six-Americans-Think-US-Ready-Female-President.aspx.

11. Debra J. Dickerson, "Colorblind," Salon, January 22, 2007, http://www.salon.com/opinion/feature/2007/01/22/obama.

12. David Nitkin and Harry Merritt, "A New Twist to an Intriguing Family History," *Baltimore Sun*, March 2, 2007, http://www.baltimoresun.com/news/nationworld/politics/bal-te.obama02mar02,0,3453027.story.

13. Roger Simon, "Relentless: How Barack Obama Outsmarted Hillary Clinton," *The Politico*, August 25, 2008, http://www.politico.com/relentless/relentless.pdf.

14. Elaine Kamarck, "A History of 'Super-Delegates' in the Democratic Party," John F. Kennedy School of Government at Harvard University, 2008 [1986], http://www.hks.harvard.edu/news-events/news/commentary/history-of-superdelegates.

15. Richard L. Berke, "House Democrats Choose Delegates," *New York Times*, April 21, 1988, D26.

16. At a conference following the 1992 election, Clinton strategist James Carville fore-

saw such a situation. "What happens is, we don't have to win. Once you have a 500-delegate margin, even if you lose a primary, you're still adding to get to the 2,145 or whatever the number is." Charles T. Royer, ed., *Campaign for President: The Managers Look at '92* (Hollis, NH: Hollis Publishing, 1994), 51.

17. Chris Cillizza and Zachary A. Goldfarb, "Democrats Tweak the Primary Calendar," *Washington Post,* July 23, 2006, A4.

18. "Deck the Halls with Politicos' Folly," *New York Times*, August 19, 2007, Week in Review, 9.

19. Joseph E. Cantor, "The Presidential Election Campaign Fund and Tax Checkoff: Background and Current Issues" (Washington, DC: Congressional Research Service, March 8, 2007), http://moneyline.cq.com/flatfiles/editorialFiles/moneyLine/reference/crs/campfin/crscheckoff.pdf.

20. Pew Internet & American Life Project, "The Internet and Campaign 2004," March 6, 2005, http://www.pewinternet.org/pdfs/PIP_2004_Campaign.pdf.

21. Public Citizen, "The Importance of Bundlers to the Bush & Kerry Campaigns: Post-Election Summary of Findings," December 2, 2004, http://www.whitehousefor sale.org/documents/postelection.pdf.

22. ComScore, "Huffington Post and Politico Lead Wave of Explosive Growth at Independent Political Blogs and News Sites This Election Season," October 22, 2008.

23. Tova Andrea Wang, "Has America Outgrown the Caucus?" Century Foundation Issue Brief, October 23, 2007, http://www.tcf.org/publications/electionreform/caucus brief.pdf.

24. Mark R. Levy and Michael S. Kramer, *The Ethnic Factor: How America's Minorities Decide Elections* (New York: Simon & Schuster/Touchstone, 1973), 51.

25. "Out of a Cocoon," *Time*, September 27, 1976, http://www.time.com/time/maga zine/article/0,9171,918352-2,00.html.

26. U.S. Bureau of the Census, "U.S. Hispanic Population Surpasses 45 Million Now 15 Percent of Total," May 1, 2008, http://www.census.gov/Press-Release/www/releases/archives/population/011910.html.

27. "A Closer Look at the Parties in 2008," Pew Research Center for the People and the Press, August 22, 2008, http://pewresearch.org/assets/pdf/933.pdf.

28. "A Closer Look at the Parties in 2008."

29. Dianne Bystrom, quoted in Emma Pearse, "Analysts Watching Female Voters in Iowa," Women's E-News, January 19, 2004, http://www.womensenews.org/article.cfm/dyn/aid/1682/context/archive.

30. U.S. Bureau of Labor Statistics, "Union Members in 2007," January 25, 2008, http://www.bls.gov/news.release/union2.nr0.htm.

31. Alan Abramowitz, "This Is Not Your Father's (Or Mother's) Democratic Party," Rasmussen Reports, May 15, 2008, http://www.rasmussenreports.com/public_content/political_commentary/commentary_by_alan_i_abramowitz/this_is_not_your_father_s_or_mother_s_democratic_party.

32. "A Closer Look at the Parties in 2008."

33. Alan I. Abramowitz and Kyle L. Saunders, "Is Polarization a Myth?" *Journal of Politics* 70 (April 2008): 546–47.

34. Gary C. Jacobson, *A Divider, Not a Uniter: George W. Bush and the American People* (New York: Pearson, 2008), 201–2.

35. "22% Believe Bush Knew about 9-11 Attacks in Advance," Rasmussen Reports, May 4, 2007, http://www.rasmussenreports.com/public_content/politics/current_events/general_current_events/president_bush/22_believe_bush_knew_about_ 9_11_attacks_in_ advance.

36. Jake Tapper, Mike Callahan, and Avery Miller, "Did Kerry Hand Republicans a November Gift?" ABC News, October 31, 2006, http://abcnews.go.com/WNT/story? id=2619383.

37. Jennifer Rubin, "A Tax-Cutting Democrat," *The Weekly Standard*, March 5, 2007, http://www.weeklystandard.com/Content/Public/Articles/000/000/013/333khsla.asp.

38. Margaret Carlson, "Richardson Meets the Press—And Melts Down," The Huffington Post, May 31, 2007, http://www.huffingtonpost.com/margaret-carlson/richardson-meets-the-pres_b_50178.html.

39. Christopher Cooper, "Edwards, Trailing Rivals, Holds Sway over Party's Agenda," *Wall Street Journal*, July 20, 2007, A5.

40. John Edwards, "The Right Way in Iraq," *Washington Post*, November 13, 2005, B7.

41. Don Carrington, "Edwards Home County's Largest," Carolina Journal Online, January 26, 2007, http://www.carolinajournal.com/exclusives/display_exclusive.html?id= 3848.

42. Leslie Wayne, "In Aiding Poor, Edwards Built Bridge to 2008," *New York Times*, June 22, 2007, http://www.nytimes.com/2007/06/22/us/politics/22edwards.html.

43. Carla Marinucci, "Edwards Charges $55,000 to Speak to UC Davis Students about Poverty," *San Francisco Chronicle*, Politics Blog, May 21, 2007, http://www.sfgate.com/cgi-bin/blogs/sfgate/detail?blogid=14&entry_id=16809.

44. Ben Adler, "Why Doesn't Edwards Appeal to Youth?" *The Politico*, December 1, 2007, http://www.politico.com/news/stories/1107/7068_Page2.html.

45. Mark Blumenthal, "Harris Interactive's Poll on Clinton," Pollster.com, March 28, 2007, http://www.pollster.com/blogs/harris_interactives_poll_on_cl.php.

46. Markos Moulitsas, "Hillary Clinton: Too Much of a Clinton Democrat?" *Washington Post*, May 7, 2006, B1.

47. Jeffrey M. Jones, "Democrats Express Decided Preference for Change over Experience," Gallup Poll, September 4, 2007, http://www.gallup.com/poll/28591/Democrats-Express-Decided-Preference-Change-Over-Experience.aspx.

48. Mendell, *Obama*, 305–6.

49. Barack Obama, "Tone, Truth, and the Democratic Party," Daily Kos, September 30, 2005, http://www.dailykos.com/story/2005/9/30/102745/165.

50. Jane Hammon, "Politics with Drawl," *Columbia Journalism Review*, July/August 2008, http://www.cjr.org/essay/politics_with_drawl_1.php.

51. CBS News Poll, "Clinton v. Obama?" January 22, 2007, http://ww.youtube.com/watch?v._letlZaf6zUw.

52. John Edwards, "Tomorrow Begins Today," December 27, 2006, http://www.youtube.com/watch?v=letlZaf6zUw.

53. Barack Obama, announcement for president, Springfield, Illinois, February 10, 2007, http://www.barackobama.com/2007/02/10/remarks_of_senator_barack_obam_11.php.

54. David D. Kirkpatrick, "McCain and Obama in Deal on Public Financing," *New York Times*, March 2, 2007, http://www.nytimes.com/2007/03/02/us/politics/02fec.html.

55. Campaign Finance Institute, "Big, $1,000 + Donations Supply 79% of Presidential Candidates' Early Money," April 16, 2007, at http://www.cnfinst.org/pr/prRelease.aspx? ReleaseID = 136.

56. Fredreka Schouten and Paul Overberg, "Upper-Income Black Donors Back Obama Over Clinton," *USA Today*, June 14, 2007, http://www.usatoday.com/news/politics/elec tion2008/2007-06-13-obama-clinton_N.htm.

57. Joshua Green, "The Amazing Money Machine," *The Atlantic*, June 2008, http://www.theatlantic.com/doc/200806/obama-finance.

58. Andrew Ross Sorkin, "Hedge Fund Investing and Politics," *New York Times*, April 22, 2008, http://www.nytimes.com/2008/04/22/business/22sorkin.html.

59. Trudy Lieberman, "Obama's Lobbyist Line," *Columbia Journalism Review*, February 15, 2008, http://www.cjr/org/campaign_desk/obamas_lobbyist_line.php.

60. Campaign Finance Institute, "Fundraising Central: Majority of Presidential Bundlers and Other Fundraisers Hail from Only Five U.S. Industries: Lawyers and Law Firms, Three Finance Industries, and Real Estate," December 20, 2007, http://www.cfinst.org/pr/prRelease.aspx?ReleaseID = 176.

61. Anne E. Kornblut and Matthew Mosk, "Obama's Campaign Takes in $25 Million," *Washington Post*, April 5, 2007, A1.

62. Kornblut and Mosk, "Obama's Campaign Takes in $25 Million."

63. Carla Marinucci, "Obama's Lucrative Internet Campaign," *San Francisco Chronicle*, April 5, 2007, A1.

64. Steve O'Hear, "Barack Obama Launches Social Network," February 10, 2007, The Social Web, http://blogs.zdnet.com/social/?p = 89.

65. Cooper, "Edwards, Trailing Rivals."

66. Democratic Presidential Candidates Debate at Drexel University in Philadelphia, Pennsylvania, October 30, 2007, http://www.presidency.ucsb.edu/ws/index.php?pid = 75950.

67. Ryan Lizza, "Battle Plans: How Obama Won," *The New Yorker*, November 17, 2008, http://www.newyorker.com/reporting/2008/11/17/081117fa_fact_lizza.

68. James Fallows, "Rhetorical Questions," *The Atlantic*, September 2008, http://www.theatlantic.com/doc/200809/fallows-debates/4.

69. Remarks of Senator Barack Obama: Iowa Jefferson-Jackson Dinner, Des Moines, Iowa, November 10, 2007, http://www.barackobama.com/2007/11/10/remarks_of_senator_barack_obam_33.php.

70. Lizza, "Battle Plans."

71. Lloyd Grove, "World According to . . . David Plouffe," *Portfolio*, December 11, 2008, http://www.portfolio.com/views/columns/the-world-according-to/2008/12/11/David-Plouffe-Interview.

72. Jonathan Weisman, Shailagh Murray, and Peter Slevin, "Strategy Was Based on Winning Delegates, Not Battlegrounds," *Washington Post*, June 4, 2008, A1.

73. Simon, "Relentless."

74. Thomas Edsall, "Obama's Debt to Harold Ickes," *RealClearPolitics*, June 3, 2008, http://www.realclearpolitics.com/articles/2008/06/obamas_debt_to_harold_ickes.html.

75. Simon, "Relentless."

76. Joshua Green, "The Front-Runner's Fall," *The Atlantic*, September 2008, http://www.theatlantic.com/doc/200809/hillary-clinton-campaign.

77. Green, "The Front-Runner's Fall."

78. Lydia Saad, "Black Democrats Move into Obama's Column," Gallup Poll, January 15, 2008, http://www.gallup.com/poll/103756/Black-Democrats-Move-into-Obamas-Col umn.aspx.

79. Brian DeBose, "Obama Needs Early Win to Get Black Vote," *Washington Times*, August 31, 2007, A1.

80. Institute of Politics, Harvard University, "The 12th Biannual Youth Survey on Politics and Public Service," April 17, 2007, http://www.rockthevote.com/assets/publications/research/iop_poll_analysis-mar-2007.pdf.

81. Marc Ambinder, "At Yearly Kos, Clinton Defends Lobbyists," August 4, 2007, http://marcambinder.theatlantic.com/archives/2007/08/at_yearlykos_clinton_defends_l.php.

82. Lizza, "Battle Plans."

83. Obama, announcement for president.

84. Paul Kane and Jonathan Weisman, "The Conventional Wisdom Defied," *Washington Post*, January 4, 2008.

85. Marc Ambinder, "Teacher and Apprentice," *The Atlantic*, December 2007, http://www.theatlantic.com/doc/200712/clinton-obama.

86. Hillary Clinton, remarks at the Iowa Jefferson-Jackson Dinner, November 10, 2007, http://www.hillaryclinton.com/news/speech/view/?id=4156.

87. Eric Appleman, "Democracy in Action," http://www.gwu.edu/~action/2008/chrniowa08.html.

88. Shailagh Murray and Peter Slevin, "Message, Method Are Behind Obama's Climb," *Washington Post*, December 21, 2007, A6.

89. Tessa McClellan, "Campaigning in Iowa," *Daily Bruin*, January 7, 2008, http://dailybruin.ucla.edu/news/2008/jan/07/campaigning-iowa.

90. Marc Ambinder, "Kucinich Urges Supporters to Choose Obama on Second 'Ballot,'" January 1, 2008, http://marcambinder.theatlantic.com/archives/2008/01/kucinich_urges_supporters_to_c.php.

91. National Election Pool, Iowa caucuses entrance poll, January 3, 2008, http://www.cnn.com/ELECTION/2008/primaries/results/epolls/#IADEM.

92. Simon, "Relentless."

93. Democratic Presidential Candidates Debate in Manchester, New Hampshire, January 5, 2008, http://www.presidency.ucsb.edu/ws/index.php?pid=76224.

94. Democratic Presidential Candidates Debate in Manchester, New Hampshire.

95. Kate Phillips, "The Clinton Camp Unbound," *The Caucus*, January 8, 2008, http://thecaucus.blogs.nytimes.com/2008/01/08/the-clinton-camp-unbound.

96. Anne Kornblut, "An Emotional Clinton Reflects on How She Does It," The Trail, January 7, 2008, http://voices.washingtonpost.com/the-trail/2008/01/07/an_emotional_clinton_reflects.html.

97. Jay Cost, "How Clinton Won," HorseRaceBlog, January 8, 2008, http://www.realclearpolitics.com/horseraceblog/2008/01/how_clinton_won.html.

98. Margie Omero, "Women Non-Working for Hillary," Pollster.com, January 10, 2008, http://www.pollster.com/blogs/women_nonworking_for_hillary.php.

99. National Election Poll, New Hampshire primary exit poll, January 8, 2008, http://www.cnn.com/ELECTION/2008/primaries/results/epolls/index.html#NHDEM.

100. Karl Rove, "Why Hillary Won," *Wall Street Journal*, January 10, 2008, http://online.wsj.com/article/SB119992615845679531.html.

101. Ben Smith, "Racial Tensions Roil Democratic Race," *The Politico*, January 11, 2008, http://www.politico.com/news/stories/0108/7845.html.

102. Lydia Saad, "Black Democrats Move into Obama's Column," Gallup Poll, January 15, 2008, http://www.gallup.com/poll/103756/Black-Democrats-Move-into-Obamas-Col umn.aspx.

103. Democratic Presidential Candidates Debate in Myrtle Beach, South Carolina, January 21, 2008, http://www.presidency.ucsb/edu/ws/index.php?pid=76271.

104. Jake Tapper, "Bubba: Obama Is Just Like Jesse Jackson," Political Punch, January 26, 2008, http://blogs.abcnews.com/politicalpunch/2008/01/bubba-obama-is.html.

105. National Election Pool, California primary exit poll, February 5, 2008, http://www.cnn.com/ELECTION/2008/primaries/results/epolls/index.html#CADEM.

106. Karen Tumulty, "The Five Mistakes Clinton Made," *Time*, May 8, 2008, http://www.time.com/time/politics/article/0,8599,1738331,00.html.

107. Thomas Edsall, "Super Tuesday Fallout: Where the Race Goes from Here," *RealClearPolitics*, February 6, 2008, http://www.realclearpolitics.com/articles/2008/02/super_tuesday_fallout_where_th.html.

108. Edsall, "Obama's Debt."

109. The 2,025 figure was the number needed to win the nomination if Michigan and Florida did not count. After it was clear that Obama would win the nomination, the Democratic National Committee decided to give half-votes to the two states, which increased the total number of delegates and raised the nomination threshold to 2,118. At the convention, the credentials committee restored the two states' full voting rights, and the threshold went up to 2,210. By that time, Obama was the presumptive nominee and the impact was purely symbolic. Similarly, the inclusion of Michigan and Florida raised the total number of superdelegates from 796 during the primaries to 852 at the convention.

110. Adam Nagourney, "Obama's Lead in Delegates Shifts Focus of Campaign," *New York Times*, February 14, 2008, http://www.nytimes.com/2008/02/14/us/politics/14dele gates.html.

111. Charles Mathesian and Richard T. Cullen, "HRC's Black Supporters Pressed to Support Obama," *The Politico*, February 27, 2008, http://www.politico.com/news/stories/0208/8734.html.

112. Justin Rood, "Clinton Camp Pushes O-Bomber Links," ABC News, February 22, 2008, http://www.abcnews.go.com/Blotter/story?id=4330128&page=1.

113. Abdon M. Pallasch, "Obama Denounces Rhetoric But Stands Behind His Pastor," *Chicago Sun-Times*, March 16, 2008, http://www.suntimes.com/news/politics/obama/844447,CST-NWS-wright15.article.

114. Remarks of Senator Barack Obama: "A More Perfect Union," Philadelphia, Pennsylvania, March 18, 2008, http://www.barackobama.com/2008/03/18/remarks_of_sena tor_barack_obam_53.php.

115. "CBS News Video Contradicts Clinton's Story," March 24, 2008, http://www.cbs news.com/stories/2008/03/24/eveningnews/main3964921.shtml.

116. Mayhill Fowler, "Obama Exclusive (Audio): On VP and Foreign Policy, Courting the Working Class, and Hard-Pressed Pennsylvanians," April 11, 2008, http://www.huf fingtonpost.com/mayhill-fowler/obama-exclusive-audio-on_b_96333.html.

117. "Clinton Plays Up Obama's 'Bitter' Quote as 'Elitist,'" Associated Press, April 13, 2008, http://www.usatoday.com/news/politics/election2008/2008-04-13-obama-clin ton_N.htm.

118. Jim Rutenberg, "Pundits Declare the Race Over," *New York Times*, May 8, 2008, http://www.nytimes.com/2008/05/08/us/politics/07cnd-pundits.html?_r = 1&hp.

119. RealClearPolitics, 2008 Democratic Delegates, at http://www.realclearpolitics .com/epolls/2008/president/democratic_delegate_ecount.html. Figures include all delegations, including those from U.S. territories and Democrats abroad. They credit Michigan and Florida with the half-votes that the DNC assigned in May. They also separate the delegates from the Texas primary from those in the state's caucuses.

120. Edsall, "Obama's Debt."

Chapter Five

The General Election Campaign

Some election campaigns really don't appear to matter very much. The 1996 contest between Bill Clinton and Bob Dole is one recent example. Bill Clinton began the contest ahead, remained in front for the whole contest, and coasted to victory in the end. Without some huge and unforeseen event, one that would have worked dramatically to the advantage of Bob Dole, it is hard to imagine how this election could have turned out differently. Other campaigns do decide the outcome. The 2000 election between George W. Bush and Al Gore is a prime case. No one knew in advance who would win, the candidates traded leads in the polls three times, and the race went down to the wire—in fact, past the wire. Tactical errors by the candidates and relatively minor events along the way affected the final results.

Where does the 2008 presidential campaign fit on this spectrum? The best answer is "in between." The "logic" of the race from the beginning strongly favored a Democratic victory. But without stretching matters too much, it is fair to say that John McCain had a shot and that for a moment it even looked as if he might take control of the race. A huge event occurred: the financial crisis, which either turned the race from where it was then heading or else restored the "logic" that would likely have reasserted itself in any case. This ambiguity makes the 2008 campaign all the more fascinating, leaving one to wonder whether in the end it was decisive or irrelevant.

ANALYZING PRESIDENTIAL CONTESTS

Every general presidential campaign has its own structure, which consists of the prevailing political conditions in the country and the known qualities and liabilities of the candidates at the time the campaign begins. The candidates and their teams survey this structure and devise their overall campaign strategies. The strategies may change with ongoing assessment of the state of the campaign and in light of important events.

The prevailing political conditions of 2008 were defined chiefly by the general dissatisfaction with the incumbent president and with anxieties about where the nation was heading. The candidates tailored their strategies in large part to deal with this situation. In Obama's case, though much adulation has been bestowed on the campaign staff for its strategic planning, that praise is woefully exaggerated as far as the general election campaign was concerned. (The primary campaign was another matter.) Obama's strategy was obvious and virtually determined by the situation. It had two components. The first was to remind the public of its dissatisfaction with George Bush and to tie John McCain to him. This effort went to exquisite lengths, as when Obama likened John McCain's attempt to separate himself from Bush to "Robin getting mad at Batman," as if the older McCain could ever have fit into Robin's taut britches. (Joe Biden, by Obama's recounting, had compared McCain's effort to "Tonto getting mad at the Lone Ranger."[1]) Other things about John McCain were thrown in along the way, such as complaints that he was out of touch and innuendos that he was too old. But this part of the strategy came down to a simple equation: McCain = Bush.

The second component of the strategy was to make every effort for Obama to clear a threshold of acceptability for the public. Given the electorate's dissatisfaction, the voters' inclination was to prefer change, or the candidate from the "out" party. Obama's job was to allow them to fulfill this inclination. On this basis, it oversimplifies matters only slightly to say that the contest boiled down to Obama running against himself. Obama had to overcome whatever reservations the electorate might have about an untested individual assuming the office in dangerous times. Obama had to convince the public to be "comfortable" with him and to show that he had the right stuff. The major tactical shift in achieving this objective came when Obama adjusted his main public image from inspirational leader to calm and sober statesman in the making.

In John McCain's case, the choice of strategy was both more open-ended and more difficult to decide. Although McCain was from the incumbent party and was the better known of the two candidates, he was—continuing the same oversimplification—the "challenger" in this race. He had to consider how to take the race away from Obama, who held the upper hand. His campaign had to incur the risks, to look for the bold stroke, the end run, and the stunning maneuver. This task fitted McCain's personal disposition as a leader, which helped. McCain was never too cautious to back off. But it may be wondered in retrospect whether this view did not become so pervasive that it substituted for a more coherent plan.

McCain's strategy had three components. First, he had to try to separate himself from George Bush, by seven degrees if possible. But in separating himself, he could not be too critical, either. None of the Republican candidates in the nomination contest, McCain included, ran an insurgency candidacy against the president, akin to the campaigns that Bobby Kennedy or Eugene McCarthy ran against President Johnson. It was never, for most Republicans, a question of repudiating George Bush, and McCain had to walk a fine line between running not as George Bush but not against him. McCain was not a part of the administration and had opposed the president on some important matters while senator. But they shared the party label, and full separation proved difficult.

Second, John McCain had to offer something that showed his superior fit to be the commander in chief. This meant demonstrating worthy qualities of his own while pointing up his opponent's personal liabilities. It meant a campaign that contrasted their characters and their deepest beliefs as they affected character. Much of the McCain campaign was therefore about Barack Obama the person, with the particular flaws charged to him changing as the campaign went on.

Finally, McCain had to present a general plan or vision, beyond differences with Obama on specific issues, of where he intended to lead the nation. It would have to be an alternative to both the Democrats and to the current Republican administration. The campaign struggled on this point. Since McCain never defined a programmatic or ideological direction—this had never been his approach or style as a leader—the plan would have to be more thematic. McCain resolved to present himself as a reformer who would "stand up" and "fight" against all the political pressures and interests that were eating at the core of the political system. Late in the campaign he also turned to denouncing Obama's ideological premises, but without offering a fully developed program of his own.

THE RACE

A look at the poll numbers over the course of the campaign provides a good basis for dividing the race into three distinct periods. In the first period, from the summer up to the Republican convention, Obama maintained a slight lead, although at a few points it dwindled to well below the margin of error. Democrats worried that Obama had not managed to "take control" of the race in the way he should have—that, to use a sports term, he was letting his opponent "hang around." Republicans complained that the McCain campaign jumped from one thing to another without articulating a coherent idea of what the race was about.

The second period ran from after the close of the Democratic convention until mid-September. McCain produced a shock—positive and negative—with the announcement of Sarah Palin as his vice presidential pick, and following the Republican convention, for the first and only time since both nominations were wrapped up, the poll lines crossed. McCain jumped briefly to a lead that was at or outside the margin of error. During this period, John McCain (now John McCain with Sarah Palin) held center stage, with others—the media and the Obama campaign—having to react to them. Was this lead a mere convention bounce, extended a little bit longer than usual, or had the race really changed? We will never know.

A third and final period began in mid-September with the onset of the financial crisis, when Obama pulled ahead and remained in front for the duration. An event of this kind and magnitude undoubtedly played to the advantage of Obama, who had been trying before—and succeeding—in making the economy the central issue of the campaign. But it was not just the event by itself that was important. It was how the candidates responded to it, and what that response indicated about their leadership capacity. Forced to take a risk (or feeling himself in this position), McCain handled the event in a way that detracted from the image of an experienced leader, while Obama showed himself to be cooler and sober. Along with the bad economic news, this image helped seal the race. By the end, the outcome—a decisive Obama victory—surprised no one.

THE L●NG SUMMER

On June third, Barack Obama strode before an enthusiastic crowd of supporters in St. Paul, Minnesota, and announced that he had secured the Democratic nomination for president. The general election campaign was underway, with no pretense made by either candidate of waiting until the decisions of the party conventions to get started. In fact, McCain jumped in the next day to invite Obama to participate in a series of ten "joint forums" over the summer. The plan, he claimed, would establish "a new tenor" for political campaigns and allow these two professedly reform-minded leaders to embrace "the politics of civility."[2] This was McCain's opening bid to open a "reform" theme in the campaign, reviving something of the spirit of the old "Straight Talk Express" bus from his 2000 primary campaign against George W. Bush.

Obama's campaign manager, David Plouffe, professed to find the idea "appealing," which was a way of saying no thanks. Ahead in the race, Obama was not about to risk a lead in order to prove his reform credentials. As the American people would soon learn, if they didn't know it already, Barack Obama was not just a high-minded idealist who intoned about change. He was a tough politician as well. And he said as much. Paraphrasing a line from *The Untouchables*, Obama said: "If they bring a knife to the fight, we bring a gun."[3]

Obama used the period after clinching the nomination for a number of important moves. One was to begin the process of mending fences with Hillary Clinton and her 18 million strong constituency (the number, roughly, that had voted for Hillary in the nomination contest). It was not as difficult as it seemed. For all the tough words between the two of them, there were no important differences on the issues. The Obama campaign needed only to use a lot of therapeutic language such as "reaching out," "understanding," and "healing"—a practice at which Democrats excel—and to rely on the extraordinary graciousness of their candidate. Among the many advantages of living in a large continental nation is the superabundance of names of geographical units that can be put to good political use. So it was that on Friday, June 27, Barack Obama joined Hillary Clinton in Unity, New Hampshire, population 1,500, for a rally, replete with pledges on Hillary's part to work for Obama. A few days later Obama was in communication with Bill Clinton, the figure whom he had just dethroned as the de facto head of the Democratic Party (and who had been accused of introducing race into the campaign in South Carolina).

Fence mending within the party was something Democrats expected. Two other moves, however, were not, and they both showed Obama as a hard-nosed politician at work. One was a repositioning toward the center, as Obama proceeded quickly to modify or abandon some previous stands to appeal to more moderate voters. Obama had earlier backed away from his call for direct talks with Iranian leaders (there would be need for "preparations"), and he now showed support (or no opposition) for the position that gun ownership was an individual right, issuing no criticism of the Supreme Court's decision that struck down the District of Columbia's ban on handguns.[4] Near the end of June, he voted for a compromise measure endorsed by the Bush administration that permitted wiretapping for national security purposes (Hillary opposed the measure), and later in the summer he withdrew his complete opposition to offshore oil drilling as part of a larger "package" to deal with the energy problem.[5] If Obama was not completely reinventing himself by these modifications, he was making clear that he was not the kind of candidate who was going to agonize over defending positions as a matter of pure principle if that was going to hurt him politically. He had run a thematic, not an ideological, campaign, and he was now availing himself of the flexibility that this approach afforded him. Obama's "adjustments" brought him some criticisms from the Left, but most commentators found little difficulty in praising him as much now for his "toughness" and "realism" as they had before for his lofty idealism.

Obama's other move was to opt out of public financing and raise all his campaign funds from private donors, a step that broke from his previous reform platform and promises. Here, Obama received slightly more heat. The *New York Times* issued what for it was the stern rebuke that since Obama's support rested "considerably on his evocative vows to depart from self-interested politics," it was unfortunate that "Mr. Obama has come up short of that standard."[6] Other reformers were no less severe in their condemnations.

McCain's campaign responded, as expected, by pressing McCain's credentials as the true reformer. But the real opening that the campaign saw was to turn the reform issue into a question about Obama's character as a leader. According to McCain's top advisor, Steve Schmidt, "he discards positions when they become inconvenient for him. When politicians say one thing and then do another, like Senator Obama has done, voters wonder about the steadfastness of the character of the person sitting in the Oval Office." McCain himself was only slightly less direct: "You know, this election is about trust and trusting people's word. And unfortunately, apparently on several items Senator Obama's word cannot be trusted."[7] This line of attack broke new ground from the characterizations emphasized by the Clinton campaign, which had charged Obama with being woolly-headed and unprepared. Now there was said to be something far more disturbing at work, a dangerous ambition that was hidden under a gloss of idealism.

Lying beneath the surface of this specific attack was a more general point that the McCain campaign was trying to drive home: just who was Barack Obama? Americans could feel that they knew John McCain, knew what made him tick, but did they really know Barack Obama? Not only was Obama new to the scene, but when the focus was placed on him he seemed elusive. There is every indication that Obama cultivated this quality, sensing that his different masks were an asset. In an earlier *New York Times* interview, he had said, "I am like a Rorschach test. Even if people find me disappointing ultimately, they might gain something."[8] The McCain campaign's objective was to raise the doubtful aspects of this chameleon-like character, hoping that Americans would prefer the tried and true.

Early in the summer, it did not seem as if McCain could bring Obama down to earth. The Democrat's nomination campaign had been brilliant, and enthusiasm for his campaign was in full flower. McCain, on the other hand, won his nomination not because he had captured the hearts and minds of Republicans, but because his party rivals had failed to do so. A good deal of

GOP support for McCain was tepid at best. Indeed, surveys suggested a wide "enthusiasm gap" between the candidates. Asked how they felt about their nominee, 50 percent of Obama supporters said that they were "enthusiastic." Just 16 percent of McCain's supporters said the same. Although more than half of McCain voters were "satisfied" with him, 15 percent said that they were "dissatisfied" or even "angry" that he was the GOP standard-bearer.[9]

By far the most important moment in the campaign during the summer was Obama's trip to the Middle East and Europe in July. Obama announced he would make this trip at the end of June, saying that it would be "an important opportunity for me to assess the situation in countries that are critical to American national security and to consult with some of our closest friends and allies about the common challenges we face."[10] Never before in a presidential campaign had there been anything like the media coverage that this trip received. The anticipation froze everything, with commentators speculating on what would happen. McCain aides complained in advance, as McCain had traveled in June to Canada, and then in late June to Colombia and Mexico, but received scant press coverage.[11] Yet McCain in truth had little reason to complain, for he had helped to set up the trip by criticizing Obama for ignoring the situation in Iraq: "Sen. Obama has been to Iraq once—a little over two years ago he went and he has never seized the opportunity except in a hearing to meet with General Petraeus."[12] McCain had dared Obama to make this trip, which seemed like a good idea at the time, but which looked different when Obama accepted the challenge. For unless one banked on the unlikely prospect that the troops would snub Obama or that he would commit a huge gaffe, how could this trip fail? Obama would be seen in shirtsleeves, eating and joking with the troops (proving that he could be commander in chief) and holding high-level meetings with foreign leaders (showing that he could be a statesman).

And this is exactly what took place. The photos were all presidential, and the press gave Obama glowing reviews. In Iraq, Obama pulled off a coup when Prime Minister Maliki seemed to endorse his sixteen-month troop withdrawal plan, providing him with valuable cover against McCain's charge that his policy would risk defeat in Iraq.[13] European leaders were said to be impressed with his grasp of the issues. For the European public, Obama recalled the image of JFK. Best of all, he was not George Bush. The grand finale was a speech in the open air in Berlin before a vast crowd in which Obama delivered a lofty message calling himself a "citizen of the world." Obamamania had gone international, and Obama's media entourage was all but ready to declare, nay crown, him president of the United States. While Obama spoke in Berlin, McCain visited a German restaurant, Schmidt's Restaurant und Sausage Haus, in Columbus, Ohio. The boy back home ploy did not seem to be working.

Or was it? McCain's campaign sensed something that others were apparently missing: that Obama had gone too far. Still just a candidate, he could be seen as presuming to be president; still seeking his party's nomination, he could be viewed as courting European and world public opinion. Former Speaker of the House of Representatives Tip O'Neill was known to remind young lawmakers of his own adage that "all politics is local," by which he meant that it was a fool's errand to court the national elite and the Washington press corps while ignoring the folks back home who control your fate by their votes. People back home, in the Kiwanis clubs and at the Schmidt's Restaurants, resent that. The same principle held here, but on a different level. Obama was seen to be playing to a world audience while perhaps forgetting the folks "back home" in America. McCain received a rousing ovation at the famed Sturgis Motorcycle Rally when he said, "As you may know, not long ago a couple hundred thousand Berliners made a lot of noise for my opponent. I'll take the roar of fifty-thousand Harleys any day."

After Obama delivered his speech, the McCain campaign ran an ad portraying Obama as a celebrity phenomenon, akin to Paris Hilton or Britney Spears. It was followed up by another ad, The One, satirizing Obama's lofty status, which included the line (from his speech declaring victory in the nomination contest) that this is "the moment when the rise of the oceans began to slow and our planet began to heal." The ad concluded with a quick video reference to a classic Hollywood movie scene, from *The Ten Commandments*, of Charlton Heston playing Moses parting the Red Sea. This pair of ads will qualify as the most memorable of the 2008 campaign. Both were a bit silly, perhaps even juvenile, but it was just this quality that enabled them to make their point without being too negative or nasty. The ads struck a chord with large parts of the electorate. In fact, The Trip was not as universally admired by the public as it was by the press corps in Obama's retinue. While 35 percent experienced a positive response to Obama's trip abroad, 39 percent held no opinion, and 26 percent reacted negatively.[14]

An even surer indication of the effectiveness of these ads than the panic in the Obama campaign was the reactions of some friends in the media. One of these was David Gergen, the self-proclaimed son of the South and moral voice of CNN, who brought out the biggest gun in the arsenal, the nuclear option, by accusing the McCain campaign of using racist appeals, all the more cleverly and insidiously for hiding it under Moses' robe: "As a native of the South, I can tell you, when you see this Charlton Heston ad, 'The One,' that's code for, 'he's uppity, he ought to stay in his place.' Everybody gets that who is from a southern background. We all understand that."

The McCain campaign was having some success in one of its primary strategy objectives: raising questions about Barack Obama as a leader and making people ask, who exactly is this man? By the beginning of August, McCain polled neck and neck with Obama in Gallup's Daily Tracking poll. As Obama gained with the press corps, he began to lose some with the American people.

Outside events, if they are significant enough, can shake up a presidential campaign, especially as they either fit into or belie existing tenets of campaign strategy. If one thinks about it in the abstract—and the campaigns strategists always do—there was one kind of event that have been helpful to McCain and another kind to Obama. For McCain, it would be a foreign policy crisis, above all a terror event, that would have boosted the salience of national security concerns in the electorate's thinking and rekindled Americans' fear. The preferred reaction of the candidates in this script, in the McCain scenario, would be one in which McCain demonstrated his experience and ability to handle the issue, while Obama looked hesitant and fell short. For Obama, the helpful event would have been a domestic problem, especially an economic downturn, and the preferred reaction, in the Obama scenario, would be for him to demonstrate his judgment and maturity, allaying any concerns that he was not ready to lead.

During the summer, each candidate got his event, though not yet in a way that would turn the campaign. In early August, Russian troops invaded Georgia's northern region of South Ossetia. McCain spoke with Georgian President Saakashvili and made clear United States' solidarity with Georgia, telling him, "I know that I speak for every American when I say . . . , 'Today we are all Georgians.'" McCain acted quickly and decisively in a way that highlighted his foreign policy experience. Furthermore, the Russian invasion brought notice to McCain's seemingly prescient long-standing suspicion of Vladimir Putin.[15] The Obama campaign waited more than a day to issue an initial statement, perhaps because Obama was on vacation in Hawaii at the time. McCain dismissed Obama's response as timid and inexperienced. McCain probably gained a slight advantage, but the bottom line was that the invasion of Georgia did not strike Americans as a major event, and it was in any case partly overshadowed by the Olympic Games, which displaced much of the political coverage for the period from August 8 to closing ceremonies on August 24.

The other "event," objectively favorable to Obama, was the cost of gasoline at the pump, which had been going up since the spring. The word *crisis* might not be too strong, as the prices approached $5 per gallon in some parts of the country. This "bad" economic news obviously was helpful to the Democrats, for this occurred under Bush's watch and could be blamed on

Bush's "failed energy policies," an expression that became a kind of Democratic mantra. Yet as prices began reaching their peak, it became apparent that one plan Bush had favored, increasing domestic oil production by allowing for offshore drilling, began to look more appealing. McCain sensed this, and though he had long opposed offshore drilling in a career of seeking environmentalist support, he changed positions and called for drilling in most areas. It was necessary now for economic independence and national security reasons. This shift proved popular, and McCain become more and more of an enthusiastic advocate, endorsing the line, "drill, baby, drill." (Getting hammered on the issue, Obama too later shifted positions, though in a nuanced way that McCain depicted as insufficient.[16]) The net result was that on the issue of the economy, on which Obama held the upper hand, McCain was able to blunt the Democrats' advantage to a considerable degree. Indeed, Republicans in general seemed to have found the issue that might serve as a life preserver in an otherwise tough year. The moral of this story is that while an event may provide an objective advantage for one side, it is impossible to know in advance how each side will respond and which side will ultimately achieve a net gain.

The final occurrence of importance before the Democratic convention was the first debate—actually a sequential appearance—of McCain and Obama at Rick Warren's evangelical Saddleback Church. Obama's performance was solid, but he seemed too academic. Evangelicals and conservative Catholics were not the only ones disappointed when Obama ducked a question on abortion, saying it was "above my pay grade." McCain's answers were crisper and more to the point, and he was widely acclaimed to be the clear winner. More important, this debate gave Republicans some confidence in their candidate, as one who might after all be able to take the race to his opponent. As the Democratic convention approached, uneasiness swept the Democratic ranks. McCain was hanging around, behind but within striking distance. It was not what Obama's followers hoped for.

In a gesture to both the new technology and to the participation of the campaign faithful, Obama promised to make known his eagerly awaited pick for the vice president by means of a mass text message. In a rare fumble for the Obama campaign, the news leaked prematurely, prompting the campaign to send the message at an odd hour. When the message arrived on August 23, at 3 a.m., the unexpected wake-up call announced the choice of Senator Joe Biden, hardly the jolt to get most out of bed. Much as George Bush had chosen Richard Cheney for his foreign policy heft, so Obama was selecting Biden for his long experience in working on issues of international affairs. Politically, Biden might also help to shore up support with working-class and

Catholic voters, especially under the campaign's projected plan to emphasize Biden's purported working-class roots in hardscrabble Scranton, Pennsylvania. (Apart from a short spell of economic difficulty, Biden's upbringing was solidly middle class.[17]) There was the known liability of Biden's reputation as a gaffe machine—which he proceeded to uphold with great honor during the campaign—but he was so well liked among journalists that they could be counted on to pass off his bloopers as merely expressions of personal idiosyncrasy. The choice of Biden was a safe one. It generated no great excitement, perhaps deliberately so, as Obama was thought to provide all the excitement that was needed. Still, with the race being much closer than most anticipated, many wondered why Obama had not gone for the bold stroke of selecting Hillary Clinton, a move that would have united the party and, as some thought, virtually guaranteed his election.

The Democratic convention was a success. To counter the concerns about elitism and cosmopolitanism, Michelle Obama's speech on the first night sketched the picture of the Obamas as a responsible family of modern middle-class values that was as American as apple pie, which was all the more striking because this was a black family. Both Clintons were given a prime speaking slot, and both gave good speeches. Bill, who had come under much fire in the spring from within his own party, was welcomed with genuine warmth and enthusiasm. So was Hillary, who endorsed Obama strongly, though some detected in her speech a greater focus on herself. The gestures made to the Clintons were generous—enough to quell any idea of a snub in not being offered the vice presidency. Most worries about disunity in the party were put to rest, and the stage was set for the huge extravaganza of Obama's acceptance speech before eighty-thousand supporters at Invesco Field. It is safe to say that if the plans for the convention had not been made before his trip to Berlin, Obama would never have chosen this venue. It now presented as many risks as advantages. Obama was in the altogether unusual situation of being forced to play down his soaring oratorical talents. His task was not, as the jargon for acceptance speeches usually says, to hit it out of the ballpark, but to keep the ball safely in play in the infield. He accomplished this feat. Obama's speech was deliberately short on inspiration, except for a peroration. The scene was impressive, and the weather, which like the press has been a reliable ally of Obama, cooperated perfectly. Obama enjoyed a post-convention bounce in the polls, as the numbers showed a six-point gap in the last week of August.

Obama no doubt hoped the nomination acceptance speech would persist as the story of the next week, but McCain acted roughly twelve hours later to steal the limelight.

EARLY SEPTEMBER: MAC IS BACK

The Democrats in 2008 chose to schedule their convention right before the Republican convention, rather than the more usual timetable where the out party holds its convention about month before the in party. This tight scheduling seems to have been a reaction to what happened in 2004, when John Kerry was damaged by a negative ad campaign in the long month following the Democratic convention. One consequence of the new compacted schedule, however, was that any afterglow from the conventions could be cut short. McCain was fully within his rights to step in just after the Democratic convention to name his VP pick: Governor Sarah Palin of Alaska.

It was less the timing, however, than the choice itself that captured the nation's attention. Prior to her selection, Palin was a virtual unknown outside of Alaska, where she had an 80 percent approval rating as governor and had taken on the state's corrupt (Republican) establishment. She was included on the McCain list of mentionables (along with Mitt Romney, Mike Huckabee, Governor Tim Pawlenty of Minnesota, Governor Bobby Jindal of Louisiana, and outside-of-the-box options like Senator Joe Lieberman and former eBay CEO Meg Whitman), but very few took the possibility seriously. The choice caught everyone by surprise. The contrast between Obama and McCain on the whole issue of the vice presidency, from start to finish, could not have been greater. Obama used the most unconventional means (the fanfare of a text messaging system) to announce a thoroughly conventional choice, while McCain used the most conventional means (an old-fashioned campaign rally) to make a completely unconventional choice. McCain was making a bold effort to show that, despite all the glitter of the Obama campaign, he was the real thing.

And to social conservatives, so was Palin. In December 2007, when she was thirteen weeks pregnant, amniocentesis revealed that her baby had Down syndrome. About 90 percent of the time, this diagnosis leads to abortion.[18] Palin, however, decided to bring the baby to term. Opponents of abortion revered her for living up to her convictions, or as the newsletter of the National Right to Life Committee put it, "The selection of pro-life Alaska Governor Sarah Palin was a twenty on a scale of one to ten."[19] As the convention got under way, Palin also revealed that her daughter Bristol was pregnant, a fact that led some to charge her with hypocrisy. It was also speculated that religious conservatives would turn against her. They did not: in fact, most regarded the Palin family situation with sympathy. Barack Obama did, too. "You know," he said, "my mother had me when she was eighteen."[20]

In other respects, the Palin pick drew mixed initial reactions, with many commentators questioning Palin's qualifications and wondering also about the allegedly hasty process by which she had been chosen. The debate that immediately commenced over Palin's qualifications turned many of the arguments made in the campaign to this point upside down. Here were the supporters of Obama decrying the choice because she was inexperienced and unprepared, while defenders of McCain were now denying that experience should be all that mattered. From one side came the refrain that McCain could no longer use the issue of experience against Obama; from the other, the retort that it was hardly a reason to vote for the Democratic ticket—its presidential nominee now had as little experience as the Republican vice presidential nominee. The Obama campaign itself initially got tied up in knots deciding whether to attack Palin's inexperience; in the end it wisely backed off and let others make the argument.

The concern with Palin's preparedness would linger for the rest of the campaign, confirming the assessment of many that this was in fact a risky choice. Yet it was clear that she brought real assets that no other choice could have. She could appeal to the conservative base of the Republican Party in a way that John McCain could not, and she could introduce an element of freshness and youth—and an appeal to women, to parents of handicapped children, and perhaps to parts of western and Middle America. With Palin on the ticket, McCain could reinvigorate his appeal as a "reformer," not just in the limited sense of favoring certain procedures, but in the broader sense of being willing to take on the big interests and the establishment. Or that, at any rate, was to be the image. And this image would help more than anything else to create the separation from Bush that McCain was seeking. Finally, despite her general unpreparedness, Palin could claim hands-on knowledge in one key policy area: energy and oil. At this point, energy looked to be one of the most important issues that would be debated throughout the campaign.

The major objection to Palin, besides the question of her inexperience, was her social conservatism, which in many areas was more evidenced in her lifestyle than in her stances on matters of public policy. Her mere presence on the ticket began to rekindle heated discussion of the issues of abortion, religion, marriage, and traditional values in a way that had not been part of the campaign to date. There is a thesis, which has much evidence to support it, that the salience of these social issues has been a major factor driving many Republican moderates from the party and making the party less attractive to independents. But the reality is more complex. A look at recent instances in which these kinds of issues have emerged will show that it is quite often the side that Americans see as pushing things immoderately that ends up losing the battle. No doubt there were segments of the population (moderate Republicans and independents) that would—and did—desert McCain because of Palin. But on the other hand, the fury with which punditocracy attacked her made many think that America's intellectual elite was fully engaged—if the word is not inappropriate—in a crusade against Sarah Palin the person. The condescension on display toward a mother of five, a former beauty queen, a moose hunter and lifelong member of the National Rifle Association, a conservative Christian, and, to top it off, someone who attended school at the University of Idaho was palpable. Here was an alien. And when fighting aliens, no rules apply. This display of prejudice could provoke a huge reaction from the other side. For every vote Palin was losing, she might win more from the other side.

If one measures the quality of a convention speech by how well the performance exceeds expectations, Sarah Palin's address was one of the most successful speeches ever given at a party convention. It was cutting, it was gentle, it was delivered with freshness and with a certain bravado. She was the first and only candidate in 2008 to have had the kryptonite to pierce Barack Obama's armor. Her criticism scored like no others had. It left her critics (temporarily) flummoxed. It looked like a star was born. From a Republican viewpoint, the most striking praise for the speech came from Michael Reagan: "Wednesday night I watched the Republican National Convention on television and there, before my very eyes, I saw my dad reborn; only this time he's a she."[21]

Oh, yes, and John McCain gave a speech, too. He told his narrative, but in a different way that made his sacrifice as a prisoner of war less the story of a hero than a personal account of lowering his own personal expectations and coming to love his country more. He evoked a sense of personal depth, authentic stature, and humility that was intended to contrast favorably with Obama. It was an old-fashioned speech that cultivated old-fashioned virtues, and it appeared to have its effect. Something, in any case, had changed. McCain surged, taking a lead outside the margin of error in a number of polls. On September 11, InTrade futures were selling McCain shares for 51.3 cents, meaning that for the first time speculators believed he had a slightly better than even chance of winning. The share of Americans identifying as Republicans rose from 26 percent just before the convention to 30 percent after it. Together with a two-point dip in Democratic identification from 37 to 35 percent, that shift cut the Democrats' advantage in party identification from eleven points to five.[22] Such a change might have been temporary, but it did suggest that McCain had a chance.

Acknowledging that Palin was a bigger draw for many Republicans than he was, McCain took the unusual step of frequently appearing at rallies with his running mate. Their crowds grew in size and enthusiasm, and Republican fundraising picked up. Numerous observers detected signs of panic in the Democratic camp, and Obama and Biden seemed to be caught off-stride, with

Obama making a slip that allowed some to think he was referring to Palin as a pig in lipstick.

Was this a mere convention bump? Or was it the opening of a different campaign, the campaign that might have been, but for the onset of the financial crisis that would shortly take place? In the race that could have been, the candidates went back to talking about the economy, with a heavy emphasis on energy. Obama was also poised to press the case that McCain, who had just admitted in an interview that he did not know how many homes he and his wife, Cindy, owned, was out of touch with hard-pressed Americans. (His spokespersons and allies in the media also began to push the line that McCain was a "liar" in response to increasingly hard-hitting advertising.) But the campaign now seemed to be opening a second front on the cultural theme. Cultural themes can go either way, but this was one in which the "friends" of Obama were serving as his worst enemies. By keeping alive the cultural dimension of Palin's small-town roots and values, they were reinserting into the campaign, without McCain ever having to bring it in, the image of Obama as enemy of the "bitter" small-town Americans clinging to their guns and their religion. In the campaign that might have been, the emphasis on Sarah Palin would have been much greater than it turned out to be. Her appearances, which offered a mixed picture, would have carried even more weight than they did. Her deficiencies would have continued to polarize, but with the assault coming from the Left, many voters might have rallied to her side.

It is impossible to say what would have happened had the campaign continued on the trajectory of early September. Polls were showing that Obama was losing his advantage on economic issues, and an article in the *Politico* quoted Democratic strategist James Carville: "I noticed the tightening on the economy. And if it stays that way, I would be damn worried."[23] The article was posted at 7:24 a.m. on the morning of September 14. Everything was about to change.

9-14

Over the summer, the nation faced a slowly deteriorating general economy combined with a highly visible spike in gasoline prices. The economy had already emerged as the top problem facing the nation in the eyes of the voters, far surpassing the Iraq War. But the financial crisis that started on September 14 lifted concern over the economy to a new and different level. From the third of Americans who cited the economy as the top problem in July, the figure rose to 47 percent in October and to 58 percent in early November, the highest level since the recession of 1980.[24] The political campaign of 2008 was now operating within a new and different universe in which only one issue mattered. The cultural aspect of the campaign became a sideshow, as did whatever was left of concern for national security issues. The way in which the economy was discussed also changed. Instead of inequality and general dissatisfaction, the overriding questions were now the financial crisis and the worsening recession. Discussion of the economy began to separate from the problem of energy—indeed, collapsing demand led prices at the pump to begin falling at a remarkable rate, though this change earned no credit for Republicans.

This crisis was the "perfect" event for Barack Obama. He also handled it perfectly—or at any rate much better than did John McCain. Following the news on Sunday, September 14, that Lehman Brothers would file for bankruptcy, McCain took the occasion on the next day to characterize the "fundamentals" of the economy as "strong," which might be the kind of statement that a president would make to try to reassure the nation, but which hardly suits a candidate. Later in the day, McCain stated that those strong fundamentals were "at great risk." In the immediate skirmishing, the Obama camp called McCain to task over his inconsistent reaction, using his first statement to claim that he was out of touch. The first phase of the economic crisis was a mirror image of the Georgia crisis, only McCain's stumble was greater and this issue was of infinitely greater magnitude of importance to the voters.

As the economic crisis deepened, it was apparent what the political fallout would be. Polls confirmed that Obama benefited from the economy's woes. As the Bush administration prepared to offer a huge bailout plan to handle the freezing of the credit markets, McCain determined that he needed to attempt the bold stroke and try to get out in front of the issue—to show he was shaping it rather than merely reacting to it. On September 24, after speaking with Obama and agreeing to sign a joint statement on dealing with the crisis, McCain abruptly announced the formal suspension of his campaign and suggested calling off the presidential debate scheduled for two days later. The economic crisis was too important. He would return to Washington, meet the next day with the president (along with other congressional leaders whom Bush had invited to the White House, including Obama) and then commit himself full-time to help arrange a bipartisan agreement to pass the bailout measure that Treasury Secretary Paulson deemed essential to the solvency of the financial industry. McCain now made himself hostage to the legislative processes, where Democrats were not about to let him score a triumph and where many Republicans had some profound reservations about the plan. Hopes for quick passage failed to materialize; indeed, some Democratic leaders may have exaggerated the prospects for quick passage and then blamed

McCain when nothing happened. Negotiations and wrangling would continue for weeks before the legislation passed.

It is a noteworthy fact about the presidential debates in 2008 that the most important thing about them never took place during the three debates themselves, which proved largely uneventful. The main drama, or melodrama, touching on the debates centered on whether McCain would show up for the first debate in Oxford, Mississippi. Obama made clear that he would be there and did so without falling into the trap of minimizing the importance of the economic crisis. As he coolly noted, "It's going to be part of the president's job to be able to deal with more than one thing at once." McCain's bid to play the statesman in this crisis began to disintegrate. He backed down, reinstated his campaign, and traveled to Mississippi. The effect of the capitulation was to undermine the image of the seasoned leader that McCain's campaign had sought to portray. Obama went on the offensive, calling McCain "erratic in crisis." (McCain also, incidentally, missed a TV appearance on the David Letterman show, for which he later apologized to Letterman: "I screwed up. What can I say?")

The first debate, which was scheduled to be on foreign policy, now was broadened to include the financial crisis. Both camps claimed victory, although the electoral dynamic shifted little as a result of the debate. The situation of the campaign following the onset of the financial crisis was now clear. Obama did not have to win this debate or any of the others on debating points (though most Americans gave him the victory in all three). Experts might pore over the videotapes and transcripts, but the real political importance of the debates has nothing to do with technical victory or defeat on the spot, but with how the debate functions inside the larger campaign. For the candidate who is trailing or in a tight race, the key becomes whether he can take away something from a debate that opens a new line of argument or attack. Because of where the campaign stood, Obama just had to avoid mistakes, give McCain no big point or issue to develop, and show that he was presidential. Obama accomplished all three of these objectives, above all the final one. The Barack Obama of this debate was as far away from the image of "The One" as Oxford, Mississippi, was from Berlin.

Meanwhile, as they say, back at the ranch, the bailout bill failed to pass the House the next week. Obama blamed McCain for having injected presidential politics in the House's consideration of the measure, while McCain complained that Democrats did not muster enough votes to pass the bill so as to embarrass his campaign. Little was to be gained for McCain in this gambit, and while he might deserve credit for trying (and actually helping), he left himself subject to matters beyond his control.

The race was now set, with Obama enjoying a clear lead. If there was any possibility of victory, McCain would need to convince the American people that he knew better how to deal with the economy. He would need to explain what went wrong, why it was not just the Republicans' fault, and what could be done to restore economic health. The problem the campaign confronted here had no solution, as it was grounded in the limitations of John McCain himself. Whatever else might be said in favor of his strengths, explaining the broad issues of the economy was simply not one of them. McCain was an honor politician, not a policy wonk or abstract thinker. It did not help that his campaign manager, Rick Davis, contended that the campaign wanted to stop talking about the economy as soon as possible; the election, Davis said, was not about issues. (It was at this point that some Republicans began privately grumbling that the economically fluent businessman Romney might have been a better vice presidential—or presidential—choice.)

Forced nevertheless to address the economy, the McCain campaign tried different things, from proposing a huge new plan to buy up bad mortgages, to assigning the blame to the government for insufficient oversight or for pushing banks to make bad loans. It never quite worked. All Obama had to do was hold tight, heeding Napoleon's apocryphal advice not to interfere with the enemy when he is in the process of destroying himself. This is not to say that Obama, any more than McCain or anyone else, actually had any idea what to do about the crisis, but he knew enough to keep his distance while McCain floundered. Throughout, his debate performances showed a quality of coolness and restraint.

The next campaign event to generate any considerable interest was the vice presidential debate, which occurred on October 2. Between the Republican National Convention in early September and the VP debate, the public had grown much warier of Governor Palin because of a lackluster interview with Charles Gibson and an inept showing with Katie Couric that projected an image of inexperience and incompetence.[25] (Behind the scenes the issue of the McCain campaign's handling of Sarah Palin became a matter of contention. They first protected her by denying media interviews, and then threw her to the lions by scheduling her only with high-profile national interviews.) In the changed climate, the one debate was unlikely to settle anything, though a poor performance by Palin would be the nail in the coffin for whatever dwindling chance McCain still had. Nevertheless, given the attacks on Palin, the human interest aspect of this debate was high, and more viewers tuned in to watch the vice presidential debate than the first presidential debate. Neither Biden nor Palin performed very competently in the debate. Palin entered with the advantage of low expectations, especially since her opponent was more seasoned. She handled herself adequately and avoided any lasting gaffes. Her performance won no converts, but it stanched the McCain campaign's Palin-related bleeding.[26] Biden made his share of misstatements, but he carried himself with confidence and was judged by polls to have won the debate.

The second presidential debate had a "town hall" format. Many commentators thought that the setting would work to McCain's advantage, since he long excelled at giving extemporaneous answers to questions from ordinary citizens. Unfortunately for McCain, the town hall debate merely spotlighted differences in style and appearance that worked in Obama's favor. Because of the torture he endured as a prisoner of war in Vietnam, he limped and had difficulty moving his arms. These limitations became obvious when he walked around the debate floor. In a just world, television viewers would have watched him and thought "war hero." In the real world, many probably thought "elderly man." Obama, as a relatively young man in apparently good health, gained from the visual contrast.

Both camps sharpened attacks and worked hardest to sway voters in October, but the polls fluctuated less than in September. The bailout bill, opposed in polls by a significant majority of Americans, finally passed, supported by both Obama and McCain. It was perhaps McCain's final chance to sever the connection with Bush and to turn the economic issue around, but switching to a no vote on the bailout, after supporting it all along, was a risk that would surely have backfired. Under these circumstances, with the debate clogged and the campaign sinking, what was McCain to do? Only one expedient was left: call the plumber. Obama provided a small opening during a response to a question posed to him by one Samuel Joseph Wurzlebacher, a plumber from a small town in Ohio. Responding to his concerns about Obama's plan to raise taxes on the wealthy (making more than $250,000), Obama responded, "When you spread the wealth around, it's good for everybody." The remark was seized on by Republicans, and in the final debate John McCain created the human character of "Joe the Plumber," a name destined to be a staple on quiz shows in years to come. (A few days later, Joe endorsed McCain and appeared with him at a rally.) The argument opened up an ideological dimension, with McCain and Palin accusing Obama of embracing a European-style system of redistribution. (Palin called it an experiment with "socialism.")

McCain kept up his attacks on Obama's likely tax increases, and he tried to reinject national security into the conversation by pointing to Biden's late prediction that foreign adversaries would create a crisis to test Obama in the first six months of his presidency. McCain also began to emphasize the danger of complete Democratic rule, that is, Democrats in control of the White House and both chambers of Congress.[27] In 1996, both Bill Clinton and congressional Republicans used such arguments to win a verdict for divided government from ambivalent Americans. In 2008, however, the danger of single-party hegemony with Obama in control did not frighten enough independents to generate support for McCain. The McCain campaign unleashed a series of attacks that decried Obama's supposed relationship with 1960s terrorist William Ayers. Along with the redistributionist charge, these attacks fed press stereotypes of the Republican base, even though the Hillary Clinton campaign had originally raised the Ayers issue. The media did not hesitate to portray such attacks as desperate flailing from a doomed campaign. Whether reasonable or not, the attacks came too late to be effective.

For his part, Obama continued assailing Bush's "failed economic policies" and McCain's health care plan; perhaps surprisingly, Obama also held McCain to a draw on the issue of taxes with his promise to cut taxes for 95 percent of Americans. (That much of this tax cut would consist of Treasury checks paid out for refundable tax credits to non-taxpayers was not emphasized.) Obama launched an advertising blitz for the month of October and outspent McCain nearly three to one. From October 15 to November 4, Obama raised $104 million. Over the same period, McCain spent $26 million to Obama's $136 million. By the end of the campaign, Obama outspent McCain by roughly four to one. McCain's numbers never kept pace. Throughout the fall, Obama not only maximized his own fundraising but tried to minimize the impact of the other side's (more meager) resources. The Obama campaign was very aggressive in threatening legal action against television stations and organizations running advertisements that it considered untruthful. The Wednesday before Election Day, Obama bought a half-hour commercial on major networks, forcing a delay in the start time of a World Series game.

At points in late October, some polls seemed to be tightening, but the phenomenon was temporary, and McCain never quite edged back to a lead even in the most favorable polls. Outside of the polls, late moves were toward Obama, who reaped the endorsements of former secretary of state Colin Powell, former Reagan staffer Kenneth Duberstein, and William F. Buckley's son, Christopher. Aside from his old friend Joseph Lieberman, who campaigned hard for him around the country, McCain enjoyed no similar crossover endorsements. Bipartisanship only carries one so far.

ENDING AND VERDICT

Obama, who was prepared for his victory, held a massive preelection rally at Grant Park in Chicago. The weather in Chicago was springlike, as Obama delivered his election eve speech. His victory a day later was greeted with euphoria not only in America, but in many other places across the world. It was both a political and cultural event. Despite the anxieties generated by the economy, the race ended with a greater feeling of hope.

The positive side of the 2008 campaign became immediately apparent in the aftermath, and not just because of John McCain's extremely gracious concession speech. For all the skirmishing, this had not been a particularly nasty campaign. Of greatest importance, the issue of race in a negative sense rarely came up explicitly, and never at all from the Republican side. There was no basis for any kind of recrimination on this question, and in this sense the nation was already becoming post-racial. It would not be very long, in fact, before the significance of Obama's race was little more than an afterthought for most Americans.

No one likes to lose. But this was an election result that both sides accepted as legitimate, not just in a legal sense but in a moral and political sense. Large parts of the opposition parties in 1996, 2000, and 2004 in some ways rejected the moral authority of the election, or saw the results as coming from dirty campaigning, trickery, or false consciousness. Though a few grumbled about Obama's unfair advantage in spending and about the media's favoritism of Obama, no one seemed to question the fundamental right of Obama to be president. And though it is a delicate subject, it is fair to ask how Democrats would have reacted to a McCain victory, had he pulled one out. Many of the explanations were already prepared: Would it have been racism? Voter suppression? Character attacks? As it turned out, these explanations could be filed away unused.

John McCain, for his part, never shied away from taking risks. Some of them worked and some did not. The Palin pick was not the huge blunder that many have alleged, but neither was it an unvarnished success. Much more problematic—and perhaps the moment that any chance of victory was lost— was the short-lived suspension of his campaign in the face of the economic crisis. McCain's weaknesses were his age, the appearance of unsteadiness, and the inability to explain economic matters in a credible way. His campaign organization never fully came together, which was a reflection in part of his own style. Nevertheless, most Republicans did not blame McCain for the loss. Although no one would nominate him again, and his campaign was flawed, there was little sentiment among Republicans that he should have won, or that another Republican would have. As some had argued, McCain was dealt a bad hand and played it poorly. Even this appraisal, however, is too severe. True, he did not play his hand perfectly—whoever does?—but even with his mistakes he came closer to winning than almost anyone expected. Indeed, McCain performed better relative to the approval rating of his party's president than any other would-be successor since 1952 (see table 5.1). In 2008, though, he had no margin for error.

Table 5.1.   Gap between Outgoing President's Job Approval Rating and the Vote Share of His Party's Nominee for President, 1952–2008

Year	President	Approval	Party's Nominee	Vote Share	Difference
1952	Truman	29.0%	Stevenson	44.3%	+15.3
1960	Eisenhower	61.3%	Nixon	49.6%	–11.7
1968	Johnson	38.8%	Humphrey	42.7%	+3.9
1988	Reagan	53.5%	Bush	53.4%	–0.1
2000	Clinton	59.1%	Gore	48.4%	–10.7
2008	Bush	29.4%	McCain	45.6%	+16.2

Note: Presidential approval is based on an average of all Gallup polls in the July 20–October 19 quarter of the election year.

Barack Obama did execute his strategy. He pulled the great tactical shift, moving from messiah to manager after overplaying his hand in Berlin. He also was never tested fully in the "behind" mode. His campaign was gearing up for such an effort when events propelled Obama back into the lead. It would have been very interesting to see what such a campaign would have looked like with McCain as the leader and Obama playing catch-up.

THE RESULTS: VOTER TURNOUT

Turnout is important not only for its political effects in helping one of the candidates, but also for the broader question of judging the health of American democracy. Slightly more than 131 million people voted in 2008, the most ever in American history. The turnout *rate*—based on considering the relation of actual voters to eligible voters—has been estimated at 61.6 percent, which was a slight rise (1.5 percent) from 2004 and represents the highest rate since 1968.[28] Turnout after 1968 tended to decline, settling in at low rates in 1996 (51.7 percent) and 2000 (54.2 percent). These rates led to widespread concern that Americans had become politically apathetic and disengaged from political life. The 2004 election was a major turning point, with more than a 5 percent jump from the 2000 election (to 60.1 percent). The continuation and consolidation of higher participation in 2008 is a significant fact that should put to rest the dire predictions about the death of civic engagement.

It is curious, however, that so little was made of this good news following the election. On the contrary, the announcement of the turnout rate was met in some quarters by expressions of disappointment. Part of the reason was that so many commentators, relying on evidence of massive increases in voter registration, had predicted a much larger turnout rate, one that would have equaled if not exceeded the rates of the 1960s. This disappointment was most keenly felt by some Obama supporters and had a political component to it. Their hope was that a huge increase in turnout, on the scale of what had happened between 2000 and 2004, would demonstrate a surge of support for Obama, proving that he was a transformative leader who had produced a political realignment: he would not only be victorious, but also become a president who brought record-setting levels of democratic participation to American politics. Despite the disappointment of not quite achieving this exalted status, the more important point is that turnout in 2008 did increase, and Barack Obama's campaign deserves much of the credit. Much of the detailed analysis on this question still remains to be done. There was an upturn, as expected, in the African American vote, and a slight rise in participation among young voters. A couple of the states that became newly competitive and that Obama won, North Carolina and Virginia, saw unusually high increases in voter turnout. On the other side, in trying to account for why rates did not go as high as many expected, it appears that many Republicans who turned out in 2004 failed to do so in 2008. They were less enthusiastic in 2008 than in 2004 and voted, as is often said, with their feet by staying home on Election Day. The irony here is that a good part of what accounts for the lower-than-expected turnout worked to the advantage of Barack Obama.

GEOGRAPHY

The history of international relations is filled with pairs of states or empires that are locked in conflicts that seem unending. It could be Athens and Sparta fighting for control of Greece in the Peloponnesian War or France and England in the Hundred Years' War. At one moment, one of the empires gains the advantage, spreading out from its home base and capturing significant pieces of territory from its adversary. Time goes on, the defeated empire regroups, and in the next phase of conflict it manages to expel the conqueror, invade its territory, and become a conqueror in its own right. And so it goes, back and forth, with each side hoping either to score the final victory or to recover what it may have lost. This scenario could just as easily describe the struggle between Republicans and Democrats over the past three elections. It has been the War of the Decade, and both sides are now already preparing for the next battle.

Geography is everything in American presidential politics because of how electoral votes are counted. All the states, expect Maine and Nebraska, award their electoral votes by a winner-take-all system. The name of the game is therefore to win states. Parties in presidential elections seek to win popular

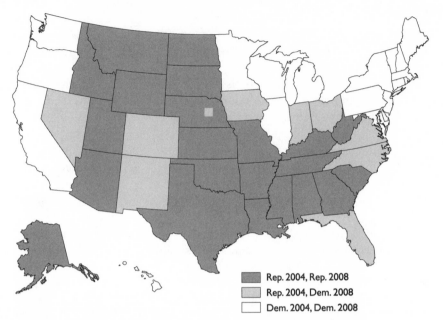

Figure 5.1. Electoral Vote Map for the Two Major Parties, 2004 and 2008

Source: Map courtesy of Steven E. Schier. From *The American Elections of 2008*, edited by Janet M. Box-Steffensmeier and Steven E. Schier (Lanham, Md.: Rowman & Littlefield, 2009).

votes in order to capture states, they do not seek to win states in order to increase their popular votes.

The map of the 2008 election bears a resemblance to those of 2000 and 2004, but obviously with the Republican empire now in retreat, having ceded huge chunks of territory to the invading Democratic forces. The result of the battle of 2008 can be expressed in three points.

First, the Democrats held their homeland. Republicans did not capture a single piece of enemy territory. Every state that John Kerry won, Barack Obama also won—and by an increased margin in every case (see table 5.2). Democrats can feel safer in their core territory than they have in a very long time. Republicans made efforts to find weak points. Early on there was a plan to target the upper-tier midwestern states—Wisconsin and Minnesota—which was the main reason why the Republican convention was held in St. Paul. The choice of Sarah Palin also raised hopes of a northern state surge, born of the rise of the "hockey moms" in Minnesota, Wisconsin, and New Hampshire. But no goals were scored. As the campaign got underway, McCain decided to focus his efforts on capturing Pennsylvania, not only

Table 5.2.   Geographical Continuity and Change in Presidential Results from 2004 to 2008

State	Electoral Votes	% Obama	% McCain	Margin of Obama Victory	Obama Margin over Kerry
States Won by Democrats in 2004 and in 2008					
District of Columbia	3	93	7	86	4
Hawaii	4	72	27	45	18
Vermont	3	68	31	37	9
Rhode Island	4	68	35	28	4
Massachusetts	12	62	36	26	0
Delaware	3	62	37	25	9
Illinois	21	62	37	25	7
Maryland	10	62	37	25	6
New York	31	62	37	25	4
California	55	61	37	24	7
Connecticut	7	61	38	23	7
Maine	4	58	41	17	5
Washington	11	58	41	17	5
Michigan	17	57	41	16	6
Oregon	7	57	41	16	5
Wisconsin	10	56	43	13	7
Pennsylvania	21	55	44	11	4
New Jersey	15	54	45	15	4
Minnesota	10	54	44	10	2
New Hampshire	4	54	45	9	4
States Won by Republicans in 2004 and Democrats in 2008					
New Mexico	5	57	42	15	8
Nevada	5	55	43	12	7
Colorado	9	54	45	9	7
Iowa	7	54	45	9	5
Virginia	13	53	47	6	7
Ohio	20	51	47	4	2
Florida	27	51	49	2	4
Indiana	11	50	49	1	11
North Carolina	15	50	49	1	6
States Won by Republicans in 2004 and 2008					
Missouri	11	49	50	−1	3
Montana	3	47	50	−3	8
Georgia	15	47	52	−5	6
South Dakota	3	45	53	−6	7
North Dakota	3	45	53	−8	6
South Carolina	8	45	54	−9	4
Arizona	10	45	54	−9	1
Texas	34	44	55	−11	6
West Virginia	5	43	56	−13	0

(*continues*)

Table 5.2. (Continued)

State	Electoral Votes	% Obama	% McCain	Margin of Obama Victory	Obama Margin over Kerry
Tennessee	11	42	57	−15	−1
Nebraska	5	42	57	−15	10
Kansas	6	41	57	−16	4
Kentucky	8	41	58	−17	1
Louisiana	9	40	59	−19	−2
Arkansas	6	39	59	−20	−6
Alabama	9	39	61	−22	2
Alaska	3	38	60	−22	2
Idaho	4	36	61	−25	6
Utah	5	34	63	−29	8
Oklahoma	7	34	66	−32	0
Wyoming	3	33	65	−32	4

because its size (twenty-one electoral votes) could make up for expected potential losses elsewhere, but also because Obama's decisive loss in the Democratic primary there, aided by his "bitter" comment, promised an opportunity. Like George Bush, who also sought the prize of Pennsylvania in 2000 and 2004, the effort came up short.

Second, the Democrats made huge gains into what had been Republican territory. Obama captured nine states that Bush won in 2004: Florida, Ohio, New Mexico, Colorado, Nevada, Iowa, Virginia, North Carolina, and Indiana. These netted Obama a swing of 112 electoral votes. (Obama also made a successful foray into Nebraska, picking up one of the "congressionally" allocated electors in that state.) Some of these states had been scenes of pitched battles in the earlier elections. Iowa and New Mexico had already changed hands once, from Democratic to Republican, between 2000 and 2004, and Florida and Ohio were disputed in both elections. The conquest of the five other states represents the Democrats' deepest foray into Republican territory. Democrats have not occupied Virginia or Indiana since 1964 or North Carolina since 1976. The conquest of Indiana, which had the largest swing from 2004 of all of these states, showed the great tactical prowess of Obama's generals. Sensing an opportunity, Obama aimed far more ammunition at Indiana than his opponent did, significantly outspending McCain there and making forty-eight campaign stops to McCain's two. As a leading war correspondent, Michael Barone, remarked from the front lines: "Organization matters. I was not sure how much the Obama organization could deliver in actual votes. The answer turns out to be a lot."[29]

Finally, Republicans held twenty-two states from 2004. These states, which make up the Republican heartland, are found in the South, parts of Appalachia, and the mountain Northwest. The territory is contiguous, in the sense that—Alaska of course excepted—it is connected by ground corridors at every point, which helps keep the supply lines open. But unlike 2004, large distances must now occasionally be traversed to avoid occupied territory. And the homeland is far from being fully secure. Montana, Missouri, Georgia, and the Dakotas are all under siege. Obama gained ground in most of these twenty-two states, though generally by less than the national average of 6.7 percent. Republicans improved or held their own in five states: Arkansas, Louisiana, Oklahoma, Tennessee, and West Virginia.

The generals planning the next war will begin by studying this electoral map. The Democratic scenario will be based on the strategy of Hold and Expand. And there are clear prospects for gains in the states mentioned in the almost or near category. But this map offers the Republicans some solace. The task looks difficult but not impossible. The GOP formula is Hold and Reconquer. Many of these states are within close reach, only a few points away, including North Carolina, Ohio, Florida, Indiana, and Virginia. These five states, currently representing 86 electoral votes, would bring the Republicans to 259, tantalizingly close to the 270 needed for victory. (Of course, the 2010 census is likely to redistribute electoral votes slightly.) Only one more medium-sized state would be needed. Another way to look at the question is to note that Obama's map, with few exceptions, was Bill Clinton's map. Colorado, Florida, Ohio, Nevada, Iowa, and New Mexico—six of Obama's nine takeaways—voted for Clinton in 1992 and/or 1996, and subsequently were reconquered by the Republicans.

Republicans face a daunting prospect in trying to make inroads in much of the Democrats' territory. Ten states and the District of Columbia gave more than 60 percent of their votes to Barack Obama, and in six of these, which were all strongly Democratic to begin with, his swing from 2004 exceeded the national average. The Democratic homeland is pure and in many places becoming purer. Regionally, New England resembles the solid South of old, with only New Hampshire (barely) competitive at the national level. Every member of the House from New England is a Democrat, as are all of its senators, except the two moderate gentlewomen from Maine, Olympia Snowe and Susan Collins, who look now like vestiges of the past. If ever the Republicans hope to reconquer New England, they will need a formidable army to enter and oust the master class of intellectuals that now holds a grip on the hearts and minds of the people of that region.

ISSUES AND COALITIONS

Much of the election was decided by overall dissatisfaction and by general themes, like the wish for change. But the exit polls also asked voters to identify the most important issue facing the country. It comes as no shock that the economy placed first, but the magnitude of the lead may still be surprising. Fully 63 percent cited the economy as the top issue, with 10 percent mentioning Iraq, 9 percent terrorism, and 9 percent health care. Add Iraq and terrorism together as the national security component of this election, and it totaled 19 percent or less than a third of the number mentioning the economy. By contrast, in 2004 34 percent listed these national security concerns first and just 20 percent the economy; 2004 was a foreign policy election, 2008 a domestic policy—and overwhelmingly economy-focused—election.

The rhetoric coming from both candidates in 2008 stressed working beyond parties, but the voting patterns told a very different story. Like 2000 and 2004, this election was one in which few partisans defected to vote for the opposition. Only 10 percent of the Democrats voted for McCain (almost the same as in 2004), and 9 percent of the Republicans for Obama (a slightly higher defection rate than the last time). If it had not been for all the talk of unity following the election, the 2008 contest might have been called a "base" oriented election that left the nation polarized.

The comparison to 2004 must, however, be qualified by one important fact. Republicans remained faithful to their party, only there were now many fewer Republicans. What was left, one might say, was the truer or harder core. The GOP experienced a huge defection from 2004, sinking—according to the exit polls—from 37 percent to 32 percent of the electorate. Meanwhile the Democrats gained slightly, moving up from 37 to 39 percent. Exit polls, because they are taken at the time people vote, are not considered to be the best measures of partisan strength. But other polls have shown similar results. Republicans have been losing large parts of their moderate wing, particularly in the larger cities and suburbs. These losses stem from a number of causes; some were for dissatisfaction with the Iraq War, and others for the party's positions and image on social issues. (Sarah Palin was no doubt a lightning rod for many of these voters.) According to David Brady and Douglas Rivers: "These voters are not lost to Republicans—yet. Most consider themselves Independents or leaning Republicans, not Democrats. They're not liberals and remain closer, on average, to Republican positions than those espoused by the Democrats. But they are up for grabs."[30]

As for the coalitions that supported each of the candidates in 2008, they also resembled the pattern of the past two elections, only with a pronounced slide in most categories toward the Democrats. Obama gained with white voters, African Americans, and Hispanics, and among all income levels and all educational levels. With the size of his victory and the swing from 2004, this kind of gain across the board was to be expected. The few categories in which John McCain made slight gains were among older voters, white Protestant voters, and union households (a predominantly Democratic group).

The Democratic coalition is what it was in 2004, only more so. Obama was strongest among African Americans, Hispanics (where he gained hugely from 2004, perhaps as a result of Republican party opposition to the immigration reform plan), unmarried men and women, Jews, and lower-income groups. Catholic voters overall, who went for Bush against John Kerry (a Catholic) in 2004, this time went slightly for Obama. Catholics represented one of the key swing groups in the election. The Democratic coalition had a large advantage in urban areas and this time, in another important swing from 2004, held a small edge over the Republicans in the suburbs. McCain's coalition was strongest among white voters overall, the married, Protestants (especially evangelicals), and Christians who "attend church weekly" (Protestant or Catholic). In terms of place of residence, McCain had strong support in rural areas and in smaller towns. For the economic base of his voters, McCain did best among the middle class, holding his own with Obama. But wealthy voters in 2008 were split evenly between Democrats and Republicans, which marked an important defection for Republicans from 2004. Likewise, in education, Republicans are now distinctly the party of the middle. Democrats do best among those with low levels of education and also among those with very high levels (professionals).

Perhaps the most interesting result had to do with age. There was a general concern across the board with McCain's age, with more voters expressing concern about McCain's age than about Obama's race. The more important fact, however, was the breakdown of voter preference by the different age groups. Every age group below sixty-five years went for Obama, with the youngest (18–29 years old) doing so by a huge margin of 2–1. One reason advanced for the position of the youngest group was that these voters rejected McCain for his stand on social issues, although this position may be at odds with the overwhelming focus on the economy by most voters of all age groups. A more general version, however, is that McCain's ideas and values were "older" or more traditional, a fact that was only accentuated by his chronological age. McCain may have been respected, but the kinds of values he emphasized—country, honor, and duty—resonated less strongly with today's youth. By contrast, Obama represented, even embodied, the deeper aspirations of this generation. Young himself (and multiracial), Obama was an emblem for the youth and was fluent in its language (including technological communication) and congruent with its general attitudes about the world.

Obama's organization was adept at contacting and organizing this group, especially in the university community and within the media outlets that communicate with the young. Youth culture became Obama culture, and it became cool, even obligatory, to support him. Arguably, the big story of this election was not race but age.

Do Republicans have any hope of cutting into the Democratic majority? To repeat what has been said, the most important answer depends on the success or failure of the performance of the Democrats in office. But as for some of the confident arguments of Democrats that demography and destiny are moving in their direction, in particular that the young and the growing sectors of American society are now a lock for the party, there are a few possible responses. Yes, the young voted for Barack Obama, but if this was largely because of his age and style (and the age and style of John McCain), there is nothing permanent in this pattern. Strange as it might seem, not all Republicans are old or square. As for Barack Obama's "post-racial" appeal, this attaches to him and not necessarily to the Democratic Party. Post-Obama, there will be other candidates and other configurations. Republicans, too, have post-racial hopefuls, such as Bobby Jindal, and there is no natural law dictating that Democrats will do as well in the future among African Americans and Hispanics. Hoping against all hope, Republicans might even imagine a day when, as in the 1980s, the climate of university campuses changes and the GOP becomes the "hot" party of the moment. Stranger things have happened.

NOTES

1. "McCain Is to Bush as Robin Is to Batman" CNN political ticker, October 26, 2008, http://politicalticker.blogs.cnn.com/2008/10/26/obama-mccain-is-to-bush-as-robin-is-to-batman.

2. Michael D. Shear, "McCain Proposes 10 Joint Forums," *Washington Post*, Thursday, June 5, 2008, A06.

3. "Obama: 'We Bring a Gun,'" *New York Times*, The Caucus, June 14, 2008, http://thecaucus.blogs.nytimes.com/2008/06/14/obama-we-bring-a-gun.

4. Janet Hook, "Obama Is Shifting to the Center," *Los Angeles Times*, June 28, 2008, A1, http://articles.latimes.com/2008/jun/28/nation/na-obama28.

5. Jonathan Weisman, "Obama May Consider Slowing Iraq Withdrawal," *Washington Post*, July 4, 2008, A01, http://www.washingtonpost.com/wp-dyn/content/article/2008/07/03/AR2008070303919_pf.html.

6. "Public Funding on the Ropes," *New York Times*, editorial, June 20, 2008, http://www.nytimes.com/2008/06/20/opinion/20fri1.html?ref = opinion.

7. Michael D. Shear, "GOP Sharpens Attacks on Obama." *Washington Post*, June 30,

2008, A04, http://www.washingtonpost.com/wp-dyn/content/article/2008/06/29/AR2008 062901878.html.

8. Michael Powell, "Barack Obama: Calm in the Swirl of History," *New York Times*, June 4, 2008, http://www.nytimes.com/2008/06/04/us/politics/04obama.html.

9. Kathy Frankovic, "Is There an Election 'Enthusiasm Gap'?" CBS News, July 18, 2008, http://www.cbsnews.com/stories/2008/07/18/opinion/pollpositions/main4273290 .shtml.

10. Dan Balz and Anne E. Kornblut, "Obama Plans Meetings with Leaders in Mideast, Europe," *Washington Post*, June 29, 2008, A07, http://www.washingtonpost.com/wp-dyn/ content/article/2008/06/28/AR2008062800985.html.

11. Balz and Kornblut, "Obama Plans Meetings with Leaders in Mideast, Europe."

12. "McCain Targets Obama for Not Going to Iraq," CNNPolitics.com, May 28, 2008, http://www.cnn.com/2008/POLITICS/05/28/campaign.wrap.

13. Charles Krauthammer, "Maliki Votes for Obama," *Washington Post*, July 25, 2008, A21.

14. See http://www.gallup.com/poll/109159/Month-Graphs.aspx.

15. See http://www.washingtonpost.com/wp-dyn/content/article/2008/08/12/AR200 8081202935.html.

16. http://blog.washingtonpost.com/the-trail/2008/08/01/obama_opens_the_door_to _offsho.html.

17. Steve Chapman, "Joe Biden's Deep (But Mythical) Blue-Collar Roots," *Chicago Tribune*, August 31, 2008, http://archives.chicagotribune.com/2008/aug/31/magazine/chi -oped0831chapmanaug31.

18. Marijke J. Korenromp et al., "Maternal Decision to Terminate Pregnancy after a Diagnosis of Down Syndrome," *American Journal of Obstetrics & Gynecology* 196, no. 2 (February 2007): 149e1–149e11.

19. Dave Andrusko, "Pro-Lifers Ecstatic Over Selection of Alaska Gov. Sarah Palin as John McCain's Vice Presidential Running Mate," National Right to Life Committee: Today's News and Views, August 29, 2008, http://www.nrlc.org/News_and_Views/Aug 08/nv082908.html.

20. "Candidates' Statements," *New York Times*, September 2, 2008, A19.

21. Michael Reagan, "Welcome Back, Dad," *Human Events*, September 4, 2008, http://www.humanevents.com/article.php?id = 28389.

22. Jeffrey M. Jones, "GOP Increase in Party ID After Convention Not Unusual," Gallup Poll, September 11, 2008, http://www.gallup.com/poll/110215/GOP-Increase-Party -After-Convention-Unusual.aspx.

23. David Paul Kuhn, "Five Reasons Why McCain Has Pulled Ahead," *The Politico*, September 14, 2008, http://www.politico.com/news/stories/0908/13422_Page2.html.

24. Lydia Saad, "Economy Entrenched as Nation's Most Important Problem," *Gallup Report*, December 10, 2008, http://www.gallup.com/poll/113041/Economy-Entrenched -Nations-Most-Important-Problem.aspx.

25. Jon Cohen and Jennifer Agiesta, "Skepticism of Palin Growing, Poll Finds," *Washington Post*, October 1, 2008, http://www.washingtonpost.com/wp-dyn/content/article/ 2008/10/01/AR2008100103600_pf.html.

26. Dan Balz, "Palin Delivers, But Doubts Linger," *Washington Post*, October 3, 2008, A1, http://www.washingtonpost.com/wp-dyn/content/article/2008/10/03/AR2008100300 074_pf.html.

27. Michael D. Shear, "McCain Gives Economy Speech in Ohio, Warning against 'Dangerous Threesome' of Democratic Leaders," *Washington Post*, October 27, 2008, http://voices.washingtonpost.com/the-trail/2008/10/27/mccain_gives_economy_speech_in.html.

28. Turnout rate has been calculated in two ways, as a percentage of the total voting age population (which includes noncitizens, felons who are not legally entitled to vote, and some other categories), and as a percentage of the eligible voting age population. The latter has been developed by Dr. Michael MacDonald of George Mason University, and is now the preferred figure by analysts in the field. The material can be accessed at the United States Elections Project Website, http://elections.gmu.edu/voter_turnout.htm#.

29. Michael Barone, "Obama's Organization Delivered Impressive Results Against McCain," *U.S. News and World Report*, November 14, 2008, http://www.usnews.com/blogs/barone/2008/11/14/obamas-organization-delivered-impressive-results-against-mccain.html.

30. David Brady and Douglas Rivers, "The Democratic Shift in the 2008 Election." Presented at the Hoover Institution, January 5, 2009.

Chapter Six

Congressional and State Elections

President Barack Obama came to office with strong Democratic majorities on Capitol Hill. Substantial House and Senate gains in 2008 followed the party's dramatic takeover of both chambers in 2006. On the House side, it was the first time in seventy-five years that either party had gained more than twenty seats in back-to-back elections. Democrats were doing well in the statehouses, too. Nevertheless, some Democrats voiced disappointment that they had not done even better in Obama's wake.

These things would have astonished a time traveler from the ancient year of 2004. After George W. Bush's reelection, Republicans seemed invincible. House Majority Leader Tom DeLay had engineered an unusual redistricting of Texas congressional seats that enabled his party to pad its narrow but persistent margin. Republicans gained several Senate seats, including that of Senate Minority Leader Tom Daschle (D-SD). Right after Election Day, three key Democratic senators—Christopher Dodd of Connecticut, Charles Schumer of New York, and Jon Corzine of New Jersey—were reportedly thinking about leaving the Senate to run for governor. Some took these reports as a "sign of growing Democratic powerlessness and despair in Washington." According to one Democratic strategist, "People are just giving up."[1]

Congressional Republicans were eager to flex their muscles. Senator George Allen (R-VA) said simply, "We know what we want to do and now we have the ability to do it. And I think we will."[2] In response to the continued threat of Democratic obstruction, Republicans pondered a maneuver by which they could stop filibusters of judicial nominations by simple majority vote. Supporters of the move apparently did not think that they would ever be in the minority under a Democratic president. (The maneuver did not take place, thanks to a bipartisan coalition that included John McCain. Some conservative bloggers called him a "traitor.")

In both parties, however, some suggested that GOP power was neither invincible nor permanent. Warned Senator Harry Reid (D-NV), who succeeded Daschle as Democratic leader: "They'd better be very, very careful what they do."[3] Representative John E. Sweeney (R-NY) cautioned party colleagues against presuming permanent majority status: "In '06, the midterm elections with a lame-duck presidency, we need make a compelling case to the American people that we deserve to be reelected."[4]

The next two years amply justified these comments. War in Iraq and the botched response to Hurricane Katrina dragged down President Bush's public support, and overall Republican fortunes sank accordingly. Bush's proposal for personal Social Security accounts gave Democrats a political target even though the plan died without congressional action. The media presented many stories of scandal in the administration, enabling Democrats to talk about a "culture of corruption." Congressional Republicans did their part to scar the GOP image. Among other things, DeLay's redistricting maneuvers led to his indictment for violating Texas election law.

Corruption issues plagued Republicans at the state level as well. The fallout was especially bad in Ohio, where Governor Robert A. Taft pleaded no contest to violating state ethics laws. His political standing fell so far that he could have envied President Bush's approval ratings: his own numbers dropped to single digits.

While Republicans were self-destructing, Democrats were shaking off their torpor. Schumer declined to run for governor and instead became chair of the Democratic Senatorial Campaign Committee (DSCC). In the House, Rahm Emanuel (D-IL) took the helm of the Democratic Congressional Campaign Committee (DCCC). Both were fierce fundraisers and pragmatic recruiters, backing candidates who could win Republican votes even if those candidates bucked party orthodoxy on issues such as abortion and gun rights. Former presidential candidate Howard Dean won the chair of the Democratic National Committee and launched a "fifty-state strategy" to build party organizations in red states as well as blue. This controversial approach got Dean into shouting matches with Emanuel and Schumer, but it ended up improving Democratic performance in seemingly unattainable territory.[5]

Democratic momentum fed on itself. Candidate recruitment got easier for Democrats, harder for Republicans. The color of "access money" turned from red to blue, as economic interest groups reckoned that they should appease the future majority party. Representative Charles B. Rangel (D-NY), who would chair the tax-writing Ways and Means Committee, started making new friends. "I don't think meeting with the chairman of General Electric has anything to do with my taking over Ways and Means," he said. "I just never realized how much they loved me."[6]

On the day of the 2006 election, the national political tide drowned Republicans. Democrats gained control of the U.S. House and Senate, a majority of governorships, and a plurality of state legislatures. For the first time in American history, the winning party did not lose a single House seat, Senate seat, or governorship that it was defending.[7] In some places, Democrats won because of superior candidates or campaign organizations. In others, Republicans simply threw away seats through individual ineptitude. Senator George Allen of Virginia, who in 2004 had confidently asserted that Republicans knew what they wanted to do, used an ethnic slur against an Indian American Democratic operative who was recording a campaign rally. The resulting video, which gave rise to the term "macaca moment," fatally wounded Allen when it went up on YouTube. The Virginia seat, once a sure thing for Republicans, was the last one the Democrats needed to get a bare majority. The throwaways on the House side were quite remarkable. Don Sherwood of Pennsylvania lost his seat after the press reported allegations that he had choked his girlfriend. (He was married.) John Sweeney of New York, who had advised colleagues to deserve reelection, convinced constituents that he did not. Stories of drunkenness and spousal abuse caused him to boot a safe GOP district.

At the start of the 110th Congress in 2007, Nancy Pelosi (D-CA) became the first woman to serve as Speaker of the House. Harry Reid became majority leader in the Senate. Practically no one thought that they would lose those posts in 2008.

THE POLITICAL CONTEXT OF THE 2008 ELECTIONS

Political scientists define "structural" factors in an election as how many seats each party must defend and where, the makeup of House districts, and the campaign finance laws that affect fundraising.

After the 2004 election, two political scientists complained: "Republicans enjoy a lead right out of the starting blocks thanks to the geographic structure of American elections. In the Senate, Republicans have a tremendous built-in edge because small states, which lean Republican, are so overrepresented."[8] But Senate races are more competitive than House races, so even though only about one-third of Senate seats are up in any election, a national tide will shift a greater share of those seats.[9] That is why Republicans simultaneously gained both chambers in 1994 and lost them in 2006.

One feature of Senate elections is worthy of note there. When a tide brings in a majority, some of the winners may be weak candidates who would have lost in a less favorable setting. Six years later, long after the tide has ebbed, these seats come up again. If times are not as good, the weaker candidates of this Senate class (and perhaps some of the stronger ones) will be in jeopardy. In 1980, for instance, the Reagan landslide helped Republicans take control of the Senate. In the midterm election of 1986, several of the GOP winners of 1980 proved unable to survive on their own, and the Democrats retook the majority.

So to understand the conditions of the 2008 Senate elections, we must look back to 2002. Midterm elections are usually hard for the party holding the White House (more so in the House than in the Senate), but 2002 was different. Republicans were still riding the surge of public support that Bush received after the attacks of September 11, 2001. Instead of losing seats, they scored a net gain of two and thereby regained the control that they had lost in 2001 with the defection of Senator James Jeffords of Vermont. Consequently, the class of 2008 had a bigger Republican "bulge" than it might have had otherwise. Republicans occupied twenty-three of thirty-five seats in play, including two in which appointed senators were running in special elections to complete their predecessors' terms. (John Barrasso of Wyoming succeeded Craig Thomas, who died; and Roger Wicker of Mississippi succeeded Trent Lott, who quit to make money as a lobbyist.) Republicans had more to lose than the Democrats.

A retirement usually hurts the party holding a seat, since its new candidate lacks the advantages of incumbency. When a minority party is facing a bad election, its members are more likely to leave voluntarily. Some want to avoid the cost and embarrassment of a reelection defeat, and others do not want to keep facing the frustrations of minority status. And as more members head for the exits, there are more open seats for the majority party to pick up, which in turn makes the minority's plight even worse. Conversely, members of the majority are more likely to stick around if they think their party will gain seats or take over the White House, since they could more easily achieve their legislative goals.

Of the dozen Democrats whose seats were up in 2008, not one retired—not even Tim Johnson of South Dakota, who was suffering from a severe brain disorder. The only one with worries was Mary Landrieu of Louisiana, where Hurricane Katrina had forced thousands of poor black people—mostly Democrats—out of the state and off the voter rolls. On the GOP side, five senators decided to leave. Two of them, Chuck Hagel in Nebraska and Larry Craig in Idaho, represented deep-red states that would probably elect Republican successors. (If he had not retired, however, Craig would have lost because of his arrest for lewd conduct in a Minneapolis men's room.) The three other seats were Democratic targets. New Mexico's Pete Domenici announced that he would not seek reelection after doctors diagnosed him with dementia. He was already in trouble over accusations of improperly influencing the Justice Department to fire a prosecutor. Wayne Allard stepped down in Colorado, which had been trending Democratic. And in Virginia, the departure of John Warner opened the way for Mark Warner (no relation), a popular former governor who stood to benefit from the state's recent Democratic revival.

From the start of the campaign, Democrats were drawing a bead on several Republican senators seeking reelection. Ted Stevens of Alaska was under investigation for graft. Despite the state's Republican leanings and his own record of bringing home mass quantities of pork, a July 28 indictment put him in grave danger. Susan Collins of Maine, Norman Coleman of Minnesota, John Sununu of New Hampshire, and Gordon Smith of Oregon all represented states that had gone for John Kerry in 2004 and would be a challenge for any Republican candidate. Other GOP senators would later find reason for fear.

House elections are different from Senate elections because members represent districts whose shapes change over time. Before 2006, many Democrats worried that unfair district lines would block a Democratic takeover. The redistricting after the 2000 census did protect House incumbents, making it harder for the minority party to score gains. Nevertheless, some commentators overstated the effect of computer-crafted districts. No matter how clever a redistricting scheme may be, demographic and political changes may blunt its impact over time. Young people and new citizens enter the electorate. Old voters die. Other voters move around or change their party preference. Such shifts were on display in New York State, where a bipartisan gerrymander had once seemed to guarantee the GOP a certain minimum of House seats. But by 2006, shrinking Republican numbers helped nudge three GOP seats into the Democratic column. Texas, Florida, and Pennsylvania had notorious Republican gerrymanders that backfired. The *Wall Street Journal* reported shortly after the election: "Republican leaders may have overreached and created so many Republican-leaning districts that they spread their core supporters too thinly. That left their incumbents vulnerable to the type of backlash from traditionally Republican-leaning independent voters that unfolded this week"[10]

Early signs pointed to continued good times for House Democrats in 2008. Never in the entire election cycle did any national poll show the GOP leading on the "generic ballot" question, asking whether respondents would vote for the Republican or Democratic candidate in their district. Democrats picked up three seats in special elections, including the district that former speaker Dennis Hastert (R-IL) had represented until his resignation. "By itself, this would not be that big of a deal, but coupled with everything else it will just deflate the [House Republican] Conference," said a House GOP staffer. "And symbolically, losing Hastert's seat is like the toppling of the Saddam statue in Baghdad for Republicans."[11]

Then came the retirements. In 2008, twenty-six incumbent Republicans either declined reelection or sought other office. Three others lost primaries, leaving a total of twenty-nine open Republican seats. By contrast, there were only seven open Democratic seats: three retirements, three runs for other office, and one primary defeat. In April, *Congressional Quarterly* found that Democrats were competitive in at least sixteen of the twenty-nine open Republican seats, while Republicans had a chance in only two of the Democratic districts.[12] One reason for the GOP's low level of competitiveness was that it had a very hard time finding "quality candidates," those who had held another office or had a high profile in their district.

Democrats played an active part in the GOP's woes. "There are two pieces to that," said DCCC Chair Chris Van Hollen (D-MD). "One is putting pressure on incumbent Republican members to make the decision to retire, and the other is to put pressure on candidates that they're trying to recruit and convince them that it's not a good idea to run against one of our incumbents." They played rough. In one case, they discouraged a prominent Republican from running by spreading details of his son's criminal record. In another, they forced a GOP candidate to drop out by supplying the *New York Times* with information about his conflicts of interest while serving on a transit board.[13]

House Democrats were also mounting strong challenges to GOP incumbents. Most notably, Christopher Shays of Connecticut had barely hung on in 2006 and was now the sole Republican House member from New England. Democrats now wanted to turn the region into a pure blue lake.

Desperate to keep hope alive, Republicans cited data suggesting that they could win some seats. Of House Democrats, sixty-one represented districts that President Bush carried in 2004, while only eight Republicans came from Kerry districts.[14] And thirty Democratic freshmen were from House seats that the GOP held in 2006.[15] Normally, such seats would have been ripe for Republican takeover: after all, if either Bush or a Republican House member had won a district in the recent past, there must be GOP support there. As of mid-2008, though, most of these seats appeared secure for Democrats. The party's "Frontline" program provided potentially vulnerable incumbents with valuable assistance in strategy and communication. As *Congressional Quarterly Weekly Report* saw things in April, Democrats were running highly competitive races for thirty-four GOP seats, while Republicans were highly competitive in only twenty-four Democratic districts. Of fifteen toss-up races, eleven involved Democratic bids for Republican seats.[16]

Republicans also pointed to polls showing public discontent with Congress. In July, Gallup asked, "Do you approve or disapprove of the way Congress is handling its job?" Only 14 percent approved, the lowest such figure in the Gallup Poll's thirty-four-year history of asking the question.[17] If Democrats controlled Congress, and if the people so strongly disapproved of the institution's performance, then would it not follow that voters were ready to oust the Democrats? Not necessarily. True, low approval ratings preceded big losses by the majority party in 1980, 1994, and 2006, but in all three cases, the same party controlled the White House and Congress.[18] In 1982, by contrast, approval of Congress was at 29 percent, but the majority House Democrats gained twenty-six seats; and in 1992, when approval was at 18 percent, they lost a mere nine. In these two cases, presidential approval was also low at the same time. So even if voters disliked the way Congress was running, they did not want to hand it to the party of an unpopular president. Unfortunately for Republicans, the 2008 election fell into this category. Furthermore, when Gallup asked about the parties in Congress, Democrats had higher approval ratings than Republicans.[19]

Campaign finance provided yet another set of numbers that favored House and Senate Democrats. As members of the majority party, their incumbents had little trouble raising money for their own war chests. Majority status also made a huge difference for the party's "Hill committees." In 2004, the National Republican Congressional Committee (NRCC) raised twice as much as the DCCC. In 2008, the DCCC raised 47 percent *more*. In 2004, DSCC outraised the National Republican Senatorial Committee (NRSC), but only by 12 percent. In 2008, it widened this advantage to 67 percent.[20] Subject to certain limits, these committees could give funds directly to congressional candidates, or undertake "coordinated expenditures." They could also make *unlimited* "independent expenditures" to support or oppose candidates, provided there was no involvement by the candidates' campaigns.

Majority status means control of congressional committees and the ability to conduct investigations. During the 110th Congress, hearings on administration scandals helped Democrats sustain the "culture of corruption" charges that had helped them to win their majority in 2006. Congressional Republicans were in a weak position to respond. Rick Renzi (R-AZ) faced federal charges in a land-swap deal, and Vito Fossella (R-NY) announced his retirement after a drunk-driving arrest and the revelation of his out-of-wedlock child. And if the Stevens investigation and Craig arrest were not enough for Senate Republicans, Senator David Vitter (R-LA) ensnared himself in a prostitution scandal.

The majority party governs the legislative agenda. Although congressional

Democrats had disappointments—especially their inability to pull troops out of Iraq—policy setbacks could work to their political profit. By forcing Bush vetoes on embryonic stem-cell research and children's health insurance, they put the GOP on the wrong side of public opinion.[21] They also avoided sharing legislative credit with Republicans, especially those in difficult races. Gordon Smith (R-OR) told *Roll Call* that Senate Finance Chairman Max Baucus (D-MT) rejected his offer to negotiate on Medicare legislation. "I had offered to be the lead Republican and help them get votes. And I was told that I was not allowed to be." A former Democratic Senate staffer explained: "This is a long-standing practice in the Senate. When elections come around, you try not to give vulnerables anything to point to."[22]

A popular stereotype contrasts the supposedly fractious Democrats with the organized and disciplined GOP. In fact, the majority Democrats maintained remarkable cohesion during the 110th Congress. In both chambers, the parties diverged on most roll call votes. On average, House Democrats voted with the majority of their party 92 percent of the time in 2008, tying the record they set in 2007. The House GOP's scores were slightly lower. Senate Democrats voted as a unified caucus 87 percent of the time, compared with 83 percent for the Republicans.[23]

Congressional Republicans not only faced a unified majority party, but they also had to grapple with the separation of powers. They were both opposition and government by virtue of being in the minority and having George W. Bush in the White House. This position meant responsibility without power. That is, they suffered from President Bush's unpopularity even though they had no chance to shape his policies. In a strategy memo, outgoing Representative Tom Davis (R-VA) identified the source of their difficulties: "It starts with the brand and the brand is Bush."[24] The frustration was even greater among House Republicans than their counterparts on the other side of the Hill: whereas senators at least have the blocking power of the filibuster, members of the House minority are legislative bystanders, often reduced to mere grumbling. As Davis wrote, "our ability to draw issue lines and force choices by Democrats is frustrated by House Rules, inarticulate and unfocused national leadership and finger pointing."

As they were taking political arrows for the White House, congressional Republicans thought that the president was showing little concern for them. In July 2008, the House leadership tried to rally members behind a threatened veto of a housing bailout package. Then the president abruptly decided to approve the measure. Republicans felt orphaned. "I'm deeply disappointed the White House will sign this bill," said House Minority Leader John Boehner. Another House Republican was more succinct: "We got nothing."[25]

Worse still, the minority party in Congress often cannot speak for itself under a president of the same party. Knowing that the real action is at the other end of Pennsylvania Avenue, the media pay scant attention to minority party proposals. When the House Republicans issued a policy agenda in the spring of 2008, press coverage ignored the substance and instead focused on its title: "Change You Deserve." By unhappy coincidence, it turned out to be the slogan for Effexor, an antidepressant.[26] Political analyst Stuart Rothenberg said: "The idea that Congressional Republicans could have redefined their party before the elections is not credible. Sitting presidents and presidential nominees define a party."[27]

In 2008, the nominees had different relationships with their congressional parties. Although some Democrats in conservative districts kept their distance from Barack Obama, many more were eager to embrace him. Pelosi spoke of an "Obama effect" on congressional races, saying Democrats would like to "exploit the opportunities he has opened up for us." She added: "We're in the attraction business. Sometimes you might never know it, but that is what we are in. And he has proven to be an attraction in politics, and we see it as very positive."[28] At midyear, it remained uncertain whether Obama was as eager to return the embrace.

John McCain was unpopular among congressional Republicans, and true to his "maverick" image, he often disregarded their interests. Although they were eager to shed the "culture of corruption" image, he spotlighted it in his acceptance speech: "We were elected to change Washington, and we let Washington change us. We lost the trust of the American people when some Republicans gave in to the temptations of corruption."[29] Congressional Republicans warned about enlarged Democratic majorities and one-party control of the federal government. Sometimes he reinforced this message, but sometimes he stepped on it. In San Francisco, he praised Pelosi as an "effective" leader he could work with, "an inspiration to millions of Americans . . . one of the great American success stories."[30]

According to a report in the *New York Times*, the problems of congressional Republicans steeled the resolve of McCain's advisors "to run a campaign that distinguished Mr. McCain from both Mr. Bush and a Congress where he has served." They said that he would "distance himself by speaking critically of what he has described as excessive spending in Washington, as well as on issues like the environment."[31] His economic plan highlighted drug reimportation and earmark reform, two issues on which he parted company with Republican congressional leaders.[32] During the fall debates, he abruptly changed course to propose a $300 billion mortgage buyout plan, which congressional Republicans neither knew about in advance nor supported afterward.

McCain's mixed messages only added to a difficult issue environment for the GOP. The party had split badly on immigration during 2007, with House Republicans favoring a tougher approach than the Senate Republicans or President Bush. By 2008, the Surge in Iraq seemed to be working, but most Americans still thought that the war had been a mistake and disapproved of the way the administration was handling it. In February, the Pew Research Center found that the Democratic Party held a double-digit edge over the GOP on Iraq, the economy, energy, education, health, the environment, and government reform. It had smaller leads on immigration and foreign policy. Terrorism was the only issue on which Americans thought that Republicans would do better, and the margin was modest: 45–38 percent.[33]

For a short time in the summer, Republicans thought that the energy issue might turn to their benefit. Gasoline topped $4 a gallon, and Americans were ready to support a greater expansion of oil drilling than many congressional Democrats wanted. During the summer recess, House Republicans unofficially took to the House floor to criticize Democratic inaction. Though House cameras and microphones were shut off for the month, the members got a fair amount of attention from the print press, and bootleg videos of their "guerrilla" sessions made it to YouTube. "Drill, baby, drill!" became the GOP's new slogan, and it seemed to be getting through. Congressional Republicans also seemed poised to capitalize on the successful GOP convention and John McCain's subsequent lead in the presidential race. On September 12, Gallup reported: "A potential shift in fortunes for the Republicans in Congress is seen in the latest *USA Today*/Gallup survey, with the Democrats now leading the Republicans by just 3 percentage points, 48 percent to 45 percent, in voters' 'generic ballot' preferences for Congress. This is down from consistent double-digit Democratic leads seen on this measure over the past year."[34]

But with the financial crisis of 9-14 and the controversial bailout of financial institutions, the Democrats were suddenly stronger than ever. In some polls, they jumped to a double-digit advantage on the generic ballot question. "It's not the bailout itself. It's the conditions leading up to needing the bailout and the difficulty in the economy that is sending voters in our direction," said DSCC Chairman Charles Schumer.[35] NRCC Chairman Tom Cole (R-OK) said: "There is no question the economic crisis, the great stimulus debate and the aftermath changed a playing field that had been improving to one that has become considerably more challenging."[36]

HOUSE CONTESTS

In the spring and summer, House Democrats worked to link GOP candidates to the Bush administration. In the fall, they also tied them to the national economic emergency. The Republican strategy was to avoid these connections. In a report for the NRCC, consultants analyzed GOP defeats in special elections. "None of the candidates nor their allies [*sic*] successfully established themselves and their local brand in contrast to the negative perception of the national GOP," their report said. "Traditional Republican messages essentially did not work in these campaigns. Nationalizing these elections as a choice between a traditional Republican and a traditional Democrat did not work in this political environment. Democrats ran candidates that were a reflection of their districts." The consultants made several recommendations: "Encourage Republican candidates to establish themselves in a personal manner, emphasizing local issues whenever possible. Candidates have to have a positive alternative vis-à-vis their Democratic opponents. Work to develop an issues matrix that is different than in years past and also shows a deep empathy towards the voters."[37]

Many Republicans tried to take this approach, but Democrats were effectively pounding national issues. And not all Republicans got the message. When television personality Chris Matthews asked Representative Michele Bachmann (R-MN) if she thought that Barack Obama had "anti-American" views, she replied: "Absolutely. I'm very concerned that he may have anti-American views. That's what the American people are concerned about. . . . I wish the American media would take a great look at the views of the people in Congress and find out, are they pro-America or anti-America?"[38] Democrats seized the comments to argue that Republicans were smearing Obama, and the DCCC started pouring money to her challenger's campaign.

For Republicans, there was also turmoil at the top. Minority Leader Boehner and NRCC Chair Cole disagreed on strategy and personnel, and stories about staff shake-ups and threatened resignations made it to the press. And in a year when things apparently could not get worse, Cole discovered that the committee's treasurer had embezzled several hundred thousand dollars, a revelation that may have discouraged contributors from giving more money.

The Democrats kept pressing their financial advantage. Just before Election Day, the DCCC had put more than three times as much as the NRCC into independent spending ($75.3 million to $22.8 million).[39] In thirty-eight House races, the DCCC spent $1 million. The NRCC reached that level in only four races. Nonparty spending was also part of the picture. Advocacy groups called 527s (after a section of the tax code), which can spend unlimited contributions in elections, collected $185 million through October. By a three-to-one margin, this money went to groups favoring Democrats. America Votes, a coalition of unions and groups such as the Sierra Club, spent $16 million to help its members with voter files, communication hubs, and get-out-the-vote efforts. There was also activity by 501(c) groups (after another section of the tax code), which leaned Republican and thus offset at least some of the 527 efforts.[40]

A few Democrats were in trouble. Tim Mahoney (D-FL), who had won Mark Foley's seat after the congressional page scandal, suffered a mortal blow when the media revealed that he had agreed to pay $121,000 to a former mistress who worked on his staff and was threatening to sue him. But for the most part, Democrats were growing more confident and Republicans were growing more pessimistic. Throughout the year, *Congressional Quarterly* reported, the number of competitive Democratic districts stayed at about 15 percent of the party's total. But the list of competitive Republican seats continued to grow, from fifty-three in April to seventy-three in October. In other words, more than one-third of GOP seats were vulnerable to Democratic takeover.[41]

The financial meltdown, Bush's unpopularity, strong campaigns by Democrats and weak ones by Republicans—all made it nearly certain that the majority party would be bigger in January 2009. Some even spoke of a Democratic pickup of thirty to forty seats. "You like to see a fair fight," said retiring Tom Davis (R-VA), "but basically we are playing basketball in our street shoes and long pants, and the Democrats have on their uniforms and Chuck Taylors."[42]

SENATE CONTESTS

"We are not going to be back in the majority in the Senate next year," said Senate Republican Leader Mitch McConnell (R-KY) in June. "The numbers make that impossible." Nevertheless, he thought Republicans could limit their losses. "I'm optimistic we can stay roughly where we are."[43] Though he was engaging in spin control, his comments did not seem outlandish at the time.

As in the House, the events of early fall radically changed campaign calculations. On the horizon loomed the possibility that Democrats could gain nine seats, and thus reach a total of sixty—the number needed to break a filibuster. If Democrats attained that goal, and if they maintained perfect unity, they could render the Senate Republicans essentially powerless. But the number sixty was not as magical as some assumed. On the one hand, a sixty-vote majority would not guarantee victory every time, since some Democrats would occasionally break ranks. On the other hand, Democrats could often stop filibusters even if they just got close to sixty, since they could usually peel off a few Republicans.

Campaigns, of course, do not traffic in such fine distinctions. In a fund-raising letter, NRSC Vice Chairman Orrin Hatch (R-UT) said: "Liberals are bent on handing Barack Obama a filibuster-proof Senate majority to rubber-stamp his radical agenda."[44] Senator Elizabeth Dole (R-NC) played a similar theme in a television ad. With ominous music in the background, a narrator said: "These liberals want complete control of government, in a time of crisis. All branches of government. No checks and balances. No debate. No independence."[45]

Although these appeals may have motivated contributors and campaign volunteers, there is no evidence that they swayed many voters. A contrast with the 1996 election is instructive. Late in the campaign season, when Bill Clinton's reelection seemed assured, the National Republican Congressional Committee ran a television spot saying, "What would happen if the Democrats controlled Congress and the White House? Been there, done that." It then showed headlines from 1993 and 1994 involving taxes, health care, and government waste. The message seemed to have some impact then, so why did a comparable argument fall short in 2008? First, memories of unified Democratic government in 1993–1994 were still fresh in 1996. By 2008, they were history. Second, in the months before the 1996 election, divided government had produced some popular results, such as welfare reform. In 2008, voters were unhappy. "Vote Republican to prevent Obama from changing too much" was a very tough sell.

Senate Democrats were cautious about predicting a nine-seat gain. They did not want to seem *too* power hungry, and they did not want to set unrealistic expectations, lest a smaller gain seem disappointing. Still, they had much to smile about. Even before the meltdown, the DSCC had nearly a two-to-one financial advantage over the National Republican Senatorial Committee.[46] Between the GOP's fundraising malaise and the worsening issue climate, NRSC Chair John Ensign had a subdued message for Republican candidates, "[J]ust run as hard as you can. There are some things that are outside of your control, so just focus on what you can control."[47]

Susan Collins of Maine seemed to be weathering the storm, but other blue-state Republicans—Smith of Oregon, Coleman of Minnesota, Sununu of New Hampshire—were in difficult fights. Sununu's situation was particularly dire. In a Democratic-trending state in a Democratic year, he was facing the state's formidable former governor Jeanne Shaheen, whom he had barely edged out even in the strong Republican year of 2002. In Alaska, Ted Stevens made a bad bet when he insisted that his corruption trial take place before the election. A jury convicted him of falsifying Senate ethics forms to hide hundreds of thousands of dollars in graft.

Other seats came into serious contention. In Georgia, where Obama's candidacy promised to motivate a large African American turnout, Saxby Chambliss had an uncomfortably small lead. In North Carolina, Elizabeth Dole faced a strong challenge from state legislator Kay Hagan. Democratic voter registration had increased, fueled by enthusiasm for the Obama campaign, especially among African Americans. With a record of Washington service dating back to 1965, Dole was vulnerable to the charge of "insiderism." One Hagan attack ad hit Dole hard and neatly encapsulated the 2008 Democratic message:

> *Narrator*: In this economy, Elizabeth Dole made her choices. Three votes against the minimum wage. Tax breaks to oil companies and corporations sending jobs overseas. Six years of putting the special interests first.
> *Hagan*: We all know this economy didn't break itself. George Bush's economic policies plotted the course. And Senator Dole voted with the special interests to put us over the edge. I'm Kay Hagan. I approve this message because middle class families have had enough, and together we can get our economy moving again.[48]

Dropping in the polls, Dole ran a spot that became an instant classic of overreach. "A leader of the Godless Americans PAC recently held a secret fundraiser for Kay Hagan," the thirty-second ad said, showing clips of the group's members talking about atheism. "Godless Americans and Kay Hagan. She hid from cameras. Took godless money," the ad concluded. "What did Kay Hagan promise in return?"[49] Though technically true (advisors to the group did host a Hagan fundraiser), it falsely implied that the group itself sponsored the event and that Hagan shared its views. Such an implication was not credible since Hagan was a Sunday school teacher and church elder. The spot prompted a surge of contributions to Hagan.

Democrats also took the opportunity to go after Minority Leader McConnell. In May, the DSCC's executive director said:

> Senator McConnell is the Republican leader in the Senate. The filibuster starts and ends with Mitch McConnell. The strategy of gridlock to prevent legislation from moving on the floor starts and ends with Mitch McConnell. This strategy that they've been aggressive with in this cycle starts directly with McConnell. Nobody in the Senate has worked more aggressively for special interests and, often, against the wants and needs of working Americans. We're going to need to make a change in Kentucky, and we can do it. There's a primary of candidates running. We encouraged Bruce Lunsford to get in this race. We think Lunsford is running a forceful campaign, and I have a lot of confidence that Bruce Lunsford could win in November.[50]

The DSCC poured millions into Kentucky, running spots saying that McConnell took Wall Street money and let the industry do whatever it wanted. The attack was part of a long-standing pattern. Since the 1980s, the national parties had often relied on "decapitation"—the strategy of taking out the other side's leaders. Sometimes decapitation took the form of ethics charges. In 1989, House Speaker Jim Wright (D-TX) had to resign because of accusations from Newt Gingrich. When Gingrich became speaker, Democrats returned the favor, resulting in a lengthy investigation for which the ethics committee docked him $300,000. At other times, decapitation has consisted of targeted efforts to beat the other side's leaders at the polls. House Speaker Tom Foley (D-WA) lost his seat in 1994, as did Senate Democratic Leader Tom Daschle (D-SD) ten years later. For Senate Democrats, beating McConnell would be payback for Daschle.

THE RESULTS

In the end, Democrats expanded their majorities in both houses. On the first day of the new Congress, they had gained at least seven Senate seats (for a total of fifty-eight), with one race still pending. On the House side, they had already gained three seats in special elections and made a further net gain of twenty-one on Election Day. Their caucus thus had 257 members, twenty-four more than two years earlier. Some preelection forecasts said that their net pickup of House seats might be twice as large. This gap led to some quiet Democratic grumbling about the "Obama effect." Wrote journalist Michael Barone: "His monster rallies in the fall resembled his monster rallies in the spring: enthusiastic and adulatory crowds inspired by this unique candidate's oratory, without much attention paid to local Democratic officeholders and office-seekers."[51]

By historical standards (see table 6.1), his victory did not bring in the kind of Democratic surge that accompanied FDR in 1932 or LBJ in 1964. He did very well for a candidate whose own margin was in the moderately competitive range, and some House Democrats, such as Paul Kanjorski of Pennsylvania, got a welcome lift from the Obama vote. But according to a study by the National Committee for an Effective Congress, Democrats in the most competitive races outperformed Obama.[52] On the Senate side, Obama probably helped boost the Democratic vote, especially in southern states with large African American populations. But long before he clinched the nomination, as we have seen, a Democratic gain was virtually assured by virtue of structural factors (a number of seats the GOP had to defend, the number of retirements, the Democratic advantage in campaign finance) and a chilly political climate for the Republicans.

Exit polls supplied the definitive temperature reading for that climate. Three-quarters of respondents thought the country was on the wrong track,

Table 6.1. Gains or Losses in the House by the Party of the Winning Presidential Candidate, 1908–2008 (in order of seat change)

		Winner's Margin (in percentages)	+/− Seats
1932	Franklin D. Roosevelt	18	93
1948	Harry S. Truman	4	75
1920	Warren G. Harding	26	63
1912	Woodrow Wilson	19	62
1964	Lyndon B. Johnson	23	37
1980	Ronald Reagan	10	34
1928	Herbert C. Hoover	17	30
2008	**Barack Obama**	**6**	**24**
1924	Calvin Coolidge	25	22
1952	Dwight Eisenhower	11	22
1944	Franklin D. Roosevelt	8	21
1984	Ronald Reagan	18	16
1972	Richard Nixon	23	12
1936	Franklin D. Roosevelt	24	11
1940	Franklin D. Roosevelt	10	5
1968	Richard Nixon	1	5
1996	Bill Clinton	9	3
2004	George W. Bush	3	3
1976	Jimmy Carter	2	1
1956	Dwight Eisenhower	15	− 2
2000	George W. Bush	− 1	− 2
1908	William Howard Taft	9	− 3
1988	George H. W. Bush	8	− 3
1992	Bill Clinton	6	− 9
1960	John F. Kennedy	0	− 20
1916	Woodrow Wilson	3	− 21

and 61 percent of them voted Democratic for the House. Sixty-two percent disapproved of the war in Iraq, and they went Democratic by a three-to-one margin. The economy overshadowed everything else: 63 percent said that it was the most important issue. Eighty-one percent worried that the economic crisis would hurt their own families, and they broke Democratic 59–39 percent.[53] Exit polls in Senate races also showed that economic issues boosted Democratic candidates.

Though Democrats fell just short of the sixty-vote "filibuster-proof" point, they won the biggest Senate majority in thirty years, and they did not lose a single seat to a Republican. They gained three of the five open Senate seats. Mark Warner replaced John Warner (no relation) in Virginia, Mark Udall succeeded Wayne Allard in Colorado, and his cousin Tom Udall took Pete

Domenici's seat in New Mexico. Both Udalls were cousins of Republican Gordon Smith of Oregon, who lost his reelection to Democrat Jeff Merkley. In that race, a conservative third-party candidate may have siphoned enough votes from Smith to change the outcome. To no one's surprise, John Sununu lost to Jeanne Shaheen in New Hampshire. On Election Night, it appeared that Ted Stevens had scored the upset of the year by winning reelection in spite of his felony conviction. But in the days that followed, additional returns came in, reversing the outcome and giving the seat to Anchorage Mayor Mark Begich.

Elizabeth Dole fell to Kay Hagan in North Carolina. Though the outcome confounded early expectations, it was not quite as shocking as some commentators suggested. North Carolina had never been a solid Republican state. Democrats controlled the state legislature and had won all the gubernatorial races since 1992. The state's other seat, held by Republican Richard Burr, had regularly changed party hands since the mid-1970s, with no one holding it for more than one term.

The Kentucky race disappointed Democrats and relieved Republicans. Though some political handicappers had rated it as a toss-up, McConnell ended up winning by the fairly healthy margin of 53–47 percent. He raised large sums and ran ads effectively attacking his opponent for having multiple homes out of state.

Two other Senate races took longer to settle. In Georgia, Saxby Chambliss won a narrow plurality over Jim Martin on Election Day, but a Libertarian kept him from topping 50 percent. When no candidate gets a majority, Georgia law requires a runoff election, which took place on December 2. This time, without Obama on the ballot to boost Democratic turnout, Chambliss won 57–43 percent. The Minnesota race was extremely close. Incumbent Republican Norm Coleman, who had won just 49.5 percent in 2002, faced comedian-commentator Al Franken. Despite vulnerabilities ranging from tax problems to vulgar columns he had written for *Playboy*, Franken was able to pull even because of his fundraising prowess and the strong Democratic wind at his back. On the day after the election, Coleman had a minuscule lead. A long and bitter recount battle ensued, and on the day before Congress reconvened in 2009, the Minnesota State Canvassing Board certified that Franken had won by 225 votes out of nearly three million ballots cast. Coleman launched a legal battle, and the result was uncertain as the new congressional session began.

On the House side, Democrats beat fourteen Republican incumbents and captured twelve Republican open seats. They gained ground in every region of the country. In Alabama, Montgomery mayor Bobby Bright took the open seat vacated by Republican Terry Everett. The conservative, mostly rural district had been in GOP hands since 1964, but Bright ran to the right and played on economic discontent.[54] In Idaho's First District, moderate Democrat Walt Minnick—a former junior aide in the Nixon White House—defeated hard-core conservative incumbent Bill Sali. Meanwhile, there were some notable GOP successes. Despite her Obama gaffe, Michele Bachmann managed to keep her seat in Minnesota. Republicans defeated five Democratic incumbents, but four of them were in Republican-leaning districts.

In only one case—an odd one—did a Republican take a heavily Democratic district. A federal grand jury had indicted William Jefferson, Democrat of Louisiana, on corruption charges in 2007. (Among other things, federal agents found $90,000 that he had stashed in his freezer.) Hurricane Gustav delayed the Democratic primary, pushing the party runoff onto the November ballot and the general election for the seat to December 6. With very low Democratic turnout, attorney Anh "Joseph" Quang Cao narrowly defeated Jefferson, becoming the only Republican to represent a majority-black district, which was now the most Democratic district with a GOP congressman.

Apart from this fluke, Republicans were far less successful in invading Democratic territory than Democrats were in taking the southern, rural, and suburban districts that the GOP had recently regarded as its base. Indeed, large swatches of the country seemed to be off-limits to the Republican Party. Ever since the 1960s, Republicans had seldom won more than 10 percent of the black vote, so they were not competitive in districts with a major African American presence. In 2008, Democrats represented thirty of the thirty-one districts where African Americans made up 40 percent or more of the population (with Cao's seat as the sole exception). Republicans also found it increasingly hard to win Hispanic votes, particularly in light of controversies over immigration. In 2008, Democrats won thirty-five of the forty-two districts that were at least 40 percent Hispanic. The few Republican victories were not signs of progress: three of the seven came from Cuban American constituencies in Florida, who have long had different voting patterns from other Hispanics.

New England was once a GOP stronghold: in the Roosevelt landslide of 1936, the only two states that went for Republican Alf Landon were Maine and Vermont. But New England Republicans have been an endangered species for years, and in 2008, one breed became extinct. With the defeat of Connecticut Republican Chris Shays, Democrats held all twenty-two of New England's House seats. The election marked the first time that the region lacked any Republican House members since the party's formation in the 1850s. For most of the twentieth century, the neighboring state of New York had a robust GOP that could even win some heavily urban areas. No more.

Of New York's twenty-nine districts, only three elected Republicans in 2008. None of the three was in New York City.

In all, 106 Democratic districts fell into one or more of these categories: black, Hispanic, New England, New York. If the GOP concedes these seats to the Democrats, then it must win nearly *two-thirds* of the remainder in order to regain a majority in the House.

STATE ELECTIONS

Eleven governorships were at stake in 2008. Only in Missouri, where incumbent Republican Governor Matt Blunt did not seek reelection, was there a change in party control. Jay Nixon, the state's Democratic attorney general, defeated Kenny Hulshof, a six-term Republican congressman. The outcome was not a surprise, as Nixon had been ahead by double digits in the polls.

In North Carolina, where Democrats had held the governor's chair for eighty-eight of the past one hundred years, Democratic Lieutenant Governor Beverly Perdue ran to succeed term-limited Governor Mike Easley. Her opponent tried to use a Democratic tactic and tag her as an "insider." The Republican Governors Association ran an ad in which two men brought a "status quo" button to Perdue and goaded her into raising taxes. She had an effective comeback: "That's why I think the 'status quo' ad is so funny. Look at me," she said. "Do you think I'm part of the status quo? I've been the odd woman out all my life."[55] Benefiting from the Democratic surge that carried Barack Obama and Kay Hagan to victory in the state, Perdue won by about three points.

Washington State saw a rematch between Democratic Governor Christine Gregoire and former State Senator Dino Rossi, who had lost four years earlier by 133 voters out of more than two and a half million. The 2008 campaign was again tough and costly, with Rossi outspending Gregoire. But Rossi had a hard time overcoming the Obama surge and voter concern about the economy. Gregoire won 53–47 percent.

In seven other races, incumbents won by substantial margins: Mitch Daniels (R-IN), Brian Schweitzer (D-MT), John Lynch (D-NH), John Hoeven (R-ND), John Huntsman (R-UT), Joe Manchin (D-WV), and Jim Douglas (R-VT). In Delaware, Democrat Jack Markell succeeded term-limited Democrat Ruth Ann Minner. Schweitzer deserves a special mention for bipartisanship: in 2008 as in 2004, his hand-picked running mate was a Republican, John Bohlinger.

Democrats won control of four legislatures: Delaware, Nevada, New York, and Wisconsin. With these victories, Democrats ran every chamber north of

Virginia except for the Pennsylvania Senate.[56] In New York, where Democrats already controlled the Assembly, they won a majority in the State Senate for the first time since 1965. Democrats last held both chambers and the governorship in 1935, when Herbert H. Lehman was chief executive.[57] (Ironically, he was one of the founders of the Lehman Brothers investment bank that collapsed as part of the financial crisis in 2008.) National Republicans once worried that unified Democratic control of New York government would lead to a gerrymander that would eliminate most of their House seats. But when Democratic dominance arrived, the GOP no longer had much cause to worry: they only had three seats left anyway.

Offsetting losses in the North and mid-Atlantic regions, Republicans won victories in the South, gaining legislatures in Tennessee and Oklahoma for the first time. And they had a net pickup of seats in the region despite a net loss nationwide of about a hundred seats.

Voters decided 153 statewide ballot propositions on issues ranging from property taxes to living space for farm animals. Nebraska voters approved a measure to ban preferential treatment based on race, gender, and national origin at public institutions, including colleges. Colorado narrowly rejected a similar measure, thus becoming the first state to do so. Voters in Colorado and South Dakota defeated sweeping curbs on abortion, while California turned down a requirement that physicians notify parents of minors before performing abortions. Massachusetts and Michigan relaxed penalties for the possession and use of marijuana.

By far the most controversial ballot propositions were bans on same-sex marriage that passed in Arizona, California, and Florida, which brought to thirty the number of state constitutions with such provisions. The fight in California was especially intense. In 2000, 61 percent of the state's voters approved a statute declaring that "only marriage between a man and a woman is valid and recognized in California." In May of 2008, the state's Supreme Court voted four to three to strike down such limits, saying that people have a fundamental "right to marry" the person of their choice and that gender restrictions violated the state constitution's guarantee of equal protection. Thousands of same-sex marriages soon took place. Opponents of the practice got enough petition signatures to put on the ballot a proposition that would insert the ban into the state constitution. The ensuing campaign battle cost more than $70 million, split about equally between supporters and opponents. It was the most expensive initiative campaign in the country, and except for the presidential campaign, the costliest contest of any kind in 2008. John McCain nominally supported the ban, and while Barack Obama said that he opposed same-sex marriage, he came out against the measure. Neither played a direct part in the initiative campaign.

It passed 52–48 percent, shocking those who thought that California—a reputedly liberal state that strongly voted for Obama—would not take a conservative stance on the issue. Race had a major influence on the outcome. Whites and Asian Americans narrowly opposed the measure, while Hispanics split 53–47 percent and African Americans voted overwhelmingly in favor: 70–30 percent.[58] Although heavily Democratic and generally liberal, Hispanics and African Americans do tend to have socially conservative perspectives on certain matters, and this issue proved to be one of them. One irony is that the Obama campaign may have unintentionally contributed to the measure's passage by spurring turnout among these two groups.

CONSEQUENCES OF THE VOTE

In response to Republican warnings about unified Democratic control of the federal government, House Speaker Nancy Pelosi said: "Elect us, hold us accountable, and make a judgment and then go from there. But I do tell you that if the Democrats win, and have substantial majorities, the Congress of the United States will be more bipartisan."[59] Early evidence was not consistent with that promise. A rigorous statistical analysis by political scientist Nolan McCarty showed that the 110th Congress was extremely polarized and that the 111th was likely to become more so.[60] One reason is that recent election losses removed a large number of moderate Republicans such as Christopher Shays. Pelosi was very liberal and in practice showed little interest in working with the minority party. As the 111th Congress started, she engineered a rules change that further reduced the minority party's influence in floor votes.[61]

Senate Majority Leader Harry Reid said that the enhanced Democratic majority would have to be "very, very careful" about overreaching—exactly the same words he applied to the Republican majority four years earlier.[62] Though he promised to reach out to Republicans, prospects for bipartisan harmony remained dim. The 2008 election confirmed the adage that when you strike at a king, you must kill him. At Reid's direction, Democrats tried to defeat Republican leader Mitch McConnell, who was displeased. A Republican official said: "The majority leader made a tactical error that could potentially cost him his job when he signed off on $6 million of attack ads the last few weeks in Kentucky. McConnell never takes political attacks personally, but he is someone who has never hesitated to repay his opposition for their courtesy." The official explained that the party would strive to find a high-quality opponent to Reid in the 2010 election.[63] Senate politics was reminiscent of a scene in *The Godfather* in which Michael Corleone is walking the empty streets of a Sicilian village. "Where have all the men gone?" he asks. His guide explains, "They're dead from vendettas."

It was not clear that the partisan rancor would have much direct impact on legislation. With strong majorities, Democrats in both chambers would be able to get their way with little Republican support. Unified control of the government meant great power but it also meant total responsibility for mistakes and failures. If things went wrong, Democrats would have nowhere to hide.

Majority parties may be more vulnerable than minorities to corruption scandals. Perhaps long tenure in power dulls the moral sense and renders majority members careless about ethics. This point, however, is hard to document. What is evident is that power gives majority members more occasions to misbehave. Interest groups seeking improper influence will focus on majority members, who in turn may face temptation to exploit their leverage. There is an ever-present danger of a too-cozy relationship between powerful members and economic interests. Debbie Wasserman Schultz (D-FL), a rising star on the majority side, candidly acknowledged that if she finds thirty messages on her desk, "of the thirty, you're going to know ten of them. Anyone is going to make phone calls to the people they know first. I'm going to call the people I know. Among the people I know are donors."[64] Minority members may also face temptations, but political impotence offers a moral safeguard of sorts. Would-be bribe artists tend to disregard lawmakers who can do nothing for them. You cannot abuse power when you do not have any.

Minority status creates obvious political difficulties. After Bill Clinton won in 1992, Republican National Committee chairman Haley Barbour said: "We're not going to get any big contributions. We ought to build the party on belief money, not access money, because we ain't got anything to give people access to."[65] In 2009, congressional Republicans would again need to rebuild their party organizations with belief money—but belief in what? That question was sure to occupy the party for some time.

As the new Congress started, all political maneuvering took place in the shadow of the gigantic economic problems that contributed to the Democratic victory. "You don't ever want a crisis to go to waste; it's an opportunity to do important things that you would otherwise avoid," said Rahm Emanuel, who was leaving the House to serve as the new president's chief of staff.[66] Members of Congress were eager to see what "important things" the Obama administration had in mind.

NOTES

1. Raymond Hernandez and Alison Leigh Cowan, "Three Senators Consider Bids for Governor," *New York Times*, November 6, 2004, http://www.nytimes.com/2004/11/06/nyregion/06dodd.html.

2. Carl Hulse, "Larger Majorities and the Itch to Stretch G.O.P. Muscles," *New York Times*, November 19, 2004, http://query.nytimes.com/gst/fullpage.html?res = 9904E4DC 113FF93AA25752C1A9629C8B63&sec = &spon = &pagewanted = all.

3. Hulse, "Larger Majorities and the Itch to Stretch G.O.P. Muscles."

4. Susan Crabtree and Jonathan Allen, "GOP Gains Strengthen Hand of DeLay, House Leadership," *CQ Weekly Report*, November 6, 2004, 2618.

5. Elaine C. Kamarck, "Assessing Howard Dean's Fifty State Strategy and the 2006 Midterm Elections," *The Forum* 4 (Issue 3, 2006), http://www.bepress.com/cgi/viewcon tent.cgi?article = 1141&context = forum.

6. Richard Simon, "Business Groups Woo Democrats; Campaign Contributions Rise for Lawmakers Who Might Hold Leadership Positions After Nov. 7," *Los Angeles Times*, October 27, 2006, A16.

7. Taegan Goddard, "Democrats Take House, Lead in Key Senate Races," *Political Wire*, November 8, 2006, http://politicalwire.com/archives/2006/11/08/democats_take _house_lead_in_key_senate_races.html.

8. Jacob S. Hacker and Paul Pierson, "The Center No Longer Holds," *New York Times Magazine*, November 20, 2005, http://www.nytimes.com/2005/11/20/magazine/20wwln _essay.html.

9. Alan Martinson, "Staggered Election Cycles and the U.S. Senate: A Study in Politics and Policy" (bachelor's thesis, Claremont McKenna College, 2004).

10. Jeane Cummings, "Redistricting: Home to Roost. How Republicans' Gerrymandering Efforts May Have Backfired," *Wall Street Journal*, November 10, 2006, A6.

11. John Bresnahan and Josh Kraushaar, "House GOP Funk Worsens," *The Politico*, March 9, 2008, http://www.politico.com/news/stories/0308/8920.html.

12. Bob Benenson, "Election 2008: With Enemies Like These . . . ," *CQ Weekly Report*, April 28, 2008, 1086.

13. Aaron Blake, "Van Hollen Using Fear as a Weapon," *The Hill*, April 23, 2008, http://thehill.com/leading-the-news/van-hollen-using-fear-as-a-weapon-2008-04-23_2 .html.

14. "The Land of the Split Decision," *CQ Weekly Report*, April 28, 2008, 1088.

15. "Cashing In, Big Time," *CQ Weekly Report*, October 27, 2008, 2880.

16. Benenson, "Election 2008: With Enemies Like These," 1086.

17. Lydia Saad, "Congressional Approval Hits Record-Low," Gallup Poll, July 16, 2008, http://www.gallup.com/poll/108856/Congressional-Approval-Hits-RecordLow-14 .aspx.

18. Mark Mellman, "Approval of Congress—The Import," *The Hill*, June 20, 2007, http://thehill.com/mark-mellman/approval-of-congress—the-import-2007-06-20.html.

19. See compilations of survey data, http://www.pollingreport.com/cong_dem.htm and http://www.pollingreport.com/cong_rep.htm.

20. Data from the Center for Responsible Politics, http://www.opensecrets.org/parties/ index.php.

21. Polls showed 64 percent opposing the embryonic stem-cell veto and 61 percent opposing the health insurance veto. Joseph Carroll, "Six in 10 Americans Favor Easing Restrictions on Stem Cell Research," Gallup Poll, June 15, 2007, http://www.gallup.com/ poll/27898/Six-Americans-Favor-Easing-Restrictions-Stem-Cell-Research.aspx; CNN, "House Fails to Override Bush Veto of Child Insurance Bill," October 18, 2007, http:// www.cnn.com/2007/POLITICS/10/18/schip/index.html.

22. Emily Pierce and Erin P. Billings, "GOP Forced to Sidelines," *Roll Call*, June 19, 2008, http://www.rollcall.com/issues/53_155/news/26094-1.html.

23. Shawn Zeller, "2008 Votes Studies: Party Unity—Parties Dig in Deep on a Fractured Hill," *CQ Weekly Report*, December 15, 2008, 3332.

24. Tom Davis, "Where We Stand Today," May 14, 2008, http://www.realclearpolitics.com/articles/2008/05/post_38.html.

25. Steven T. Dennis, "Bush Undercuts GOP on Housing," *Roll Call*, July 24, 2008, http://www.rollcall.com/issues/54_12/news/26982-1.html.

26. Carl Hulse, "Republican Slogan Borrowed from Antidepressant," *New York Times* blog, May 12, 2008, http://thecaucus.blogs.nytimes.com/2008/05/12/gop-slogan -borrowed-from-anti-depressant.

27. Stuart Rothenberg, "In This Case, It's Fair to Blame the Messenger," *Rothenberg Political Report*, December 10, 2008, http://rothenbergpoliticalreport.blogspot.com/2008/ 12/in-this-case-its-fair-to-blame.html.

28. Christina Bellantoni, "Democrats Ride Obama's Surge," *Washington Times*, June 17, 2008, http://www.washingtontimes.com/news/2008/jun/17/democrats-ride-obamas -surge.

29. John McCain, acceptance speech at the Republican National Convention, St. Paul, Minnesota, September 4, 2008, http://www.realclearpolitics.com/articles/2008/09/ john_mccains_acceptance_speech.html.

30. Carla Marinucci, "McCain Extends Olive Branch to Pelosi, Gore," *San Francisco Chronicle*, July 30, 2008, http://www.sfgate.com/cgi-bin/article.cgi?f = /c/a/2008/07/29/ MN0I121CI9.DTL.

31. Adam Nagourney and Carl Hulse, "Republican Election Losses Stir Fall Fears," *New York Times*, May 15, 2008, http://www.nytimes.com/2008/05/15/us/politics/15re pubs.html.

32. Jackie Kucinich, "McCain, Republican Leaders Differ on Solutions to Fix Ailing Economy," *The Hill*, July 7, 2008, http://thehill.com/leading-the-news/mccain-republican -leaders-differ-on-solutions-to-fix-ailing-economy-2008-07-07.html.

33. Pew Research Center for the People and the Press, "Obama Has the Lead, But Potential Problems Too," February 28, 2008, http://people-press.org/report/398/obama -has-the-lead-but-potential-problems-too.

34. Lydia Saad, "Battle for Congress Suddenly Looks Competitive," Gallup Poll, September 12, 2008, http://www.gallup.com/poll/110263/Battle-Congress-Suddenly-Looks -Competitive.aspx.

35. Julie Hirschfeld Davis, "Financial Woes Boost Democrats in Congress Races," Associated Press, October 11, 2008, http://www.usatoday.com/news/politics/2008-10-11 -692623334_x.htm.

36. Carl Hulse and David Herszenhorn, "GOP Facing Tougher Battle for Congress," *New York Times*, October 9, 2008, http://www.nytimes.com/2008/10/09/us/politics/09 cong.html.

37. Mike Allen, "GOP Reps Advised to Avoid Party Brand," *The Politico*, June 27, 2008, http://www.politico.com/news/stories/0608/11402.html.

38. Chris Matthews, "What Is Meant by Anti-American?" Hardblogger, October 20, 2008, http://hardblogger.msnbc.msn.com/archive/2008/10/20/1572959.aspx.

39. Campaign Finance Institute, "A First Look at Money in the House and Senate Elections," November 6, 2008, http://www.cfinst.org/pr/prRelease.aspx?ReleaseID = 215.

40. Campaign Finance Institute, "Outside Soft Money Groups Approaching $400 Million in Targeted Spending in 2008 Election," October 31, 2008, http://www.cfinst.org/pr/prRelease.aspx?ReleaseID = 214.

41. "The Growing Field," *CQ Weekly Report*, October 27, 2008, 2869.

42. Carl Hulse, "Republicans Scrambling to Save Seats in Congress," *New York Times*, November 3, 2008, http://www.nytimes.com/2008/11/03/us/politics/03cong.html.

43. Jessica Rummel, "McConnell: Senate GOP 'Won't Be in the Majority' Next Year," CNN, June 29, 2008, http://politicalticker.blogs.cnn.com/2008/06/29/mcconnell-senate -gop-won%E2%80%99t-be-in-the-majority-next-year.

44. Carolyn Lochhead, "Senate Dems Aim for Filibuster-Proof Majority," *San Francisco Chronicle*, October 27, 2008, http://www.sfgate.com/cgi-bin/article.cgi?file = /c/a/ 2008/10/27/MNMC13LJ78.DTL.

45. Carl Hulse and David Herszenhorn, "Democrats See Risk and Reward if Party Sweeps," *New York Times*, October 26, 2008, http://www.nytimes.com/2008/10/26/us/ politics/26congress.html.

46. Campaign Finance Institute, "A First Look."

47. Davis, "Financial Woes."

48. Kay Hagan for U.S. Senate, "Kay's New Ad Highlights the 'Choices' Elizabeth Dole Made on Behalf of North Carolinians during her Six Years in the U.S. Senate," November 3, 2008, http://www.kayhagan.com/press/kays-new-ad-highlights-the-choices -elizabeth-dole-made-on-behalf-of-north-carolinians-during-her-six-years-in-the-us-sen ate.

49. Jody Kraushaar, "Dole Still Keeping the Faith," October 29, 2008, http://www.poli tico.com/blogs/scorecard/1008/Dole_still_keeping_the_faith.html.

50. "Exclusive Interview with DSCC Executive Director J. B. Poersch," Senate Guru, March 27, 2008, http://www.senateguru.com/showDiary.do?diaryId = 74.

51. Michael Barone, "Obama May Be an Aloof President," RealClearPolitics.com, December 27, 2008, http://www.realclearpolitics.com/articles/2008/12/obama_may_be _an_aloof_presiden.html.

52. Carl Hulse, "Not All Democrats Rode an Obama Tide," *New York Times*, December 6, 2008, http://www.nytimes.com/2008/12/07/us/politics/06web-hulse.html.

53. National Election Pool exit poll of 16,521 respondents, November 4, 2008, http:// www.cnn.com/ELECTION/2008/results/polls/#val = USH00p4.

54. Greg Hitt, "The New Southern Strategy," *Wall Street Journal*, August 7, 2008, http://online.wsj.com/public/article/SB121807022975219007.html.

55. Benjamin Niolet, "Perdue Aims to Be a Gutsy Governor," *The News & Observer*, October 19, 2008, http://www.newsobserver.com/102/story/1260733.html.

56. Tim Storey and Edward Smith, "Election 2008—Making History," *State Legislatures*, December 2008, http://www.ncsl.org/magazine/articles/2008/08sldec08_making history.htm.

57. Storey and Smith, "Election 2008—Making History."

58. California General Exit Poll, November 5, 2008, http://media.sacbee.com/smedia/ 2008/11/05/18/prop8.source.prod_affiliate.4.pdf.

59. Mark Matthews, "Pelosi Debunks Triple Threat Rumor," KGO online, October 28, 2008, http://abclocal.go.com/kgo/story?section = news/politics&id = 6473426.

60. Nolan McCarty, "Polarization," December 24, 2008, http://blogs.princeton.edu/ mccarty/2008/12/polarization.html.

61. The rules change curbed motions to "recommit" a bill to a committee for new amendments. In practice, that motion often meant a lengthy delay or even a de facto defeat for the bill. Motions to recommit would still be possible, but the full House could reconsider the bill at once.

62. Bob Cusack and J. Taylor Rushing, "Reid: Dems Must Be 'Very Careful' About Overreaching," *The Hill*, January 6, 2009, http://thehill.com/leading-the-news/reid-dems -must-be-very-careful-about-overreaching-2009-01-06.html.

63. John Stanton, "Senate Leaders' Rapport in Tatters," *Roll Call*, November 20, 2008, http://www.rollcall.com/issues/54_59/news/30337-1.html.

64. John Harwood and Gerald F. Seib, *Pennsylvania Avenue: Profiles in Backroom Power* (New York: Random House, 2008), 85.

65. Major Garrett, *The Enduring Revolution* (New York: Crown Forum, 2005), 57.

66. Jeff Zeleny and Jackie Calmes, "Obama, Assembling Team, Turns to the Economy," *New York Times*, November 6, 2008, http://www.nytimes.com/2008/11/07/us/poli tics/07obama.html.

Chapter Seven

The Future of American Politics and Institutions

At the end of *The Odyssey*, Odysseus finally makes it back to Ithaca, kills his wife's unwanted suitors, and lives happily ever after. In November 2008, the election brought one epic journey to a close, but it also marked the beginning of another longer, more complicated, and more consequential journey for the winner: governing amid extremely adverse national circumstances and facing the prospect of innumerable contingencies. Confronting an unexpected financial meltdown as a candidate is one thing; dealing with it as president is something else altogether. It is as if Odysseus were being asked immediately to set out on another voyage to the gates of the Atlantic Ocean.

Future politics and policy are not, however, the only questions to emerge from the election. Every presidential contest has the potential to raise important institutional issues about the way the nation selects its chief executive. The extremely narrow margin between the main contenders in 2000 focused public attention on many of these issues, ranging from the casting and counting of votes to the viability of the Electoral College itself. The size of Obama's victory in 2008 provided much less reason for people to focus on these questions. But beneath the surface there were a number of institutional controversies that arose, and they will undoubtedly attract greater attention over the next four years.

AMERICAN ELECTORAL INSTITUTIONS

The 2008 election probably laid to rest, at least for the time being, some of the institutional issues that were highlighted with the 2000 election and remained a matter of conversation, if not deep concern, after 2004. Chief among these was the role of the Electoral College. In 2000, for only the second time in the nation's history, the clear winner of the plurality in the nationally aggregated popular vote lost the election in the Electoral College.[1] Through 2008, critics of the Electoral College continued their efforts to change the system, either by formally amending the Constitution to abolish the College or by devising an informal mechanism to work around it. A constitutional amendment (the "Every Vote Counts Amendment") to replace the Electoral College with a direct national popular vote was introduced in Congress in 2004 and again in 2007. But the chances of success for such an amendment were always slim, and these attempts went nowhere. An alternative, informal movement began in several states to form a "compact" in which the participating states would together assign their electoral votes to the winner of the national popular vote rather than to the winner of the state's popular vote. The "National Popular Vote Interstate Compact" would go into effect once approved by enough states to reach 270 electoral votes, the majority needed to elect a president. This scheme would leave the Electoral College formally intact but would replace it in practice with a national popular vote. Four states had approved the compact by November 2008, representing fifty electoral votes, and it had been introduced in another forty-one states. The momentum was stalled, however, when California's governor Arnold Schwarzenegger vetoed his legislature's passage of compact legislation, preventing addition of the nation's most populous state.

Whatever the merits of a direct popular election of the president, the compact proposal is a flawed vehicle. For one thing, its lack of a runoff provision would allow a candidate in a multicandidate race to win with only a narrow plurality of the popular vote. For another thing, the Constitution (Article 1, section 10) specifies that interstate compacts must be approved by Congress, a provision that many analysts believe would apply to the popular vote compact proposal. Yet requiring approval by Congress brings us back to one difficulty facing the formal amendment—passage in Congress. Of course constitutional amendments require a two-thirds majority and approval of a compact only a simple majority, but a filibuster would increase the Senate requirement to sixty votes.

Is this movement to change the Electoral College system likely to continue in the next four years? Reform dies hard, and one advocate of the compact wrote shortly after the 2008 election that "It's time to junk the Electoral College," which he criticized as "anti-democratic by design."[2] But the decisive margin of Obama's 2008 win takes much, if not all, of the steam out of current efforts, formal or informal, to overhaul the Electoral College.

The 2000 election also revealed fatal flaws in punch-card voting (the infamous "hanging chads" in Florida) and, more generally, in the inadequacy of recount procedures in some jurisdictions. In response to these difficulties, Congress in 2002 passed the Helping Americans Vote Act (HAVA). It provided incentives to the states for replacing punch-card voting systems, sought to establish minimum and consistent standards for the administration of elections across jurisdictions, and created the Federal Election Assistance Commission to facilitate these goals. Though some touted electronic voting as a panacea, it soon turned out to have problems of its own. These led to pre-election concern about the potential failure of voting machines and the lack of a paper trail for votes cast. Despite these concerns, vote-casting problems receded as a matter of intense public concern in 2008, again because the presidential results were not close enough to have been affected by irregularities. This is not to say the issue is resolved: the Minnesota Senate race showed that optical-scan ballots are no cure-all, either, and it also highlighted continuing worries about ballot security and recount procedures.[3] In a country with half a million elected officials, plus numerous state and local ballot measures, ballots will often be long and complicated, making problems inevitable. Another close race for the presidency could return many of these problems to the forefront of national attention.

In the meantime, however, other institutional issues gained in prominence—perhaps none so much as campaign finance, as a result of both the nomination battles and the general election contest in 2008. In the nomination phase, all the major contenders in both parties, with the exception of John Edwards, eschewed use of federal matching funds. John McCain flirted with public financing for the nomination but put this to rest following his New Hampshire win. The collapse of public financing in the primaries, and the unprecedented amounts of money raised in that stage of the campaign, led a number of scholarly experts on campaign finance to ask, "Is the campaign finance regime dead?"[4] If not quite dead, it was clear, at the least, that the system was on life support. From 1974 until 2000, only two candidates—Republican John Connally in 1980 and Steve Forbes in 1996 and 2000—had rejected public financing in the primaries in order to free themselves to raise unlimited funds. In 2000, George W. Bush became the first successful candidate for a major party nomination to do so. In 2004, Bush took the same tack, and Democrats Howard Dean and then John Kerry followed suit. The public financing norm in the nomination phase was so thoroughly shattered that in 2008, almost everyone who had a realistic shot at the nomination, and some who did not, opted out. It is difficult to believe, absent a significant change in the public financing rules, that any major candidates will ever again subject themselves to the restrictions attached to public financing.

If analysts were shocked in the primary phase, they were even more amazed in the general election. As one might expect from an outspoken advocate of campaign finance regulation, McCain, like all major party candidates since 1974, accepted public financing in the general election, a lump sum of federal funds that amounted to $84 million. Obama, having awakened to his own enormous fundraising potential, became the first major party candidate since 1974 to reject both the money and the restrictions tied to general election public financing, despite having previously declared his fealty to it. Perhaps as importantly, his reversal paid off, and he paid little political price for it. In the end, according to the Center for Responsive Politics, Obama raised $742.6 million (including $657.6 million from individuals). He was consequently able to outspend McCain by at least 3–2 in North Carolina, 2–1 in Ohio, 4–1 in Virginia, and 7–1 in Indiana. McCain's campaign manager, Rick Davis, estimated that Obama outspent McCain by $100 million in the last week of the campaign.

On one hand, Obama's record-breaking intake was widely praised (especially by Obama supporters) as further evidence of the breadth and depth of his support. However, the degree to which his fundraising was driven by small contributions was often exaggerated; the nonpartisan Campaign Finance Institute reported that 74 percent came from donations over $200 and about half came from donations of at least $1,000.[5] Furthermore, critics alleged that a number of irregularities were connected with the massive inflow of funds to Obama via the Internet, including illegal foreign contributions, contributions made with purloined credit cards or credit card numbers, and aggregate contributions which far exceeded the maximum allowed for donors (donors evaded disclosure by making multiple small contributions). Late in the race, it became clear that the Obama campaign had disabled fraud prevention mechanisms in its Internet fundraising system.[6] And, while Obama barred lobbyists from his transition team, he was less reluctant to include his bundlers: five of the twelve members of his transition advisory board were bundlers who had raised at least $50,000 for his campaign.[7]

All in all, the campaign finance picture at the end of 2008 was murky indeed. It seemed likely that public financing in the primary stage was dead, and very possible that its role in the general election stage was not far behind. Optimistic supporters of public financing pointed out that Obama was a unique candidate, and that it was far from obvious that anyone else in the near future would be able to replicate his fundraising capacity. Others noted that future candidates need not believe that they can raise $743 million in order to follow Obama in opting out of the system, all they have to believe is that they can raise more than they would get from public financing, which in 2012 is likely to be around $90 million. Karl Rove argued starkly that "Mr. Obama's victory marks the death of the campaign finance system."[8] At the least, the taboo is now broken, and the moral weight of opprobrium is no longer part of a candidate's calculus.

At the same time legislators will have to think about whether and how to deal with the collapse of public financing, they will have to come to terms with the fact that major portions of the 2002 Bipartisan Campaign Reform Act (BCRA) have been ruled unconstitutional, including the "millionaires amendment" that loosened fundraising restrictions on candidates facing wealthy, self-financed opponents, and a prohibition on issue advertising by outside groups sixty days before an election. As in 2004, but with less fanfare, so-called 527 and 501(c) groups—organizations that raise and spend money on political activities under section 527 or 501(c) of the Internal Revenue Code—remain generally unregulated and roam the land at will, launching barrages of ostensibly uncoordinated attacks.[9] And both parties learned how to exploit a loophole in BCRA that allows presidential candidates to establish joint fundraising committees with national and state parties accepting $70,000 or more from big donors.[10]

The meltdown of the campaign finance regime brings to a head the perennial questions of whether free political speech has precedence over attempts to stifle corruption or the appearance of corruption, and whether the best way forward is deregulation of campaign finance coupled with complete and transparent disclosure or a more thorough regulation that seeks to plug the holes in the current system with ever-tighter rules. Democrats, who now control both ends of Pennsylvania Avenue, have long favored the regulatory approach, but they were also the prime beneficiaries of its breakdown. A number of campaign finance advocacy organizations demanded after the election that regulation of fundraising "bundlers" be tightened and that the amount of public funding offered to major party candidates in the general election be increased to give them a greater incentive to forgo private fundraising. On the other side of the debate, advocates for deregulation of campaign finance contended that "If the election showed anything, it's that the answer isn't layering more regulations and limits on top of the ones that have already failed. The better road is starting to strip some of them away."[11]

A second tightly wound set of issues that came to the fore in the 2008 campaign revolved around voter registration, voter fraud, and voter suppression. Some observers have argued that voter fraud has been on the upswing in the United States for years, facilitated by looser voter registration standards and the proliferation of absentee and other mail-in ballots.[12] In April 2008, the U.S. Supreme Court ruled by a 6–3 vote in *Crawford v. Marion County Election Board* that states could require voters to present government-issued photo identification as a fraud prevention measure. The decision was widely praised by conservatives as a defense of the sanctity of the ballot and criticized by liberals as endorsing a means of disenfranchising the poor.

As it turned out, the debate over *Crawford v. Marion County Election Board* was merely a dress rehearsal for an issue that exploded in the fall, when it became clear that of the 1.3 million voter registrations collected by the community organization ACORN in 2008, a very large percentage were fraudulent. At a minimum, at least 30 percent of registrations were faulty, and one former ACORN organizer testified under oath that perhaps only 40 percent of ACORN registrations were legitimate.[13] In Nevada, Missouri, Ohio, Pennsylvania, and other key states, ACORN was exposed as having registered "Mickey Mouse," the starting lineup of the Dallas Cowboys, and other improbable electors. One Ohio man, Freddie Johnson, claimed that ACORN organizers had helped him register seventy-three times in exchange for cigarettes and cash, a story that turned out to be less than unique.[14] In October, the FBI confirmed that it was engaged in a national investigation of ACORN for voter registration fraud in up to a dozen states, and Nevada's Democratic secretary of state requested a raid of ACORN's Las Vegas office by state law enforcement agencies.[15] Overall, election officials nationwide rejected hundreds of thousands of ACORN registrations as invalid. The episode was generally troubling, but also had the potential to affect a close election. Far from being a neutral voter registration organization, ACORN was a group of "community activists" whose affiliates had endorsed Obama, received $832,000 from the Obama campaign to run a primary election voter turnout drive, and had a long history of involvement in electoral fraud schemes. For his part, Obama's days as a community organizer in Chicago had involved a voter registration drive in 1992 that may have been in coordination with ACORN.[16]

The issue became large enough that McCain made it a centerpiece of his campaign for a period in October. In the final presidential debate, McCain argued that ACORN was "now on the verge of perpetrating one of the greatest frauds in voter history in this country, maybe destroying the fabric of democracy." Republicans ran radio ads in Ohio asking, "Could Ohio's election be stolen?" Obama backpedaled from ACORN with all possible speed, but Republicans remained convinced that there was collusion between the campaign and ACORN. Of course, voter registration fraud is not the same as voter fraud, and a significant number of ACORN's fraudulent registrations seemed to have been the result of lazy organizers desperately trying to meet their quotas and bring in the promised cash.[17] However, large-scale registration fraud left the door wide open for large-scale voter fraud later, in 2008 or beyond. Republicans, in response, tried to crack down on any sign of inaccurate registration. In the most notable case, they sued in Ohio to have 200,000 flawed voter registrations invalidated, but lost when the U.S. Supreme Court ordered the state not to purge the registrations. In Indiana, Republicans sued to shut down early voting in four counties due to widespread voter registration fraud. In four states, including Florida, state election officials applied a rigorous "no match, no vote" standard, denying ballots to those whose registration information did not match information found for them in other government records. In Georgia, registration lists were examined for possible noncitizens, though federal courts later ruled that such inspections had to receive Justice Department approval.[18]

In Ohio and elsewhere, where Republicans saw fraud favoring Democrats, Democrats saw voter suppression by Republicans.[19] (It also bears noting that voter registration fraud was a temptation to both sides; a Republican contractor was accused in California of tricking voters to change their registration from Democrat to Republican.[20]) The Obama campaign and a variety of advocacy groups set up telephone numbers to receive reports of unreasonable voter suppression, and the resultant Election Protection Hotline received more than 20,000 calls from people around the country reporting that, having showed up at the polls, they found that they were not on the registration rolls. They also launched lawsuits in Colorado, Florida, Michigan, Montana, and Wisconsin asking courts to disallow aggressive efforts by election officials to cull voter registration lists; Colorado, Louisiana, and Michigan were found to have dismissed people from the voting rolls improperly.[21] In Mississippi, New Jersey, South Carolina, and Tennessee, complaints were raised by the Justice Department and others alleging misconduct related to minority voting. In Pennsylvania and Virginia, civil rights groups sued the state, alleging insufficient preparation for increased voter turnout. Some analysts called Republican fears of fraud overblown, arguing that there was very little prospect that "Mickey Mouse" would dare show up at the polls to vote. ACORN itself claimed that only 1.5 percent of its registrations were fraudulent and ran an ad on cable television accusing Republicans of trying to intimidate black voters.[22]

Altogether, it is a fair bet that if the election had been closer—say, decided by Ohio, with Obama 30,000 votes ahead—those 200,000 registrations would have received as much scrutiny after the election as before. Just as the campaign finance issue ultimately revolves around the tension between free speech and prevention of corruption, so this complex of issues revolves around the tension between maximizing participation and preventing fraud, whether organized or not. After the election, calls were made for reforms to the voter registration process, administered at either the state or national level, so as to regularize the process and take it out of the hands of third-party organizations (such as ACORN). Some suggested that same-day registration, already used in eight states, be expanded, while others proposed a universal registration system in which the federal government would be responsible for automatically registering every eligible voter, a reform which advocates argued would solve the problems of both registration fraud by outside groups and excessive purging of the registration rolls by election officials.[23] R. Doug Lewis, executive director of the National Association of Election Officials, indicated that the members of his organization might welcome federal incentives for voter registration reforms, but cautioned, "It's true that in most developed democracies the government takes on this role and it's a top-down system. But ours has been a bottom-up system because our founders were suspicious of centralized election authority."[24]

Another mechanism aimed at maximizing participation raised questions in 2008: early voting. Since the mid-1990s, an increasing number of states have allowed voters to vote two or three weeks before Election Day, either by mail absentee ballot or at walk-in early voting stations. Always touted as a convenience for voters, these schemes have also been criticized for a number of shortcomings. These include the possible compromise of the secret ballot and the resultant potential for intimidation, increased potential for voter fraud (at least among mail ballots), and the disadvantage for those who vote early that their ballots are cast before the completion of the campaign, leaving them unable to take into account late-breaking developments.

Analysts have always questioned whether early voters should be seen as additional voters or (more likely) merely as redistributed voters, reliable voters who would have voted anyway but are simply "banked" before Election Day by their preferred candidate.[25] In 2008, the Obama campaign poured extraordinary organizational energy into promoting early voting by identified supporters. These voters were banked against contingencies such as bad weather that might have depressed turnout on Election Day. The scale of early voting secured by these efforts was a great organizational achievement by Obama, but it is not clear that his overall vote totals expanded as a result. Where Obama may have benefited was among early voters who were less firmly anchored to their candidate and not mobilized by the campaign, but simply decided to vote early out of personal convenience. Exit polls showed that John McCain actually narrowly won the voters who made up their minds in the last week of the campaign. It is conceivable that he might have gained a few percentage points in early voting states if voters had not been allowed to vote early—or even as early. In essence, Obama was able to freeze into place a certain portion of his vote share when it hit its highest point. Some analysts also argued that, by spreading out the organizational task of getting voters to the polls, early voting maximized the impact of Obama's "ground game."[26]

Again, the final margin was large enough that no one could contend that early voting made the difference. However, yet again, a closer result would likely have led to more serious questions. Aside from early voting itself, additional controversy was added by some polling firms which tried to conduct exit polls of early voters to track who was ahead in that phase of the race. Many of these early voting polls were severely flawed, depending on very small and nonrepresentative samples, yet they fed the insatiable media desire for "scientific" data and affected media assessments of how the "horse race" was going.

Altogether, the neutrality and general desirability of early voting has not yet been established. Nonetheless, its trajectory appears to be moving forward, even beyond the state level. In 2007, a bill was drafted in Congress that would have established early voting nationwide. Although it did not advance, a new Congress may be better disposed to it. As with a federal effort to impose national automatic voter registration, any attempt by Congress to impose early voting as a national mandate raises questions of federalism.

Federal and state regulations dealing with campaign finance and voter registration were not the only institutional issues raised in the course of the campaign. The rules and operations of the parties themselves were also brought to the forefront.

Not least, in the nomination phase, the primary calendar became enough of an issue that the parties will likely address it sometime in the next four years. The closely related phenomena of primary front-loading and increasingly early starting points drew considerable concern in 2008, with the starting date for the delegate selection season barely prevented from reaching back into 2007. Beginning on January 3 (the Iowa caucuses), more than half of the delegates in both parties had been selected by February 5. Many Democrats cast a critical eye toward their party's use of superdelegates, the important role played by caucuses rather than primary voters in Obama's victory, and their party mandate that states allocate their elected delegates by proportional representation, a rule that undoubtedly contributed to the drawn-out character of the Democratic nomination contest.

Concerns about front-loading have led Republicans to examine their nominating rules three times since 1996. Most recently, on the eve of the 2008 Republican convention, the party's Rules Committee rejected two competing proposals to establish some order on the 2012 primary calendar. The "Ohio Plan," like the "Delaware Plan" that was nearly adopted in 2000, would have required the least populous states to vote first and the most populous states last, in hopes of lengthening the competitive portion of the race. The alternative "Texas Plan" called for rotating regional primaries.[27]

It is nevertheless conceivable that the extended nature of the Democratic campaign in 2008 may lead to some organic back-loading, with some states regretting their decision to schedule their contests early in the nomination schedule. In a classic example of the "grass is always greener" phenomenon, one set of political analysts opined ten days after the California primary that the state's early primary date had proved a mixed blessing: "We end up getting a lot more campaign visits, which was a big part of the goal. But now we're looking longingly at the late primary states, who may get the final say on the Dem side."[28] Indeed, many early-voting states ultimately looked to Pennsylvania or North Carolina with envy. We now know that under some circumstances even the current system does not inevitably result in early nomination decisions, and some states may respond to that reality by voluntarily moving their primary dates back in 2012.

Moreover, both parties indicated a willingness to reexamine their nominating rules in the future. The Democratic National Convention established a thirty-five-member Change Commission charged with that task, and the Republican convention authorized its national committee to establish a similar commission with permission to change the Republican nominating rules prior to 2012. This is important because in past cycles, while Democrats could change their rules between conventions, Republicans could only do so at their convention. That obstacle to cooperation between the parties has now been removed.

At a minimum, the parties seem likely to work together to push the starting point of the nominating season to a later start. The Republican convention voted to prohibit states other than Iowa, New Hampshire, and South Carolina from scheduling their 2012 contests before the first Tuesday in March (the three exceptions may not vote before the first Tuesday of February). Key Democrats also envisioned a window for most states starting in March. An equally important question is whether the parties will build on the partial success that they had in 2008 firmly enforcing their windows, despite the bitterness engendered in the Michigan and Florida fights.[29]

Some scholars contend that a promising way to prevent excessively early nominating decisions, and hence to provide some incentives for back-loading, would be to require states to use proportional representation in early primaries and some form of winner-take-all in later primaries.[30] This could take the form of statewide winner-take-all contests, as many Republican states use, or district-wide winner-take-all, as Democrats permitted in 1984 and 1988. Democrats may have become more receptive to such a change, judging by their apparent disillusionment with the proportional representation mandate at the height of the 2008 nomination contest. Republicans have generally left such allocation decisions to the states, and might resist such a policy on the grounds that it violates the party's tradition of intraparty federalism. To achieve interparty coordination, the GOP would have to move in the opposite direction from Democrats, using proportional representation more rather than less often and disallowing early winner-take-all states.

The 2008 contest also exposed the dilemma facing the superdelegates in any close Democratic nomination contest—they must either hew to the popular choice and render themselves redundant, or they must contradict the people's selection and face charges of antidemocratic action. Those who created superdelegates in the 1980s thought that they would perform a deliberative function, reasoning on the merits of the candidates without necessarily bowing to the results of the primaries. That is a small-*r* "republican" position. The small-*d* "democratic" position is that they ought to follow their constituents, except in rare cases where more than two candidates were viable and the convention was headed for deadlock. If that is their proper role, and if a deadlock scenario is highly unlikely (no convention has gone to more than one ballot since the 1950s), then what is the point of having superdelegates at all? Obama's campaign expressed an expectation that the Democratic Change Commission would work to reduce the number of superdelegates, but it was unclear what magnitude of change was anticipated.

Democrats also expected the Change Commission to review procedures in the caucus states, where Obama had swept Clinton and where Clinton supporters often complained about unfairness.[31] Caucuses have, over the years, been intermittently controversial. Critics point out that participation rates are much lower in caucuses than in primaries; that participation is often skewed against those whose jobs, family responsibilities, or disabilities keep them from attending the hours-long caucus process; and that there is no secret ballot in caucuses. Caucuses can also be controlled by a relatively small number of committed (critics say extreme) activists.[32] Caucus defenders argue that this method puts a premium on organization over money, allowing passion and commitment to a candidate to come to the fore. They go on to claim that caucuses promote retail politicking, enabling voters to directly connect with the candidates (or at least campaigns). Finally, they argue that caucuses (unlike primaries) can reflect second choices.

The creation of reform commissions does not guarantee actual reform, however. In the end, the parties might conclude that front-loading, proportional representation, and the role of superdelegates are not the great problems they seemed to be at the time. Complacency, instead, may reign.[33] And, of course, it is always unusual for both parties to become strongly interested in procedural changes at the same time. After all, one side just won, and it is unlikely to be enthusiastic about changing the system that got it there. In particular, it is not clear what incentive Barack Obama would have for any kind of major overhaul. His commitment to political change may not be matched by an equal commitment to institutional change.

Furthermore, it is always important to observe the cautionary note that a set of political reforms, no matter how well intended, will not always accomplish the ends for which it was adopted. The history of nominating reforms over the past century is riddled with unintended consequences. Front-loading itself was the unintentional consequence of a combination of prior reforms, and trying to fix it could easily lead to a new set of undesired side effects. Parties embarking on a path of major reform should reflect carefully on the potential for those reforms to go awry. Despite these caveats, Democratic Senator Carl Levin contended when the Change Commission was formed that "[T]here's clearly greater momentum" to rationalize the primary schedule than there was after 2004.[34] There were strong signs that both national parties' leadership understood that some coordinated assault on front-loading was necessary and desirable.

Although the parties are arguably the proper agents for change of the nominating system, the issue will also undoubtedly continue to be discussed in Congress as a possible cause for federal action. Even before the primary voting started, in September 2007, a Senate committee held hearings on a bill that would have established a national system of rotating regional primaries, a favorite solution of the National Secretaries of State Association and some reformers. Others in Congress have long wanted to impose a national primary through federal legislation. Such efforts, if they proceed beyond the hearings stage, will face two sources of opposition. One will focus on substantive shortcomings of the proposals. In particular, critics argue that either innovation will exacerbate most of the problems associated with front-loading, including a high "entry fee" for presidential aspirants, early nominating decisions, and limited opportunities for voters to exercise second thoughts. The regional primary idea would also likely lead to the de facto disenfranchisement of entire regions which vote late. Although the plan specifies that no single region would always be the last to vote, the order of regions could have a huge impact on particular nomination races. The other source of opposition will focus on the question of whether Congress even possesses the constitutional authority to legislate a national party nominating system; while there is no consensus among scholars, a good case can be made that it does not.[35]

THE FUTURE OF AMERICAN POLITICS

Although institutional development is a critical question, it is almost always subsumed in the popular imagination by the question of where American politics and government are headed. The election of 2008 was no exception.

Almost instantly upon receiving the results, the nation's political commentators were engaged in a dash to divine what it all meant.

The election failed to clarify a number of important issues. In the end, Iraq was a nonfactor in the campaign. Obama's withdrawal plan became broadly acceptable, not because things were going so badly that we had to withdraw—the reason that it had been offered in 2007—but because things were going so well that we no longer needed to stay. The economy was the decisive issue, but it was futile to look for clarity there, either. Obama won in a campaign aimed against George W. Bush's "failed economic policies," but he emphasized tax cuts for most Americans, admitted that his tax increases for the "wealthy" might have to be postponed if there were a recession, and ended up voting for Bush's bailout solution to the defining economic crisis of the fall.

Some things about the aftermath of 2008, however, were clear. Democrats were handed an enormous opportunity to implement policies to their liking. Fred Barnes worried openly in an Election Day column that "We could be in for a lurch to the left." Obama will govern, at least for his first two years, with a bigger Senate majority than any president has enjoyed since Jimmy Carter in 1977 and with a much larger incoming House majority than either party has held since 1993. Moreover, the Democratic Party is more homogeneous now than it was in 1977 or 1993, and its majorities are thus more consistently liberal than they were in previous Democratic heydays. The interest groups and advocacy networks backing the Democrats are more effective, and the return of the openly partisan press makes it less likely that most of the major media will challenge Obama.[36] Only an occasional Senate filibuster, infighting within the administration or between the administration and Congress over priorities and tactics, or a tide of public opinion will slow the juggernaut. That is, unless Obama himself calculates that it is better to proceed with some caution.

Three facts might lead one to temper this appraisal. First, while Democrats are more unified than in 1993 or 1977, they are arguably less homogeneous than in 2005. Democrats gained their congressional majorities in the elections of 2006 and 2008 by paying an ideological price: winning with relatively moderate candidates in states and in rural and suburban districts that voted for George W. Bush in 2004. While some of the new winners were unapologetic liberals such as Sherrod Brown of Ohio, more were in the mold of Jim Webb of Virginia, Jon Tester of Montana, Jeanne Shaheen of New Hampshire, and a spate of rural House members such as Heath Schuler from such places as Indiana, North Carolina, Louisiana, and Mississippi. It is an open question whether Democrats, even with their numbers swelled, would have a majority without these putative moderates. So far, with winds blowing the

Democrats' way, this abstract heterogeneity has not translated into a decline of party unity scores in Congress.[37] The actual voting records of the Webbs and Shulers in 2007–2008 were not significantly different from those of Brown or Pelosi. But what will happen if the breeze shifts a little?

Second, as Republicans discovered after 2004, there are distinct disadvantages to holding unified control of the elected branches of the federal government. In the wake of the 2008 election, Democrats hold responsibility for governing, in a comprehensive and highly visible manner, and they do so in a very difficult environment. While this itself presents opportunities—any improvement in fact or perception can bring big benefits—it also presents challenges. As one commentator noted, "With the election of Barack Obama and huge Democratic majorities in Congress, liberals must now practice something other than the politics of nostalgia and what-if": The nation has arrived at a "liberal No Excuses moment."[38] A worsening economic situation, a new terrorist attack inside the United States, slippage in Iraq or Afghanistan—Democrats will own them all, fairly or unfairly. And a statute of limitations on blaming the Bush administration for the nation's ills will be imposed at some point.

Finally, while Democrats have a ready-made list of policy departures that they want to pursue, it is not clear that they have developed an intellectual framework to hold it all together and to successfully prioritize the pent-up demands. Past eras of major policy innovation were characterized by a combination of events that propelled innovation with an intellectual groundwork that had been laid over a number of years. The New Dealers had a half century of populist, progressive, socialist, and liberal thinking to draw upon. The architects of the Great Society had John Kenneth Galbraith, Michael Harrington, and Rachel Carson. The Reagan Revolution could draw from a deep well of thinking from luminaries such as Friedrich Hayek, Milton Friedman, George Gilder, and Russell Kirk. Today's Democrats have yesterday's Democrats and today's invective-filled blogosphere. Perhaps it will be enough, or perhaps Obama will use his considerable gifts to impose some intellectual coherence. If he does not—and it is worth pointing out here that the biggest single influence on Obama was Saul Alinsky, who was all about strategy and tactics, not policy—Democrats may find an upper limit on their achievements.

Republicans face, as all minority parties do, the dilemma of whether to compromise or to confront. This choice, never simple, will be further complicated by the care that Republicans must take so as not to appear overly hostile to America's first black president or overly obstructionist to proposals made in the midst of economic crisis. To regain a positive definition in the electorate, Republicans will have to avoid "me-tooism." By any indication that might be gleaned from the debate over the federal bailout to automobile companies during the lame-duck session of Congress in November and December 2008, congressional Republicans are not inclined to pursue this option. Indeed, shorn of the remnant of its northeastern wing, the Republican contingent in Congress will be more conservative than before. At the same time, Republicans (both in Congress and in the country at large) must avoid falling into the sort of deranged opposition that infected some Republicans in the Clinton years and some Democrats during the George W. Bush years. Derangement as a political strategy has had uneven success; it has never served the country well.

For their first major opportunity to mount a comeback, Republicans will look ahead not to 2012 but to the midterm elections in 2010. In the last century, the president's party has lost seats in the House of Representatives in every midterm election but three—1934, in the midst of the New Deal realignment; 1998, in the midst of the impeachment battle; and 2002, in an election framed by the 9-11 terrorist attack. In most midterm elections the president's opponents have also gained seats in the Senate, state governorships, and state legislatures. The 2010 elections at the state level will be particularly important for how they will influence congressional redistricting following the 2010 national census.

Organizationally, Republicans will undoubtedly look for revival at the state level. Democrats sought to break out of the stalemate of the past decade by adopting a fifty-state strategy of party organization. With a big assist from events and a talented candidate, it worked. Republicans will look to their state parties, as well, and to technology and tactics. They beat Democrats at the ground war in 2004 with the adept use of technology and targeting strategies, combined with Karl Rove's highly effective Get Out the Vote (GOTV) effort, the "72-Hour Project." Democrats won the ground war in 2008 with innovative use of the Internet and their own methodical GOTV drive. Historically, the party to come out on top becomes complacent, while the party that was defeated at the mobilization game is hungrier and anxious to try new approaches. After 2006 and 2008, there is no question that Republicans will be hungry.[39]

New tactics without a compelling message, however, will be insufficient. While all elements of the Republican party can agree on the need for better mobilization of supporters, they cannot agree on exactly what that message should be. "Compassionate conservatism," as a package and a label, is probably dead, although some individual elements of it will doubtless survive. The stock market wipeout of 2008 has likewise put an end to serious talk of personal accounts in Social Security, and the economic crisis has, in general, raised questions about the Republican loyalty to "deregulation." Before the election was even finished, the debate among Republicans had begun. As the outside party at the federal level, Republicans will be particularly dependent on their governors to find an appealing approach.[40] This debate will probably intensify, although if Democrats overplay their hand Republicans may unify more quickly than many now think possible. In any event, conservatives seemed to welcome the opportunity to rethink the direction of their movement.[41]

As always, the debate over where to go next is highly conditioned by the debate over who is to blame. In one corner, some argue that Republicans were waylaid primarily by bad luck—a war gone awry and a financial meltdown that occurred eight weeks too soon (or eight months too late). No radical change is necessary. In another corner, the *National Review*'s "full spectrum conservatives" criticize Bush's substantial domestic departure from limited government conservatism; some also criticize his foreign policy as too visionary. The solution, from this standpoint, is to restore the theme of limited government. Patrick Buchanan, long submerged, has resurfaced, promising a battle to win the party back for a doctrine of economic and foreign policy nationalism, including protectionism and retrenchment abroad. Perhaps the most strident of the critics are the voices that attribute Republican troubles to the party's three-decade-long embrace of social conservatism. For example, Christine Todd Whitman and Robert Bostock argued in the pages of the *Washington Post* that "Unless the Republican Party ends its self-imposed captivity to social fundamentalists, it will spend a lot of time in the political wilderness."[42]

Of all of the critiques, the last seems in many ways the most curious. It is far from clear how social conservatives could have cost Republicans the election in a year when an overwhelming majority of voters indicated that economic issues were their top concern and when the Republican standard-bearer, who had an uneasy relationship with the religious right, was known above all for his national security credentials. Moreover, as conservative writer Ramesh Ponnuru pointed out, the dubious logic of Whitman and Bostock's position "is that if a group of voters has stayed with Republicans during a rout, the party should respond by driving them away, too."[43]

As Republicans begin the work of trying to reconstruct a winning message and a winning coalition, it is worth noting that they have never won at any point in the past four decades unless they held together economic, cultural, and national security conservatives. When they have allowed the relationship among those groups to become unbalanced, trouble arrives. They may be able to win in the future on a different basis, but trying to do so would represent a major gamble. At the same time, certain demographic realities intrude. Republicans will have to do better among the young and minorities, particularly Hispanics, if they hope to succeed. If, as columnist David Frum argues, appealing to the young will require deemphasizing social conservatism, it is no less true that an appeal to Hispanics, Asians, and even blacks requires a continued emphasis on it. Recall that Proposition 8 in California, reversing the state supreme court's pro–same-sex marriage ruling, passed with big black and Hispanic majorities.

Questions of message invariably become entangled with questions of messenger and messenger style. Republicans have already split into pro– and anti–Sarah Palin factions, both of which cut across ideological boundaries. Whatever message and political style Republicans settle on, the political fallout from the Bush years may convince them of the need to place greater weight on identifying articulate spokespersons. Arguably, whatever the other strengths of their more recent leaders, no prominent Republicans since Ronald Reagan in the presidency and Newt Gingrich in Congress have shone as public promoters of the ideas Republicans purported to endorse. Now in the wilderness again, the GOP may well put a new premium on the art of persuasion.

The 2008 election advanced several possibilities for the future of American politics. On the hopeful side, it hardly bears repeating that Barack Obama was the first African American elected president of the United States. As many commentators have noted, his election may serve to reduce racial tensions and open the way for progress by African Americans in other fields. Stereotypes may be whittled down—white stereotypes of the shiftless (or dangerous) young black male, and black stereotypes of "racist" white America. Indeed, the election offered a test of two competing worldviews on the subject of race in America. One view, common in college classrooms, civil rights organizations, and the Reverend Wright's pulpit, has long held that America is a doggedly racist country, indeed a country defined by its racism more than anything else. The other view, held by a majority of white Americans, is that America is a fundamentally decent country where race is an occasional but diminishing problem. The election of 2008 may not by itself succeed in ending that debate, but Obama's success despite his other shortcomings of national security credentials and experience generally seems to give a strong edge to the latter view. Ironically, notwithstanding his personal support for racial preferences, his election may in the long run undercut the argument for affirmative action. Certainly, whatever else Obama may do, his election may help to transform the jaundiced view of American racial relations held by many abroad. Of course, Obama himself could inadvertently stoke new racial difficulties if his presidency is disastrous or if he attempts to quiet opposition by crying "racism," as he and his supporters did at some junctures in the campaign.

Second, if Obama's presidency becomes transformative in a programmatic, rather than just political, way, it will probably be in the direction of making America more like Europe. This is true not only in ways that were widely discussed during the campaign, such as Obama's promise to raise taxes on upper income earners and his hope to "spread the wealth." If Obama's platform is implemented, everything from transportation policy to environmental regulatory policy to health care to wage policies such as comparable worth will move away from a free market model and toward a model found in European social democracies. There will be more economic security but less freedom, more equality of condition but, arguably, less opportunity. This is a trade-off Europeans made decades ago, and many Americans will be pleased to do the same. Many will not, however, and will mourn the loss of America's unique model of democratic development, one which has tended to place more responsibility—for better and worse—in the hands of individuals. Economic troubles and massive deficits may derail some of Obama's plans, but this transformation, if accomplished, will be momentous indeed—probably more momentous than most voters on either side recognized when they cast their votes.

Third, the full-blown reappearance of the partisan press raises important questions about American politics and governing. If unabated, this trend has the potential to skew future elections, especially in cases where the favored candidate also enjoys a fundraising advantage. It is in between elections, though, that the greatest dangers lie. Tilted reporting might be counteracted during campaigns by clever advertising or an appealing candidate, but can the country count on the media to hold their favorite accountable after the election? And if it can't, what price might it pay? Will scandals, policy failures, or episodes of abuse or malfeasance be ignored, either out of pure preferential treatment or out of embarrassment for having so openly facilitated the favorite's rise?

Another question mark has to do with Obama's theme of "unity." Will Obama take meaningful actions to bridge the political and cultural divide in America? And what sort of unity does he aim for—genuine compromise, or surrender by his opponents? Not too long ago, George W. Bush vowed to end hyper-partisanship in Washington by being "a uniter, not a divider." Bill Clinton likewise promised a "third way" that would find common ground. Yet neither succeeded. At least in Clinton's and Bush's presidencies, these aims were buffeted by crosswinds from the increasing partisan polarization of the electorate and the increasing nationalization of congressional elections. Where once it was considered common, if inflated, wisdom that most congressional elections were decided on the ground race by race, six of the last eight congressional elections have arguably been "nationalized," or driven foremost by national issues and trends (1994, 1998, 2002, 2004, 2006,

2008).[44] Will Obama change this dynamic, harness it to his aims, or be overwhelmed by it? As president, will he confirm or refute the charge raised by McCain during the campaign, that Obama may speak the language of unity but is actually, as shown by his record, a straightforward liberal and partisan?

Finally, while Obama's election would seem to offer America a sort of redemption for past sins, it also raises a more troubling prospect. The losing side in presidential elections has often blamed its defeat on the charisma of the winner. Barack Obama's victory, however, reached a new level in the elevation of charisma and what the Founders feared as "the popular arts." Taken individually, Obama Girl, mass stadium speeches to eighty thousand in mock Greek temples, a personalized pseudo-presidential seal, children's choirs singing the praises of The One, and college students announcing adoption of Obama as their personal messiah, might be seen as isolated instances of strange excess in a high-stakes campaign. Taken together, the picture is one of a cult of personality that is not, in the long run, easily compatible with the necessary norms of a free republic. Fouad Ajami gave expression to these concerns when he wrote less than a week before Election Day that "America is a different land, for me exceptional in all the ways that matter. In recent days, those vast Obama crowds, though, have recalled for me the politics of charisma that wrecked Arab and Muslim societies. A leader does not have to say much, or be much. The crowd is left to its most powerful possession—its imagination."[45] To the extent that Obama's win, and his presidency, move America markedly farther in the direction of a politics of personalism, sober caution is in order from Americans of all political persuasions, for once unleashed one can never know in what direction this kind of politics will take us.

At the beginning of 2008, most observers of American politics saw a destination looming in the November elections—a Democratic sweep at all levels. When the journey was over, that destination had been reached. But almost nothing about the particulars of the journey met the expectations of the observers. The race included two surprise nominees; record-breaking spending on the campaign; only the second female vice presidential nominee in American history; one convention featuring an acceptance speech to eighty thousand spectators and another shortened by a hurricane; and a remarkable shift of focus over the course of the long campaign from the Iraq War to energy policy to economic disaster. Contingency (or was it fate?) made itself felt on a regular basis, including an assassination in Pakistan that happened just in time to help John McCain in the Republican primaries and a financial meltdown that occurred just in time to help Barack Obama erase McCain's post-convention lead. Was the predictability of the destination the controlling factor? Or was it the contingency of the voyage?

Whatever the cause, the result of the journey was a new president, Barack Obama, backed by a solid majority of Democrats in Congress and around the country. Between 2004 and 2008 Americans cast their lot with the Democratic Party. What Democrats do with their prize, and what events do with them, will be what ultimately determines the meaning of the 2008 election. The journey continues. The Straits of Gibraltar are next: That way monsters be. How the voyage ends—in fame or infamy—remains to be discovered.

NOTES

1. The other time was 1888, when Grover Cleveland won a majority in the nationally aggregated popular vote but lost in the Electoral College to Benjamin Harrison. Three other elections—1824, 1876, and 1960—arguably represented such cases, but are clouded by ambiguities.

2. Jonathan Soros, "It's Time to Junk the Electoral College," *Wall Street Journal*, December 15, 2008.

3. See http://minnesotaindependent.com/16777/problem-plagued-ballot-scanners-could -impact-coleman-franken-recount and Trent England, "The Minnesota Recount Folly: We've Been Down That Road," *Wall Street Journal*, December 31, 2008, A9.

4. The April 9, 2008, edition of the online journal *The Forum* focused on issues of campaign finance, asking the question, "Has the American Campaign Finance Regime Collapsed?"

5. "Reality Check: Obama Received about the Same Percentage from Small Donors in 2008 as Bush in 2004," Campaign Finance Institute, November 24, 2008, http://www .cfinst.org/pr/prRelease.aspx?ReleaseID = 216.

6. One donor, who listed his name only as "Good Will," made enough small contributions by Internet to total more than $11,000; one "Doodad Pro" similarly managed to contribute $17,130. The legal limit is $2,000 in the primaries and $2,000 in the general elections. See Neil Munro, "FEC Rules Leave Loopholes for Online Donating Data," *National Journal*, October 24, 2008, http://www.nationaljournal.com/njonline/no_2008 1024_9865.php; Michael Isikoff, "Obama's Good Will Hunting," *Newsweek*, October 4, 2008, http://www.newsweek.com/id/162403.

7. "The $639 Million Loophole," *Wall Street Journal*, November 17, 2008, A18.

8. Karl Rove, "McCain Couldn't Compete With Obama's Money," *Wall Street Journal*, December 3, 2008, http://online.wsj.com/article/SB122835139848377873.html.

9. In comparison with 2004, in 2008 527 activity was reduced considerably and 501(c) activity was up considerably. See http://www.opensecrets.org/527s/index.php and http://www.cfinst.org/pr/prRelease.aspx?ReleaseID = 214.

10. See David Arkush and Craig Holman, "Campaign Finance Reformers Open the Floodgates," Public Citizen Watchdog Blog, posted June 5, 2008, http://citizen.typepad .com/watchdog_blog/2008/06/campaign-financ.html. Also Christopher Cooper, "'Independent' Ads Tout McCain's Energy Policies," *Wall Street Journal*, July 7, 2008, A5.

11. "The $639 Million Loophole."

12. See John Fund, *Stealing Elections: How Voter Fraud Threatens Our Democracy*, revised edition (San Francisco, CA: Encounter Books, 2008).

13. Katharine Q. Seelye, "McCain's Warning about Voter Fraud Stokes a Fiery Campaign Even Further," *New York Times*, October 27, 2008, A19; Mario F. Cattabiani, "Fired ACORN Employee Testifies," *Philadelphia Inquirer*, October 30, 2008, B1.

14. Annabel Crabb, "Even a Homeless Mickey Mouse Can Vote in Ohio; Registration Capers—The Race for Power," *Sydney Morning Herald*, November 3, 2008, 7.

15. Tom Leonard, "FBI Investigates Alleged Voter Registration Fraud in Up to a Dozen States," *The Daily Telegraph*, October 18, 2008, 15.

16. "Obama and Acorn," *Wall Street Journal*, October 14, 2008, A20.

17. See http://www.factcheck.org/elections-2008/acorn_accusations.html.

18. See Carol J. Williams and Noam N. Levey, "Campaign '08: Race for the White House; Vote Watchdogs Warn of Trouble on Election Day," *Los Angeles Times*, October 30, 2008, A1.

19. For an example of this line of argument, see Adrienne T. Washington, "Early Voting Sign of Civic Health," *Washington Times*, October 19, 2008, A4.

20. Evan Halper and Michael Rothfeld, "Voters Say They Were Duped; A Firm Hired by the GOP Is Accused of Using Petitions to Trick People into Switching Party Registration," *Los Angeles Times*, October 18, 2008, B1.

21. Williams and Levey, "Vote Watchdogs Warn of Trouble"; Ian Urbina, Katharine Q. Seelye, and Sean D. Hamill, "Push to Expand Voter Rolls and Early Balloting in U.S.," *New York Times*, November 7, 2008, A25.

22. Ben Arnoldy, "Are Voter Fraud Fears Overblown?" *Christian Science Monitor*, October 20, 2008, 25; Michael Saul, "Experts See Little Risk of Voting Fraud," *New York Daily News*, October 19, 2008, 7; Michael Falcone, "ACORN Strikes Back," *New York Times*, October 30, 2008, A28.

23. Charles Stewart III, "Get a Grip on Elections," *Los Angeles Times*, October 27, 2008, A17; "Restore Trust in Voter Rolls," *Christian Science Monitor*, October 22, 2008, 8; Urbina, Seelye, and Hamill, "Push to Expand Voter Rolls."; David G. Savage, "A Call to Overhaul Nation's Voter Registration Process; Election Reformers Say Switching to a 'Universal' System Would Expand the Rolls and Prevent Fraud," *Los Angeles Times*, November 10, 2008, A14; Robyn Blumner, "It Should Be Easy to Register to Vote," *St. Petersburg Times*, November 23, 2008, 5P.

24. Savage, "A Call to Overhaul Nation's Voter Registration Process."

25. Commission on Federal Election Reform, *Building Confidence in American Elections: Report of the Commission on Federal Election Reform*, 2008, 33, http://www.ameri can.edu/ia/cfer/report/CFER_section4.pdf.

26. Urbina, Seelye, and Hamill, "Push to Expand Voter Rolls."

27. Marc Ambinder, "Ohio Plan Advances In RNC Rules Deliberation," *The Atlantic*, August 19, 2008, http://marcambinder.theatlantic.com/archives/2008/08/post_6.php; Ralph Z. Hallow, "GOP Panel Rejects Proposal to Spread Out 2012 Primaries," *Washington Times*, August 28, 2008, A12; "For 2012, the Same Old Mess," *USA Today*, September 3, 14A.

28. *Political Pulse: The Newsletter of California Politics and Government,* February 15, 2008, 2.

29. "GOP Adopts Rules, Platform on Both Sides of McCain," *AP News*, September 1,

2008, http://townhall.com/Common/PrintPage.aspx?g = f4364elc-4894-46e8-ab5a-fa14a 0c94153&; Dan Balz, "Obama Looking to Diminish Superdelegates," *Washington Post*, August 20, 2008, http://voices.washingtonpost.com/44/2008/08/20/obama_clinton_look ing_to_dimin.html.

30. Ronald B. Rapoport and Walter J. Stone. "To: RNC Advisory Commission on the Presidential Nominating Process," *Nominating Future Presidents: A Review of the Republican Process* (Washington, DC: Republican National Committee, 2000), 139–47.

31. Balz, "Obama Looking to Diminish Superdelegates"; Stephen Ohlemacher, "Democrats to Review Nominating Process," *AP News*, August 20, 2008, http://ap.goog le.com/article/AleqM5igrYLRhG3P61Ibs2E&pSH0bxhvgD92M8QSG0.

32. See Kathryn Pearson, "Caucuses Are Voices of the Few," *Minneapolis Star-Tribune*, February 10, 2008, http://www.startribune.com/opinion/commentary/15453976 .html.

33. Liz Halloran, "Too Early, Too Long, Too Divisive," *U.S. News & World Report*, July 7/July 14, 21.

34. "Both Parties Need to Improve the Nominating Process," *Detroit Free Press*, August 31, 2008, http://www.freep.com/apps/pbcs.dll/article?AID = /20080831/OPIN ION01/808310363.

35. William G. Mayer and Andrew E. Busch, "Can the Federal Government Reform the Presidential Nomination Process?" *Election Law Journal* 3, no. 4 (2004): 613–25.

36. Fred Barnes, "We Could Be in for a Lurch to the Left," *Wall Street Journal*, November 4, 2008, A19.

37. See *Congressional Quarterly Weekly Report*, December 15, 2008, 3338.

38. Bret Stephens, "'No Excuses' for Liberals," *Wall Street Journal*, November 18, 2008, A19.

39. Karl Rove, "History Favors Republicans in 2010," *Wall Street Journal*, November 13, 2008, A17.

40. Christopher Cooper, "Republican Governors Take a Hard Look at How to Rebuild Party after Big Losses," *Wall Street Journal*, November 13, 2008, A4.

41. The December 1, 2008, *National Review* gave its cover and thirteen separate essays to the topic of "Renewal," represented visually by a sun on the horizon. Whether setting or rising was not clear.

42. Christine Todd Whitman and Robert M. Bostock, "Free the GOP: The Party Won't Win Back the Middle As Long As It's Hostage to Social Fundamentalists," *Washington Post*, November 14, 2008, A19.

43. Ramesh Ponnuru, "Scapegoating the Social Right," *National Review*, December 15, 2008, 36.

44. Gary C. Jacobson has long held that national factors drive congressional elections, but primarily indirectly, through the mechanism of candidate recruitment and fundraising. Here, we are referring to a more direct sort of impact.

45. Fouad Ajami, "Obama and the Politics of Crowds," *Wall Street Journal*, October 30, 2008, A19.

Index

About the Authors

James W. Ceaser is a senior fellow at the Hoover Institution, Stanford University, and professor of politics at the University of Virginia. He has written several books on American politics and American political thought, including *Nature and History in American Political Development* (2006), *Reconstructing America* (1997), and *Liberal Democracy and Political Science* (1990).

Andrew E. Busch is professor of government at Claremont McKenna College, where he teaches courses on American government, politics, and public policy. He is author or coauthor of eleven books, including *The Constitution on the Campaign Trail: The Surprising Political Career of America's Founding Document* (2007), *Reagan's Victory: The 1980 Election and the Rise of the Right* (2005), *Red Over Blue: The 2004 Elections and American Politics* (2005), and *The Front-loading Problem in Presidential Nominations* (2004). He received his Ph.D. from the University of Virginia.

John J. Pitney, Jr., is professor of government at Claremont McKenna College. He received his Ph.D. from Yale in 1985. Professor Pitney is the author of *The Art of Political Warfare* as well as numerous articles on Congress, the presidency, and party politics. He is coauthor with William F. Connelly, Jr., of *Congress' Permanent Minority? Republicans in the U.S. House*. He has also written many essays for newspapers, magazines, online publications, and blogs.